The
College Student's
Guide to
Mental Health

"Having worked with Mia Nosanow for over ten years, I know she is the real deal. Generations of students were supported by her compassion, intuition, and experience, and I'm sure this book will benefit many more."

— **Jim Hoppe, PhD**, vice president and dean for student life at Emerson College

"*The College Student's Guide to Mental Health* is the book that students going to college and in college need to read! The focus on staying mentally healthy in college will also help students after college. The skills and tools gained by applying what the author says will surely provide a pathway for students to engage in their college journeys with joy."

— **DeMethra LaSha "Sha" Bradley, EdD**, vice president for student affairs and dean of students at Scripps College

"Young adults often assume that everyone else has these things figured out, and feel flawed or deficient when they struggle. This book is just the resource that many students have been seeking! Mia Nosanow has decades of experience developing trusting relationships with students and helping them navigate the challenges of being human. Her insights and guidance will provide readers valuable opportunities to build skills and increase confidence."

— **Robin Hart Ruthenbeck, EdD**, dean of student development at Kenyon College

"This book could not come at a better time for the many American college students who struggle with mental health issues. Mia Nosanow's decades of experience, graceful prose, and easy-to-follow format make this the perfect companion for any student heading off to or already in college."

— **Dan Buettner**, #1 *New York Times* bestselling author, National Geographic Fellow, and founder of Blue Zones

"An incredibly helpful and thoughtful resource for those wishing to better understand mental health during a time of constant transition. This is a must-read for not only students, parents, and families, but also those who work at colleges and universities. There are many right answers for solving the same challenge. This book is the permission everyone needs to begin that discernment process and focus on personal well-being."

— **Carolyn H. Livingston, PhD**, vice president for student life
and dean of students at Carleton College

"If you want clear and effective tools to stay balanced and focused, and even to thrive, during college, then include *The College Student's Guide to Mental Health* on your reading list. It is highly recommended!"

— **Henry Emmons, MD**, author of
The Chemistry of Joy and *The Chemistry of Calm*

"Mia Nosanow knows college students and knows how to help them thrive in college. This book will be a huge asset for students trying to live their best lives while in college."

— **Holly B. Rogers, MD**, cofounder of the Mindfulness Institute
for Emerging Adults, author of *The Mindful Twenty-Something*,
and former staff psychiatrist at Duke University
Counseling and Psychological Services

The College Student's Guide to Mental Health

Essential Wellness Strategies for Flourishing in College

MIA NOSANOW, MA, LP

New World Library
Novato, California

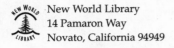 New World Library
14 Pamaron Way
Novato, California 94949

The material in this book is intended for education. It is not meant to take the place of diagnosis and treatment by a qualified medical practitioner or therapist. No expressed or implied guarantee of the effects of the use of the recommendations can be given or liability taken.

All the student quotes in this book are by real college students. However, their names have been changed to preserve their anonymity. In some cases, the experiences of multiple students have been combined into a single composite person or quote.

Text design by Tona Pearce Myers

Library of Congress Cataloging-in-Publication Data

Names: Nosanow, Mia, author.
Title: The college student's guide to mental health : essential wellness strategies for
    flourishing in college / Mia Nosanow, MA, LP.
Description: Novato, California : New World Library, [2024] | Includes index. | Summary:
    "This comprehensive guidebook covers every factor that can influence the mental
    health of college students, providing clear guidance for maintaining a healthy and
    successful lifestyle as students navigate their new life away from home"-- Provided
    by publisher.
Identifiers: LCCN 2023049393 (print) | LCCN 2023049394 (ebook) | ISBN 9781608689019
    (paperback : alk. paper) | ISBN 9781608689026 (epub)
Subjects: LCSH: College students--Psychology. | College students--Mental health. |
    Adjustment (Psychology) | Self-care, Health.
Classification: LCC LB3609 .N68 2024 (print) | LCC LB3609 (ebook) | DDC 616.8900835--
    dc23/eng/20231121
LC record available at https://lccn.loc.gov/2023049393
LC ebook record available at https://lccn.loc.gov/2023049394

First printing, February 2024
ISBN 978-1-60868-901-9
Ebook ISBN 978-1-60868-902-6
Printed in Canada on 100% postconsumer-waste recycled paper

 New World Library is proud to be a Gold Certified Environmentally Responsible
Publisher. Publisher certification awarded by Green Press Initiative.

10   9   8   7   6   5   4   3   2   1

For my former clients

Contents

PART IV: YOUR EMOTIONS

PART V: YOUR RELATIONSHIPS

PART VI: YOUR TIME

Introduction

How This Book Can Help — and How to Get the Most Out of It

*Mental health is a state of well-being in which every individual realizes
his or her own potential, can cope with the normal stresses of life,
can work productively and fruitfully, and is able to make
a contribution to her or his community.*

— THE WORLD HEALTH ORGANIZATION

I have written this book for students who are curious about how to be
a healthy person in college — which is much more complicated than
simply getting straight As or having a good time partying like a rock star.
Most, if not all, students struggle in some way with how to develop a
balanced lifestyle that supports their mental health, and my hope is that
this book provides many different ways to cope and thrive.

If this struggle speaks to you, you are not alone. In 2022, the American
College Health Association found that 41 percent of undergraduates'
academic performance was negatively impacted by anxiety,
while 77 percent of undergraduates were experiencing moderate to
serious psychological distress (see the ACHA National College Health
Assessment).

We often measure success in college by what we learn — such as how
to write a thesis statement or solve a differential equation — and by what
we achieve, like good grades and various accolades. But success is also

measured in equally important, if more intangible, ways: by how well we accept ourselves, handle emotions, and approach relationships.

We have such high expectations for ourselves in college: We seek to find our passion, learn as much as we can, make lifelong friends, have great internships and career-related experiences that turn into great jobs, and maybe even change the world. But too often, we take for granted, or don't seem to value or care about, our growth as a whole person.

For twenty years as a mental health counselor at Macalester College, a small Midwestern liberal arts college, I've spoken to thousands of students about their mental health. One thing I've found is that college students often need to be given permission to even focus on their personal well-being. Sometimes they also need to understand the rationale for doing this work, or why it's important, and then of course they need help learning the life skills for achieving mental and emotional wellness. Most of the students I've counseled do not have a diagnosable mental illness. Rather, they've been young adults struggling with the same mental health issues common to almost all college students, regardless of what type of college they attend.

This book can help. Here are its core messages:

- You can learn a set of skills that will help you live a healthier life, support your work as a student, and help you feel better about yourself.
- These skills are slightly different for each person.
- You can choose how you do things in ways that increase your mental health throughout college and make positive changes in your life.
- The popular or accepted way of doing things might not be what works for you.
- It takes practice to get good at something, including healthier behaviors.
- Making small, incremental changes, compounded over time, can lead to significant, lasting positive change.

When they first meet me, some students respond by saying: *Isn't this selfish? I'm in college — shouldn't I only be focusing on learning, so that I can get a good job, help others, or contribute to my field of study?*

Actually, no. To me, the best metaphor is the instructions we get when flying on a plane: We need to put on our own oxygen mask first before we can help others with their masks. *Learning how to take care of yourself, know yourself, have healthy relationships, and manage your time effectively is necessary in order to live the life of your dreams and give back to the world.*

I encourage all the students I counsel to value their mental health as much as they value all the other aspects of collegiate life, such as their achievements and outward success. Taking our mental health seriously is, in fact, what supports everything else.

HOW TO USE THIS BOOK

As you read this book, use what appeals to you or works for you, and skip what doesn't. This book includes a wide range of issues and advice, but not every issue applies to every person, and not every tool works for everyone. Often, there are many right answers for solving the same problem. The "right way" is the one that helps you best. Explore and experiment and stick with whatever is productive. But if something isn't broken, don't fix it.

That said, don't be too quick to decide that something isn't working or helpful. Remember, *it takes practice to get good at something, including healthier behaviors.* Athletes and musicians know this already: The only way to improve performance is through practice and training.

When it comes to mental health in general, one essential practice that I recommend for everyone is *journaling.* Journaling means writing down our thoughts, goals, positive messages, experiences (and more) so we can reflect on them and keep track of them. Journaling helps us express our inner thoughts and build self-awareness. A journal is a safe place to be honest about our feelings, especially difficult ones we might not want to share with others. Conversely, writing about positive experiences and gratitude is a way to combat negativity and foster healthier self-talk; writing about positive behaviors helps strengthen those messages in our brain. In this book, I provide many different ways to approach journaling (for instance, see appendix B).

Every chapter explores a different topic and how it particularly im-pacts college students, and then it includes two important sections: First, a strategies section provides a range of tips, ideas, and practices to try. This often includes writing exercises, which can be kept in a journal. As part of the strategies material, I also include a section titled "When to Seek Professional Help." This provides guidance for recognizing a more serious problem or when the strategies in this book are not helping enough.

The other important section in every chapter is resources. Here you'll find a selection of places to turn for more information or help, such as on-campus organizations, books, websites, and apps. Each chapter provides resources for that specific topic, and some resources appear throughout, since they help in many ways. In particular, always explore the student resources your college offers.

Ready to start? Turn the page and let's dive in.

Part I

YOUR BODY

We need to do a better job of putting ourselves higher on our own "to-do" list.

— MICHELLE OBAMA

What is the foundation of mental health? Actually, it's something that isn't in our minds at all.

Often, improving our physical health will *immediately* improve our mental health. Many areas of cutting-edge research continue to provide data about how the body impacts the mind. It is a regularly acknowledged, science-backed, and self-evident truth that self-care is a necessary element of mental health.

Yet across the country, college counseling centers are seeing a crisis in student self-care. Students are routinely undersleeping, and sleep disorders are on the rise. Students are often under- or malnourished, with the resultant loss of energy and motivation, or they may overeat. Not all students exercise at appropriate levels; some are extremely inactive while others overexercise. College binge drinking and drug use are at high levels, and abuse of prescription meds is an epidemic.

Students rarely incorporate daily quiet time into their hectic schedules. This includes meditation or just time away from electronic devices. Many don't know how to relax or be alone and comfortable in their own skin without input of some kind. Other important areas of self-care that students can struggle with include personal hygiene and getting appropriate medical care.

The term *self-care* is itself a problem. Many associate it with getting mani-pedis or taking lavender-scented baths. There is nothing wrong with those things, but self-care is much larger than that. It refers to our whole self, our entire physical wellness, and the foundational ways that we take care of ourselves. Genuine self-care isn't always supported by our productivity-oriented culture. Lack of adequate self-care is one reason many students complain of being stressed out, tired all the time, and not as motivated as they would like to be. The good news is that self-care is often easy to improve, and when we improve one area, it's often beneficial in numerous ways to other areas.

Here are the main messages of part 1: Self-care needs to happen every day, not just occasionally. Everyone needs to practice it. And self-care is the foundation of mental health.

SELF-CARE ≠ SELFISH

When some students hear this, their first response is "I don't have time for self-care." Yet when they experiment with a new behavior — such as eating protein at breakfast or sleeping eight hours a night — they almost always report back, "It works!"

The best part of self-care is that learning — the whole point of college — becomes easier and more efficient. Self-care ends up saving time and allowing students to do a better (and smarter) job at what they are trying to do in the first place.

Even so, it can be very challenging to make time for self-care on a daily basis. You don't have to do it all at once; remember that starting small and practicing over time adds up to positive change.

We humans are a diverse bunch. An exercise routine that's appropriate for an athlete will be very different from an exercise routine that works for an exercise-averse gamer. There is no one perfect way to do self-care. That means you get to be creative.

When it comes to taking care of your body and mind, think like a scientist. Check out what others are doing, and then experiment with self-care techniques until you find what works best for you.

Chapter 1

Sleep

"I'm doing okay. I get five to six hours of sleep a night. No one here who's a serious student gets more than six hours. There's no way I could get all my work done if I sleep more than six hours a night."

"When I lie down, it usually takes me one to two hours to get to sleep. I can't shut my mind off."

"During the week I don't sleep well. Then I catch up on the weekend and sleep twelve hours a night."

"I'm tired at midnight, but that's when I get caught up with TikTok, and I can get lost in that for a couple of hours, which then causes me to wake up late the next day. I know I'm setting up a bad pattern."

"I'm embarrassed to tell my friends I go to bed at eleven. They don't think I'm working hard enough when I say I've gotten eight hours of sleep."

The jury is in on sleep: We must have quality sleep — and enough of it — to perform at our best. Studies show that most of us need seven to nine hours each night. Even if we feel we can get by on less than seven hours, research shows that we perform worse on tests with this level of sleep. We need a full seven to nine hours to experience the right amount of REM and deep sleep. These latter stages of sleep are when our brain works on consolidating learning and memory, and it's when our body makes repairs, regrows tissue, and improves our immune system.

Another reason to be protective of sleep: Sleep issues are considered the gateway to mental illness. Inadequate sleep doesn't always or necessarily lead to full-blown illnesses like depression or anxiety, but being exhausted easily dampens mood and increases irritability, and it makes it tougher to cope with the daily frustrations of life. Of course, being tired is synonymous with low energy, which is the opposite of what students need to get their work done.

While it may not be cool or easy, getting a good night's sleep on most nights is actually one of the most important things you can do for your mental health.

WHY SLEEP IS A CHALLENGE

In our 24/7 culture, getting a good night's sleep is both sought after like the holy grail and the easiest thing to slip to the bottom of our priority list. Sleep is taken for granted and viewed as something that should just happen whenever we lie down at night. But many people find that getting a good night's sleep takes intentional planning and discipline.

Many factors can get in the way of good sleep: daytime stressors, a disruptive environment, lack of a healthy sleep routine, a desire to stay up because we finally have some time to ourselves, drug or alcohol use, or changes in health. Traveling or changing time zones can also interfere with sleep patterns. Did you know there is a 17-percent increase in traffic deaths on the Mondays following the change to daylight saving time in the spring, when we "spring ahead" and lose an hour?

Some of the biggest hallmarks of college life — dealing with tons of homework, living in noisy dorms or apartments, and having fluctuating routines — are all direct challenges to getting a good night's sleep. But those issues alone would be pretty easy to solve.

The biggest threat to sleep is our antisleep culture. It is almost a badge of honor to be exhausted or to be "doing fine" on six hours of sleep. It has become a deep part of college culture to accept being sleep deprived and to disregard the importance of a refreshing night's sleep.

What's happening with sleep today is similar to what occurred during the cigarette-smoking culture of the 1950s and 1960s: Everyone's skipping sleep because it's cool and everyone else is doing it. The group mentality is ruling, and no one wants to face just how damaging this bad habit is to their mental and physical health.

This has created a sleep problem of almost epidemic proportions.

The second biggest threat to sleep is a combination of stress and media use. If we are on our phone for a couple of hours before we try to go to sleep, our brain has been jumping from item to item at a very fast rate, and we have been on alert for our ... alerts. All of this activates our fight-or-flight system, which arises when we might be in some type of danger. Sleep won't come as easily or be as restful if our body is on high alert. On top of the stressful content, research on how blue light affects mental health would scare anyone out of phone use at night — that is, if we weren't all addicted to our phones.

On the flip side, some students oversleep, staying in bed ten to twelve hours a day or more. Having a long sleep once or twice a week is typical for students and not a problem. However, if you find yourself unable to get out of bed and/or feel exhausted on a daily basis, this is a sign that something is wrong.

STRATEGIES

Decide to Value Sleep

Adopt a mindset that prioritizes your body, rather than giving in to the unhealthy social norm. This is half the battle.

Create a Sleep Schedule

Set a (moderately) consistent sleep schedule. Yes, college is a time to work hard and play hard. That often means irregular schedules and late nights, whether to study or to party. That's not wrong, and to a degree, it comes with the territory of college life. But if you aren't feeling good, and want to feel better, sleep is really and truly the first place to start.

In a perfect world, go to sleep and wake up at the same time every single day, even on weekends. For example, head to bed at 10 p.m. if you need to wake up at 6 a.m., or go to bed at midnight if you can sleep until

8 a.m. But since the world is far from perfect, simply aim for a regular sleep schedule.

Research shows that even waking up one hour later than usual may cause the groggy feeling of jet lag. Our bodies operate on circadian rhythms as well as more complex neuron-based clocks in our brains.

If you have stayed up having a ton of fun with friends and not gotten to bed until 2 a.m., you have two choices: (1) Get up a little earlier than you'd like the next day in order to try to keep to your schedule, or (2) let yourself sleep late to get those eight hours of sleep. In the latter case, try to head to bed earlier the next night to get back on your schedule. It's all about being aware of what's going on and striving to keep that consistent sleep routine without getting overly rigid.

Countless students prioritize getting their homework done over getting a good night's sleep. While that work ethic is commendable, it often backfires. Skimping on sleep not only negatively affects academic performance, but it is also linked with anxiety. When students commit to a routine cutoff time for homework each night, and thus get enough sleep, their anxiety lessens. It might not resolve completely, but it lessens. And with a proper night's sleep, students are able to work more efficiently and feel more motivated to get their work done during the day.

Sleep When It Is Dark

We need sunlight to feel good, which is why it's better to sleep from midnight to 8 a.m. than from 4 a.m. to noon, when we've lost half our daylight. People who are night owls (which is about a quarter of the population) can push their regular sleep schedules back to 1 or 2 a.m. to 9 or 10 a.m.

Acknowledge the Impact of Night Shifts

If you work a regular late shift or need to take care of siblings or family at night, it's important to not deny that night-shift schedules and responsibilities impact your sleep. Give yourself kind self-talk; telling yourself, "I should be able to do it all," is never helpful. And experiment with all the techniques listed here to see what works for you to get enough restful sleep.

Include a Buffer Zone

Many students make the mistake of studying or rushing around until the moment they head to bed for sleep. Then they settle in while holding their cell phone or placing it next to them on the bedside table.

If this works for you, and you are getting a restful night's sleep and feel refreshed the next day, then it's not a problem. However, if you are struggling with insomnia or frequent waking, or you don't feel rested in the morning, then adopt this important bedtime strategy: Enforce a buffer zone.

A buffer zone means intentionally shutting down busy activities for twenty minutes to one hour before the actual time you want to go to sleep. So if you are sticking to an 11 p.m. to 7 a.m. schedule, start your buffer zone between 10 and 10:40 p.m.

One helpful technique is, once study time is over, to write a to-do list for the next day (for more on this, see chapter 34). A to-do list serves several functions:

- It's a ritual to let go of and end your workday.
- It provides a place to contain your worries about what work you have left to do.
- This practical tool helps you get started a bit more quickly the next day.

Its main role here is to help you let go of your stressful day so you can relax, get high-quality rest, and be ready to tackle it all again tomorrow.

A core buffer zone strategy is to use *no social media* or electronics during this time. Some people wind down and relax by watching a couple of episodes of a favorite TV show, but put away your computer and your phone. Let all your best friends know that you won't be looking at texts or chatting via electronics once your buffer time starts each night.

Here are some other useful specifics:

- Put your computer and phone somewhere that they won't be constantly tempting you, such as in a dedicated phone box, a drawer, or a shelf or desk that you don't see.
- Put your phone into airplane mode or Do Not Disturb before you get into bed. (Your alarm clock will still work in airplane mode.)
- Studies show that any light in a room will interfere with sleep, so make sure all the blinking charging lights are covered.

It is not just the reflected blue light from electronic devices that interferes with sleep, however. Social media and internet use cause two main issues: They create a potential emotional roller coaster (unreturned texts or negative Instagram comments, anyone?). And quick focus shifting activates the brain just when it should be quieting down.

What should you do during your buffer time? Any unplugged, quiet activity can work well.

Read purely for pleasure. This type of reading can be an important part of self-care — something you look forward to every day — and a helpful transition to deeper, more restful sleep. But pick up a real book instead of a backlit device, and choose books with content that isn't so alarming it will interfere with sleep (like horror).

You might choose a fine-motor activity such as drawing or knitting, working on a relaxing puzzle or game, writing in a journal, listening to soft music or an audio book, or chatting with roommates. Taking a warm shower can be a great sleep inducer. You can also generate relaxation by gentle stretching or yoga. *Gentle* is the operative word; this is not the time for a workout. See also chapter 5, "Quiet Time," for more ideas.

Calm a Racing Mind

No matter what we do, there will always be some nights when we lie down exhausted but our thoughts turn on and won't let us sleep. Here are some ideas for when you struggle to turn off your brain once you crawl into bed for the night (see appendix A for these and other techniques).

Square Breathing

Picture a square. Breathe in as you count to four (the first side of the square), hold your breath for a four count (the second side), exhale slowly to a count of four (the third side), and hold your breath for a four count (the fourth side). Then repeat this sequence as many times as needed until your relax.

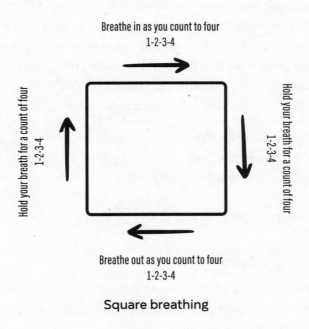

Breathe in as you count to four
1-2-3-4

Hold your breath for a count of four
1-2-3-4

Hold your breath for a count of four
1-2-3-4

Breathe out as you count to four
1-2-3-4

Square breathing

Nature Visualization

Imagine a favorite place outdoors. It can be a place you've visited many times, or a place you've only been to once but was very memorable. It can be a familiar hike in the woods, watching the ocean waves from the beach, a dock on a quiet lake, a well-lit and safe city park, a path to a cabin, or a flowering garden. Generally, choose a place that inspires a sense of awe or calm, not excitement or danger. It's helpful to imagine slowly walking through or sitting comfortably in this place. For example, as you lie in bed, imagine slowly walking through a park. Notice the colors of the trees and the grass. Feel the warmth of the air on your face. If your racing thoughts come back in your head, no worries! Gently notice the thought and then bring yourself back to your nature visualization. Stick with the visualization until you fall asleep.

Creative Calming Visualization

Similar to the nature visualization, you can come up with any creative visualization that helps you find peace of mind when trying to sleep. I know students who've tried all sorts of things. The technique is the same: Imagine doing the calm activity, and focus on your sensory awareness — what you see, feel, hear, and so on. When racing thoughts return, gently notice them and bring your attention back to the calming activity. Keep doing this until you fall asleep. Here are some ideas:

- Walking to a favorite cafe
- Browsing a bookstore
- Watching penguins slide down a hill
- Ice skating
- Sitting on a porch swing and slowly swinging

Create a Morning Routine

Besides having a consistent wake-up time, which is an important part of a sleep schedule, a morning routine can paradoxically offer many opportunities to improve sleep the night before.

Waking up in the morning is a challenge for many students. Here are some physical strategies to help wake up in an ideal way:

- Set your alarm at a midrange volume, so that it wakes you but doesn't startle or rattle you.
- Place your alarm clock or phone farther away, such as on your desk rather than on your nightstand. That way, you need to get out of bed to turn it off. Also, put your charger on your desk, so you will be reminded to leave the phone there.
- Set a backup alarm with a different ringtone, and set it to go off right after your original alarm.

- Disable the snooze function.
- Open your blinds and turn on your bedside light as soon as your alarm goes off.
- Drink a whole glass of water as soon as possible after waking up.
- If possible, work with your roommate to help each other get up at the optimal time.

It can be easy to become anxious or negative first thing in the morning. Here are ways to avoid slipping into those unhelpful mindsets:

- Don't look at your phone until you're dressed and out of your bedroom.
- Give yourself some positive messages for the day by reading a prayer or daily affirmation or by writing in a gratitude journal.
- Make time to do something you enjoy in the morning, even for five minutes, such as listening to some favorite music while getting dressed or reading an article from your favorite news source.

Create a Restful Bedroom Environment

This strategy can be tough, since most students don't have full control over their dorm room or student apartment, or their bedroom at home if shared with a sibling. However, talk to your roommates and neighbors about how to create the best environment for sleeping. Doing so could help everyone prioritize sleep, which would be great.

First, and hardest, is to save your bed for sleep (and for sex; see chapter 31). Many students love to sit in bed to work on their reading assignments, or their desk is right next to their bed, where they do their challenging, stressful homework. If this is your situation, and you have no problem sleeping and feel energized every day, then there's no reason to change anything. But if sleep and feeling refreshed is a problem, consider studying somewhere besides your room, and especially not on your bed.

When many students make this change, they find that they actually study more efficiently in the library or some other study area. Also, returning to their room signals to them that it is time to relax, which sets them up to sleep better. This is one of the simplest and most successful changes I've seen students make.

If you can control your thermostat, the optimal temperature for sleeping is around 60 to 65 degrees Fahrenheit.

Many studies have shown that darkness is essential for quality sleep. This can be very challenging for students with roommates who stay up later than them. If this is your situation, ask your roommate to study in the lounge or with a lower light after you go to bed. Using a sleep mask is a very inexpensive option, and it has the added benefit of blocking any stray light from electronic devices.

Last is finding quiet. This is also hard in dorms and communal living situations. Even if your room is quiet, activity outside your door can be impossible to stop. To block noise, many students find it helps to use a white noise machine or a fan, earplugs, or sleep headphones.

Move Your Body Daily

Getting moderate exercise each day, such as twenty to thirty minutes of walking, has been shown to help sleep. It doesn't have to be done all at once, so if you aren't an exercise fan, don't worry — you don't have to hit the gym. Just find a way to take two or three ten-minute walks each day around campus.

If you do exercise regularly, congratulations. However, it's best to work out during the day or early evening. A vigorous workout right before bed can be stimulating and make sleep more challenging.

Eat Wisely

Eating habits can affect sleep. Eating three nourishing meals a day helps set us up to sleep better at night, mainly because we feel more even and regulated in general. When we don't eat enough, our bodies rely on energy sources such as adrenaline to keep us going, and this can work against sleep.

Many students are hungry before bed. If you can sleep well after eating pizza at night, go ahead and enjoy. However, for many students, a small carb or protein snack — such as a small bowl of whole-grain cereal with milk, a banana or apple with nut butter, a protein bar, or yogurt — works better. This is especially true for students who are anxious, as this seems to regulate blood sugar and evens out their mood in the morning.

Avoid indulging in candy bars or sweets late at night. Refined sugar will rev you up and then cause your blood sugar to crash. This makes waking up in the morning very hard. Again, everyone is different, so experiment and see what works best for you.

Limit Your Chemical Intake

Chemical habits affect sleep.

- **Caffeine:** The most common chemical sleep disruptor is caffeine, a stimulant, which stays in our system for eight hours. Experiment with how much and how late in the day you can have caffeine. If you find you are sensitive to caffeine, cut it out altogether, or consider avoiding caffeine eight to ten hours before bedtime. Herbal tea before bed can be calming, but for some students, having to get up to use the bathroom doesn't make drinking tea right before bed worth it.
- **Alcohol:** Alcohol is falsely seen as a sleep aid. Yes, it does make people drowsy at first; however, it interferes with getting the deep sleep that is essential to feel rested. Don't use alcohol to get to sleep; instead, eat a small snack.
- **Nicotine:** Cigarettes or vaping before bed provide a boost of stimulating nicotine, which interferes with deep sleep.
- **Cannabis:** Cannabis, like alcohol, might seem like a sleep aid. But like alcohol, it has some unintended side effects, such as loss of motivation to work hard or feeling foggy headed or low energy.
- **Chemical sleep aids:** Do not use sleeping pills or other chemical sleep aids, even those available over the counter, without medical supervision.

Take Short Naps

Judicious use of short naps can be a lifesaver. A short nap — that is, twenty to thirty minutes — taken early in the afternoon has been shown to reenergize people for the second half of their day. So long as naps (of any length) don't interfere with a restful night's sleep, enjoy them.

However — and this is a big however! — if you are struggling with insomnia or with getting yourself to stick to a regular sleep schedule, a nap can get in the way, and so should be avoided. Many students take a nap too late in the day and then sleep for hours, undercutting their nighttime sleep schedule — not to mention their social life.

The most important sleep goal is to keep to a routine as much as possible. So experiment with naps to see what works for you.

WHEN TO SEEK PROFESSIONAL HELP

If you have tried the above steps on your own but continue to have trouble falling or staying asleep — or if you feel exhausted every day — it is important to see a medical professional. You could have a sleep disorder — or perhaps your poor sleep could be a symptom of a larger mental health issue.

Depending on your health insurance, first call your nurse line or stop by your college health center. They will refer you to the appropriate next steps, such as an appointment with a sleep specialist.

"I always try to pull an all-nighter before an exam because that is the image that I have of college students, and I thought that was the right thing to do! When I learned that it would actually help my test taking to get a good night's sleep the night before a test, even if I wasn't totally finished with studying, I was surprised. I decided to experiment with implementing a cutoff time that would give me eight hours of sleep before my next exam, even though it would reduce my so-called study time. I was nervous about this, but my test scores hadn't been that good lately, so I really did not have much to lose. I was amazed that I did better on this exam than I had on any so far this semester, with the added benefit that I wasn't strung out and exhausted. Sleep is so foundational that people overlook it."

— JONAH

Here are some other sleep-related problems that might warrant a trip to the doctor:

- Ongoing irregular breathing or loud snoring
- Increased movement while sleeping
- Physical sensations of tingling in your arms and legs

- Frequent morning headaches
- Regular nightmares
- Inability to get to sleep easily, frequent waking in the middle of the night, and/or waking up too early in the morning
- Oversleeping, which means being in bed more than ten hours per day every day
- Feeling tired every day, even though you get enough sleep

RESOURCES

On Campus

- College wellness center: Many colleges offer free sleep workshops and/or sleep items (such as earplugs or eye masks).
- College residence staff: Residence hall staff have usually dealt with sleep issues before and can provide support, such as facilitating talks with a noisy roommate or finding ways to darken a room.
- College counseling center: Counselors can help assess if sleep difficulties are part of a larger issue (such as anxiety or depression) and give referrals to off-campus providers. They may be able to help support changing habits to get a more restful night sleep.
- College medical center: Medical personnel can assess sleep issues and prescribe medication, as well as offer referrals to off-campus resources.

Websites

- National Sleep Foundation (www.thensf.org): This national nonprofit provides information on most sleep-related topics,

"I'm not sure I'm a good fit for college. I feel crabby and I'm just not that excited about anything here. I stay up late and get up early. I want to meet people who hang out in the hall late at night, and I'm also nervous about studying, so I get up early to eat breakfast before I head to the library. So I'd say I get five to six hours of sleep per night. I didn't realize that the right amount of sleep per night could have a big impact on my mood. After sleeping eight hours each night for a few days, I could feel the difference. I was much less crabby with people, and it was easier to be excited about all the new things I'm trying. The difference was like a miracle!"

— DONNA

describes sleep disorders, and offers many useful solutions for sleep issues.

Books

- *Why We Sleep: Unlocking the Power of Sleep and Dreams* by Matthew Walker: This book gives the most thorough explanation of what sleep does for us, how it significantly improves our health and well-being, and the catastrophic results of not getting enough sleep. This book is the standard that experts recommend.

Chapter 2

Nutrition

"I never get up in time for breakfast, and I never feel like eating in the morning."

"I'm so sick of the dining hall."

"I know I rely on food as a quick way to soothe myself. I can't break the habit."

"It's easier to grab food from a vending machine rather than cook."

"I wish there was a place to get free healthy lunch on campus. I usually skip lunch because I can't afford it, but I know that is making me too hungry to study as well as I could."

Mental health is greatly enhanced with healthy eating, especially eating what's right for our body and not someone else's. Healthy eating means eating the right variety and amount of food to keep us healthy, energized, and functioning at our best. No single food plan is right for every person. Eating a balanced traditional, paleo, vegetarian, or vegan diet can all be good choices.

This is one area where you can find as many opinions as there are experts. However, certain basics stay the same, which is to consume a balance of veggies, carbs, protein, fruits, fats, and a moderate number of extras (dessert has its place).

Proper nutrition and digestion lead to more energy, which in turn leads to more effective learning and studying — so it ends up being vitally important to create food habits that work for you. Conversely, not eating well can cause the body to break down in various ways or lead to increased anxiety.

In addition, sharing mealtimes with others is an opportunity to socialize and build community, which is another important goal.

WHY NUTRITION IS A CHALLENGE

In our modern world, it's a challenge to eat three healthy meals every day. It takes a lot of work, time, money, and energy to plan, buy, prepare, and eat healthy food. On top of that, we face a constant barrage of misinformation and conflicting advice about what constitutes a healthy diet. Nutrition research has been notoriously unscientific.

College students are pressed for time, have limited financial resources, and are often reluctant to slow down enough to eat a healthy meal — whether in the school's dining hall or preparing their own food in an apartment. When schedules are busy and money tight, healthy eating is often the first thing cut from the day. Even for students on a meal plan, eating in the dining hall can undermine developing a healthy eating routine, from the lack of control over meals to feeling overwhelmed by crowds and social stressors.

STRATEGIES

Value Eating Nutritious Food

First, value the importance of healthy eating and prioritize nutritious food. In your mind, repeat the mantra: *Eating healthy is important, and every day I will choose to eat as well as I can.*

Focus on a Balanced Diet

The USDA's MyPlate program (see resources at the end of this chapter) provides a good template for what makes a balanced diet: about half the plate should be vegetables and fruits, about a quarter protein, about a quarter complex carbohydrates, and a small amount of healthy fats.

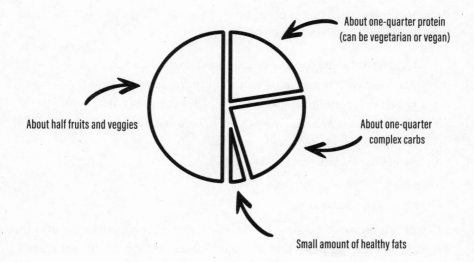

About one-quarter protein
(can be vegetarian or vegan)

About half fruits and veggies

About one-quarter
complex carbs

Small amount of healthy fats

Plate representing a healthy diet

Each meal, aim for this without being rigid or trying to be perfect (which can lead to eating disorders). Be flexible, but try to include these foods as the building blocks of your diet:

- **Vegetables:** carrots, celery, lettuce, corn, asparagus, cabbage, mushrooms, peas, turnips, kale, spinach, broccoli, and many more
- **Fruits:** apples, oranges, bananas, plums, peaches, pears, grapes, coconut, strawberries, blueberries, blackberries, and many more
- **Protein:** chicken, fish, beef, pork, eggs, milk, yogurt, cheese, beans, tofu, nuts, nut butters, and more
- **Complex carbohydrates:** whole-wheat bread, whole-wheat pasta, brown or wild rice, barley, quinoa, sweet or white potatoes, and more
- **Healthy fats:** olive oil, avocados, butter, mayonnaise, and more

Minimize Processed Foods and Sweets

In general, we feel better if processed and packaged foods are an occasional indulgence and not the foundation of our diet. Again, this isn't about being perfect or never eating chips or drinking soda, but minimize these things:

- Industrial foods, especially packaged snacks and canned or frozen food with ingredients you can't pronounce
- Foods that contain a lot of added sugars (a little is okay)
- Artificial sweeteners, unless you have a health reason to avoid regular sweeteners
- Sweetened drinks and soda

Create a Meal Schedule

If you are prone to missing meals, block out time on your calendar for meals. Include the place you will eat and the folks you will eat with, if that helps. (For more on time management, see chapter 34).

Be Aware of How Certain Foods Affect You

Pay attention to fluctuations in mood and energy and try to identify whether these are related to what you eat. Certain foods may not agree with us, but since everyone is different, you need to get to know your body. Here are some common system irritants:

- Dairy
- Wheat or other grains
- Nuts and seeds
- Deep-fried foods

Eat Breakfast

Many college students skip or put off breakfast, but this results in lower blood sugar, which can affect mood. Many students resist this suggestion; they complain they just aren't breakfast eaters. Yet I've found that when reluctant students agree to experiment with eating something to start their day, they always report experiencing a better mood — not just early on, but throughout the day. Breakfast doesn't have to mean a visit to the dining hall or cooking a full meal at home. Try some of these items, which you can keep on a bookshelf or in a minifridge:

- Protein bars
- Higher-protein, lower-sugar yogurt
- Hummus and baby carrots
- Peanut, sunflower seed, or another nut butter
- Fruit
- Milk or vegan milk
- Leftovers, like cold pizza

Visit the Dining Hall at Slower Times

If eating in a busy dining hall overwhelms you, try eating at off-times so you can feel more relaxed and it's easier to get the food options that are best for you. Of course, class and work schedules do not always allow this, but eating even a few serene meals each week may be beneficial.

Cook in Batches

If you're cooking and eating in an apartment, consider batch cooking: planning out and cooking a week's worth of food on the weekends. That way, you have plenty of healthy choices ready to go during the week when you have less time for meals.

Slow Down While Eating

Eating at a slower pace allows food to be digested properly and helps give our bodies the nutrition they need. In addition, using our senses to savor each bite of food is a wonderful mindfulness practice.

Gather with Others at Mealtime

Aim to eat at least one meal each day with friends or family. Socializing over food helps build community.

WHEN TO SEEK PROFESSIONAL HELP

"I usually feel run down by 2 p.m., and it gets in the way of my afternoon study plans. I'm skipping lunch because I'm pressed for time, and my classes are at the other end of campus from the dining hall. However, I started picking up a bag lunch after breakfast, before I head out to the science building. Now that I've started eating lunch again, my energy has bounced back in the afternoons."

— ANNIE

Eating Disorders

The latest research from the National Eating Disorders Association (see resources below) shows about one in three women and one in four men struggle with some type of disordered eating: restricting food intake, purging food calories through a variety of means (including severe overexercise with somewhat normal eating patterns), binge eating, emotional eating, and more. Eating disorders can reemerge or be exacerbated by the stressors of starting college and one or more challenging eating situations, such as a crowded dining hall, others watching what you eat, endless choices that don't seem healthy, and others talking about diet or body image issues (such as on social media). Eating disorders *must be treated by a specialist* and with a team approach (which might include a psychologist, psychiatrist, nutritionist, group therapy, medical care, and so on). College is a great time to get a handle on this illness — young adults are gaining more and more independence and developing the ability to take charge of their life and their health.

Food Insecurity

Though accurate statistics are hard to confirm, the American College Health Association estimates that one in five college students do not have reliable access to a sufficient quantity of affordable, nutritious food. Students are usually hesitant to make this fact known and reach out for help. Subsisting on ramen and mac and cheese isn't enough. If this is an issue for you, please reach out to a trusted staff member at your college to ask about food resources on campus.

RESOURCES

On Campus

- College health center: Many health centers have nutrition and food bank resources.
- College counseling center: Counselors can help identify the symptoms of an eating disorder, and they can recommend off-campus resources for treatment.
- College athletics department: College athletes usually have access to nutrition consultation.

"I used to reward myself with cheesy fries when I reached certain study goals because that's what everyone was talking about. But I noticed that I felt bloated and low on energy for a couple of hours after eating. I've brainstormed some other ways to treat myself for studying hard, such as watching a favorite show or going for a quick walk with a friend. My body is thanking me."

— DIEGO

Websites

- USDA MyPlate (www.myplate.gov): This USDA program provides lots of nutrition advice and suggestions for healthy eating.
- USDA Food and Nutrition (www.usda.gov/topics/food-and-nutrition): This site covers many areas of interest around nutrition, including basic nutrition recommendations, healthy recipes, and safe food storage.
- National Eating Disorders Association (www.nationaleatingdisorders.org): This resource includes an online screening tool, a helpline with phone and text options, and up-to-date resources on all types of eating disorders.
- Food Pantries (www.foodpantries.org) and Feeding America (www.feedingamerica.org): These organizations maintain lists of local free food banks.
- Food Empowerment Project (www.foodispower.org): This advocacy organization "seeks to create a more just and sustainable world by recognizing the power of one's food choices." They focus on abuse of farm animals, impacts on natural resources, unfair working conditions, and access to food in low-income areas.

Books

- *Intuitive Eating: A Revolutionary Anti-Diet Approach* by Elyse Resch and Evelyn Tribole: This book urges people to reject diet culture and to respect and listen to our bodies.
- *The Chemistry of Joy Workbook* by Henry Emmons, Susan Bourgerie, Carolyn Denton, and Sandra Kacher: This workbook includes a thorough chapter on improving diet for mental health.

Movies

- *Super Size Me*: This 2004 documentary by Morgan Spurlock examines the influence of the fast-food industry on society and personal health. For one month, Spurlock consumed only McDonald's food and documented the impacts on his body and mental health.
- *Fed Up*: This 2014 documentary by Stephanie Soechtig examines the role that sugar plays in our diets and how big business has downplayed the health risks of excess sugar consumption.

Chapter 3

Movement

"I want to exercise but I don't have time."

"I'm intimidated by all the jocks in the gym."

"I know I should exercise but I hate it."

"I don't feel okay if I don't exercise for two hours every day."

"I've been working out but my knees really hurt."

Physical movement, when done appropriately, is a critical component of mental and physical health. More and more research confirms that people need to move to be healthy. For example, with adequate physical exercise, our brains can focus better, we can fight the common cold more effectively, and we purge stress hormones and release calming hormones.

Like proper nutrition, exercise is a subject that generates almost as many opinions as there are writers. Most agree that there are three basic types of exercise: cardiovascular, strength, and flexibility. That said, the best exercise is the one that people will do regularly. No one agrees on what "regularly" means, but the general recommendation is to move in some manner on a daily basis and include a more rigorous workout one to three times per week.

WHY MOVEMENT IS A CHALLENGE

Our culture values being fit, but as a society, we don't make it easy for folks to get exercise. People are chronically overscheduled, even kids in grade school, leaving little time to dedicate to moving our bodies.

Exercise can also raise emotional issues, particularly related to body type, overall fitness, and body image. Those who don't have the "perfect" body (by whatever standard), struggle to stay fit, or don't like "typical" forms of exercise (going to the gym, playing sports) often struggle with discouraging self-judgment. Many health advocates are trying to change this, but cultural attitudes are difficult to shift.

In college, the main obstacle for students is carving out time in their packed schedules. Finding time to exercise absolutely takes dedication and creativity. However, no student has ever said, "Wow, regular exercise really doesn't help me." More often, I hear students say, "Regular exercise is the thing holding me together." I can't emphasize the importance of regular exercise enough.

Another roadblock is thinking there is a "right way" to exercise — that if we don't work out like a varsity athlete, it doesn't count or isn't legitimate. This is false.

Finally, pain also discourages students from exercising. This can be either physical or emotional pain. Feeling shame about our body or skills will naturally prevent us from finding the type of movement we enjoy. Meanwhile, physical issues, such as bad knees or a disability, obviously present a challenge to getting adequate exercise, but it can be done. It just may take more effort to find a strategy that feels good and is sustainable.

STRATEGIES

A note to athletes: If you are an athlete, you probably put in a ton of hours working out during your sport's season. However, don't ignore exercise during the offseason, or when you don't have mandated workouts. For one thing, it negatively impacts mental health to go from full activity to zero activity. Of course, it's also not healthy to maintain a heavy, in-season workout routine year-round, but during training breaks, consider walking or other less strenuous movement, such as some of the strategies below.

Prioritize Movement

Even on a busy day when you have a lot to do, moving for a few minutes can make a world of difference in your mental health. Continually look for ways to stay active in between and in the middle of other activities, even studying (see "Quick Stretches to Do While Studying," pages 320–21).

Ditch Perfectionism

You don't need to follow a rigid exercise schedule to get enough movement every day. In fact, many experts recommend getting in daily exercise through everyday movements, such as gardening, cleaning, or walking. Going to the playground with your kids or a family member counts! Be kind to yourself and put more movement in your life without being a drill sergeant.

Start Small

Starting small is especially important if you haven't been exercising at all. If walking is comfortable for you, take a brisk walk around campus between classes or before heading to the library. Commit to one walk per day. Then, if that goes well, try to take two walks a day. Many studies show that just a few minutes of walking each day can make a big difference to health and well-being. If walking is uncomfortable, consider what other form of gentle movement is available to you. Pick something and start there, with a small amount of movement every day.

Use the Buddy System

Setting up a regular exercise date with a friend makes it much more likely to happen. Commit to meeting up for a walk or a workout in the gym, or go dancing or take a yoga class together. Exercising with a friend also provides great social benefits.

Pick the Time of Day That Works Best for You

Be curious and experiment with exercising at different times of day. When feels best for your body? What is the best time for your schedule? Everyone is different. Some students love the morning; others squeeze

> "I thought the only legitimate exercise was working out in the exercise center! Now that I realize I can count salsa dancing — something I love — as exercise, I have joined the salsa club and a weekly dance class. I feel great and I'm making a great group of friends, too."
>
> — NELLY

in exercise during their lunch break; some like to exercise before dinner; and some prefer the early evening. Once you find the best time, make it your routine.

Plan Ahead and Set Reminders

Schedule movement the same way you schedule classes and meetups with friends. Add planned times to your calendar. Then build in reminders so you are prepared and don't forget. For instance, you might lay out your workout clothes the night before if you are going to exercise in the morning, or bring your gym bag with you to a morning class if you plan to exercise afterward. Set an alert on your phone with a cute emoji. Use your creativity.

Take an Exercise Class

Every campus offers a variety of physical education classes for students, either for credit or for recreation. Registering for an exercise class helps many people show up when they might otherwise put off exercising. There are also social benefits to exercising with others on a regular basis.

Exercise in Diverse Ways

The stereotypical vision of exercise includes heading to the gym, running on the treadmill, and lifting weights. That is great for folks who love those activities, but there are many other wonderful ways to get your body moving. If you have a disability or physical pain (unrelated to exercise), consider moving in water or any other activity that fits your mobility. Moving is moving, and it is important to do what works for you and what you enjoy. Here are some alternative ideas:

• Dance for ten minutes alone in your room (or invite friends!).
• Walk around or through campus or your neighborhood (choosing a safe route).

- For every fifty minutes of studying, walk around or stretch for ten minutes.
- Join a social dance club.
- Join a martial arts club.
- Go bike riding (see if your campus has free rental bikes).
- Play a movement-oriented video game, like Dance Dance Revolution, Wii Sports, or Pokémon Go.
- Play intramural sports.
- Follow a prerecorded dance or stretching routine online.

Establish a Routine

All these strategies are great, but best of all is creating a consistent exercise routine every week. Once you identify the types of movement you prefer, adopt them as your regular strategy for getting enough movement in your life. When regular exercise becomes automatic, it's much easier to maintain, since the habits become ingrained. Plus, you don't have to think about it, leaving more brain space for studies.

"I'm the type of person that needs more of a goal for my fitness because I can tell that I don't get out there enough without a goal. Not exercising is causing me to feel more stressed. I brainstormed with some friends and picked running in a local 5K race that is a few months away. Of course, my friends said they would run with me. This has focused my running and kept me motivated to keep a regular schedule, with the benefit that I often go out running with friends, besides my main goal of stress reduction being achieved."

— LUYEN

WHEN TO SEEK PROFESSIONAL HELP

If your body is in pain when you walk or exercise, please seek medical attention. Start with your campus health center. Similarly, if you have a physical disability or can't find a form of movement that is comfortable, seek advice through campus resources, such as the health center, athletic center, or disability center.

Conversely, if exercising itself is causing anxiety or stress — such as if missing a workout causes intense fear of getting out of shape or gaining weight — consider seeking counseling. There might be underlying anxieties that exercise is bringing up.

RESOURCES

On Campus

- College health center: Come here to have staff assess any medical issues that are interfering with exercise.
- College disability office: If you have a disability, this office will help you find appropriate forms of movement. They can also help find access to needed assistive technology.
- College counseling center: If exercise is causing anxiety or stress, counselors can help assess what the issue is (such as an eating disorder).
- College athletics department: Many college athletic facilities have staff who help students design an exercise routine and are a great source of advice.

Websites

- Blue Zones (www.bluezones.com/2018/01/what-exercise-best -happy-healthy-life): This organization provides advice and information based on the types of physical activities done by the longest lived people around the world.
- "The Spoon Theory" by Christine Miserandino (www.butyou dontlooksick.com/articles/written-by-christine/the-spoon -theory): Miserandino has written a wonderful explanation of what it is like to live with a hidden disability, and how hard it can be to find the energy to exercise.
- World Health Organization, "Physical Activity." (www.who.int /news-room/fact-sheets/detail/physical-activity): The World Health Organization provides facts and research about physical activity and suggests recommended activity levels.

Books

- *Physical Activity Guidelines for Americans* by the US Department of Health and Human Services (www.health.gov/sites/default

/files/2019-09/Physical_Activity_Guidelines_2nd_edition.pdf): This is a comprehensive guide on the benefits of and strategies to getting physical activity. It's available free online as a downloadable PDF.

Chapter 4

Substance Use

"I can't relax and socialize at a party unless I'm drunk."

"I smoke weed before bed because that's the only way I can get to sleep."

"I buy Ritalin in the library to use as a study drug. It works great, but then I get depressed when it wears off."

"I'm anxious and jittery all day after I have my Starbucks."

"I can't remember to take my meds every day. I think I'm taking them five out of seven days."

The substances we put into our bodies affect our mental health. By "substances," I'm referring to alcohol, cannabis, nicotine, caffeine, party drugs, study drugs, and also prescribed medications.

All of these substances change our brain chemistry. For instance, alcohol is a depressant; cannabis can make the brain fuzzy; study drugs speed us up, then let us down; and psychotropic meds help stabilize mood, but only if taken as directed. Today, about one in four students is taking, and needs, a mental health med. While these medications can be incredibly helpful, it is important to take them correctly (as directed, and at the same time each day) and to avoid substances that interact with the meds.

Just as with other topics in this book, self-awareness is essential when it comes to how substances affect us. With recreational substances, some students discover they can drink socially on the weekends and see no ill effects to their academic or social life; for them, drinking is just something that's fun to do. Other students know they can't drink or smoke anything because it interacts with their health in a negative way. With prescribed medications, especially mental health meds, some students do better taking their meds in the morning, while some find that taking them before bed works best. Sometimes, the only way to learn what is right for you is to be curious and experiment.

Some people choose to avoid substances altogether, but especially those who have a family history of addiction or have already fought for their sobriety.

WHY SUBSTANCES ARE A CHALLENGE

Our "instant society" supports instant solutions, and alcohol and cannabis are typically regarded as quick, easy ways to reduce stress and relax. These substances also "do the job," though not necessarily in a sustainable or healthy way. A couple of drinks in, and we may find it easier to forget our troubles or talk more comfortably to a stranger. But while these substances may provide a short-term reprieve from anxiety, stress, or any uncomfortable emotion, they are not productive solutions that resolve the source of those feelings. Rather, being "under the influence" more often covers up or masks the real issues, which need to be dealt with; these issues might include low self-esteem, social anxiety, or a lack of social skills. Further, as most know, long-term or heavy use of drugs and alcohol can lead to addiction and be very harmful.

Our culture sometimes regards college as synonymous with a "four-year party." This attitude can make it hard for students to stick to their own values and choices. If everyone around us appears to be partying as hard as possible, we can feel an urge to join them in order to fit in. Research shows that binge drinking is "contagious" among peers, and following the crowd can create a greater risk of drinking alcohol or smoking cannabis at dangerous levels.

For students, living in close quarters with others and having multiple opportunities to socialize means that deciding whether or how much to drink or smoke is an ongoing, continual issue. Each occasion where substances are present necessitates making a choice about them.

Meanwhile, substances like caffeine, nicotine, and "study drugs" provide a boost of energy so students can stay awake longer and study more. These substances can seem necessary to succeed at college or get straight As. This mindset can lead students to use Ritalin or Adderall — even though they have not been prescribed these medications to help with a diagnosed condition — to aid their productivity. These substances can sometimes mask an unhealthy or imbalanced lifestyle (one lacking adequate sleep and nutrition). However, "what goes up must come down," and the rebound effect after taking these substances can make fatigue worse, producing a painful cycle.

Finally, it's important to acknowledge that, even when students have a condition that warrants their use, mental health medications are a complex challenge in themselves. They can be overprescribed or underprescribed, and students may find it difficult to develop and maintain a consistent daily routine that allows them to take medications regularly as prescribed.

STRATEGIES

Below, I address each type of chemical separately, and for each, I address these issues:

- Identifying your values related to the substance
- Developing self-understanding about the reasons for use
- Being self-aware of how the substance affects you
- Deciding on the safest strategy for using the substance
- Overviewing the negative consequences associated with the substance
- Knowing the warning signs of abuse or addiction

Alcohol

In a journal, write about your experiences with and values related to alcohol use. Reflect on how your values around alcohol might contrast with cultural values at your college.

- **Reasons for use:** If you drink, reflect on why you do. What attracts you to drink alcohol? Here are some common reasons:

  - To have fun
  - To make socializing easier
  - To be cool or part of the crowd
  - To cope with loneliness or emotional pain
  - To be independent from family
  - To experiment and learn about oneself

- **Effects and habits:** Be curious about how alcohol affects you. What are your alcohol use habits?

  - How many drinks make you feel relaxed? When is drinking the most fun?
  - How often do you drink "too much," or past the point of having fun? Does "pregaming" (drinking before going out) or binge drinking cause problems?
  - Do you feel a desire to drink every night, every weekend, or regularly?

- **Strategies:** If you choose to drink, develop safe strategies for drinking. These can include the following:

  - Know how many drinks is your limit.
  - Ask a friend to look out for you.
  - Drink a full glass of water between each alcoholic beverage.
  - Bring your own cup to a party, so you can control what you drink.

- **Negative consequences:** Do you notice any negative consequences from drinking?

  - Are you hungover and unable to study the day after drinking?
  - Do you engage in behaviors while drinking that are at odds with your values (such as hooking up or fighting)?
  - Has drinking negatively affected your grades or activities?
  - Have you been written up by your college and lost campus privileges for excessive drinking?

- **Warning signs:** Here are some warning signs of abuse or addiction:
  - You regularly drink more than you planned.
  - Your tolerance has gone up, so you regularly drink more to feel the same effect.
  - You are regularly missing assignments or skipping class.
  - You regularly drink more than your friends do.
  - You feel you need to drink in order to be okay.
  - You are shaky in the mornings after drinking, or you feel anxious or irritable when you aren't drinking.
  - You black out frequently when you drink.

Cannabis

In a journal, write about your experiences with and values around cannabis. How do your values around cannabis contrast with cultural values at your college?

- **Reasons for use:** If you smoke pot, reflect on why you do. What attracts you to use cannabis? Here are some common reasons:
  - To feel relaxed and minimize anxiety
  - To cope with loneliness or emotional pain
  - To socialize and connect with friends who also smoke
  - To be cool or part of the crowd
  - To be independent from family
  - To experiment and learn about oneself

- **Effects and habits:** Be curious about how cannabis affects you. What are your cannabis use habits?
  - How much do you smoke to relax and have fun?
  - At what point do you smoke "too much," or past the point of having fun? Are there any other negative impacts, like trouble getting a deep sleep?
  - Do you feel a desire to smoke every night, every weekend, or regularly?

- **Strategies**: If you choose to use cannabis, develop safe strategies for use. These can include the following:
    - If possible, discern the potency of the cannabis before you smoke or ingest it.
    - Take one hit, then wait and see how it affects you. That might be all you need.
    - Use safer smoking devices, such as glass or brass pipes.
    - Take "vacations" from cannabis use in order to avoid developing a tolerance.

- **Negative consequences**: Do you notice any negative consequences from cannabis use?
    - Are you groggy or unmotivated the day after smoking?
    - Do you engage in behaviors while high that are at odds with your values?
    - Have your grades or activities been negatively affected?

- **Warning signs**: Here are some warning signs of abuse or addiction:
    - You become irritable or anxious if you don't smoke daily (or multiple times a day).
    - Your tolerance has gone up.
    - You are regularly missing assignments or skipping class.
    - You have insomnia and in general are more fidgety or agitated.
    - You have low motivation or often feel bored.

Cigarettes and Vaping

In a journal, write about your experiences with and values around nicotine use, whether smoking cigarettes or vaping. How do your values around cigarettes/vaping contrast with cultural values at your college?

- **Reasons for use**: If you smoke nicotine, reflect on why you do. What attracts you to smoking? Here are some common reasons:
    - To relax and reenergize
    - To take a break during work or studying

- To make friends with other smokers
- To enjoy a pleasant ritual
- Smoking feels natural and familiar, since your family smoked

- **Effects and habits:** Be curious about how nicotine affects you. What are your cigarette/vaping use habits?
  - How much do you need to smoke to relax and reenergize?
  - When do you feel the urge to smoke/vape (such as walking to class or after meals)?
  - Do you most often smoke/vape by yourself or with others?

- **Strategies:** If you use nicotine regularly, understand that there are no "safe strategies" for use. The jury is in and definitive: Smoking cigarettes is hazardous to your health. While some still maintain that vaping is "better" than cigarettes, the data is growing that vaping is also harmful, and the industry is unregulated.

- **Negative consequences:** Do you notice any negative consequences from smoking/vaping?
  - Does the expense of smoking impact your budget?
  - Does smoking get in the way of socializing or activities?
  - Have you noticed any negative health effects, such as breathing difficulties or frequent respiratory illness?

- **Warning signs:** Here are some warning signs of abuse or addiction:
  - You have tried to quit or reduce your use and can't.
  - Even when you are sick, you still smoke/vape.

Study Drugs

In a journal, write about your experiences with and values around study drugs — that is, any over-the-counter stimulant or nonprescribed use of Ritalin or Adderall. How do your values around study drugs contrast with cultural values at your college?

- **Reasons for use:** If you use study drugs, reflect on why you do. What attracts you to taking a study drug? Here are some common reasons:

- ○   To stay focused
- ○   To improve productivity
- ○   To be able to work or study when you are already tired or want to put off sleep

- **Effects and habits:** Be curious about how study drugs affect you. What are your study drug use habits?

  - ○   Do you use a study drug daily, weekly, or whenever a big assignment is due?
  - ○   When you take the drug, are you able to focus better than usual?
  - ○   Do you have a specific study goal before you take the study drug?
  - ○   Are your grades better, or are they the same or lower, when you use these drugs?

- **Strategies:** If you choose to use study drugs, understand that there are no "safe strategies" for use. Studies show that college students get better grades without taking nonprescribed Ritalin or Adderall, so students are actually better off not using them.

  If you take these drugs because you believe you have undiagnosed and untreated ADHD, then seek professional medical help.

- **Negative consequences:** Do you notice any negative outcomes from taking study drugs?

  - ○   Do you feel jittery or distracted after taking study drugs?
  - ○   Have you ever felt like you needed to go to the ER due to heart palpitations?
  - ○   Have you struggled to get a restful night's sleep after taking study drugs?
  - ○   Are these drugs expensive, and do they impact your budget?
  - ○   Are you using medication that a friend with the prescription needs?

- **Warning signs:** Here are some warning signs of abuse or addiction:
  - ○   You are developing a tolerance.
  - ○   You notice withdrawal symptoms — such as depression, confusion, or irritability — if you don't use.

- o   Your friends comment that you are overly talkative or sociable.
- o   You feel invincible or a heightened mood.
- o   You have consistent physical symptoms like dry mouth, nausea, and vomiting.
- o   You experience heightened nervousness, anxiety, and panic.
- o   Much of your day is spent finding sources for the drug and/or recovering from taking it.

Caffeine and Sugar

In a journal, write about your experiences with caffeine and sugar, which includes caffeinated beverages — such as coffee, tea, sodas, and energy drinks like Red Bull or Monster — and sugary food and drinks intended as stimulants. What are your values around these, and how do they contrast with cultural values at your college?

- **Reasons for use:** If you consume excess caffeine or sugar as a stimulation, reflect on why you do. What attracts you to caffeine and sugar? Here are some common reasons:
  - o   They are delicious treats that also give quick energy.
  - o   They are often part of fun activities with friends.
  - o   They are part of important daily rituals.
  - o   They are part of family traditions.

- **Effects and habits:** Be curious about how caffeine and sugar affect you. What are your caffeine or sugar use habits?
  - o   How much coffee or tea do you typically drink in the morning to wake up?
  - o   Do you rely on an energy drink to get you through certain classes or times of day?
  - o   Do you have a balanced meal before you have a sugary treat?
  - o   How do you feel after a caffeine or sugar treat? Do you notice anything special?

- **Strategies:** If you drink caffeine or eat sugary treats, be mindful of how much you consume, and set limits, either overall per day or in particular situations. Overindulging is what can lead to problems. However, everyone's body is different, so you might not be able to consume the same amount as others without negative effects.

- **Negative consequences:** Do you notice any negative consequences from caffeine or sugar intake?

  o   Do you feel jittery or struggle with insomnia? Excess caffeine, even as little as one cup, can cause symptoms that mimic anxiety in some people.

  o   Does caffeine or sugar consumption actually give you less energy than when you don't consume them?

  o   Is buying regular fancy drinks or sugary treats expensive and impacting your budget?

- **Warning signs:** Here are some warning signs of abuse or addiction:

  o   Whenever you reduce your caffeine intake, you get a headache or become irritable. These are withdrawal symptoms, and if they arise, reduce your consumption more slowly.

  o   Eating too much sugar (in any form) is undermining a healthy diet.

Prescribed Medications

To be clear, if someone is taking prescribed medications to treat a diagnosed condition (of any kind), they should take those medications. However, be aware of any negative symptoms they might be causing (emotional or physical) and discuss them with a medical professional. The amount or type of medication might need adjusting.

College students often find it a challenge to develop a routine for taking daily medications consistently as prescribed. Here are some ideas for developing a routine and for avoiding missed doses:

- Pick the time of day for taking meds that you feel you can be most consistent with.
- Tie your meds to an established habit, such as brushing your teeth.

"I admit that I smoke cannabis daily, especially at night to help relax, socialize with friends, and let go of the day. I know it's getting in the way of going to bed on time, and also I've been struggling to wake up every morning. I often miss my first class, which makes me spiral down, sometimes missing all my classes and even causing me to be unable to do any homework. I thought I would try to take a total break from smoking at night. Though it was very difficult for me, I told my friends and they supported me. I started playing my guitar at night and that helped. I was able to wake up much more easily, which started my day in a radically better way. This included attending class and being motivated to study."

— FRED

- Create a visual cue in your space that will help you remember, such as leaving the bottle of pills where you can see it, or writing yourself a note.
- Use an app or an alarm on your phone to cue you.
- Schedule the time for your med on your online calendar, which can send you reminders via alert or email.
- In a daily planner, use a grid to check off when you take your medicine every day.
- Use a weekly pill box, and make a ritual of refilling it on the same day each week.
- Develop a buddy system with someone else who is also taking a med. You can both agree to check in with the other as a reminder (via text and so on).

WHEN TO SEEK PROFESSIONAL HELP

If you have concerns about your use of any chemical or substance, it is important to seek the advice of a trusted mentor or medical professional. If your college has a good health center, start there.

In general, here are some signs and symptoms that might warrant a trip to the doctor:

- Your tolerance for the chemical has increased.
- You are preoccupied with using the substance.
- You use by yourself.
- The substance is changing your life in a negative way.
- You notice more anxious or depressed feelings and think they may be tied to substance use.

RESOURCES

On Campus

- College wellness center: These usually have online modules about substance use and abuse and local recovery referrals.
- College counseling center: Counselors can help assess whether negative chemical use has become addictive or not. They can provide support for changing habits and recommend referrals to off-campus providers for longer-term addiction treatment.
- College medical center: These can provide advice about general health and mental health issues and help with taking prescribed medications appropriately. They can also provide referrals to off-campus providers.

"I love my daily extra-large espresso mocha drink with whipped cream. It truly motivates me. However, I noticed that my anxiety about school was ramping way up, and a friend suggested it was connected to my caffeine and sugar use. I agreed to try one less pump of syrup and substitute decaf for a few days to see if it made a difference. It did. I am much less jittery and my heart is not racing. I still worry about school, but I am able to deal with it in a calmer way."

— TAHARI

Websites

- ULifeline (www.ulifeline.org): This online resource is focused specifically on college mental health. ULifeline offers a text and phone line for immediate help. Resources include general information and a "self-evaluator" that helps you evaluate your issues.
- The Jed Foundation (www.jedfoundation.org/mental-health -resource-center): This national nonprofit foundation promotes emotional wellness for teens and young adults. They have a robust section on alcohol and substance use.
- Substance Abuse and Mental Health Services Administration (SAMHSA; www.samhsa.gov, 800-662-4357): This federal organization runs a confidential, free, 24/7 hotline for anyone dealing with mental health or substance use issues. They provide referrals to local treatment facilities, support groups, and community-based organizations.

Books

- *Sober Curious: The Blissful Sleep, Greater Focus, Limitless Presence, and Deep Connection Awaiting Us All on the Other Side of Alcohol* by Ruby Warrington: This book is a conversation starter about what life might be like without alcohol, and it's a counterpoint to the drinking culture of college (and after college).
- *Buzzed: The Straight Facts About the Most Used and Abused Drugs from Alcohol to Ecstasy* by Cynthia Kuhn: If you want to know how a substance works and how it affects your body, this book is thorough and fact-based.

Chapter 5

Quiet Time

"I feel really anxious and have a lot of negative self-talk....I'm scheduled from 8 a.m. to 11 p.m., and I really have no time to myself, but everything I'm doing is really important and I don't want to let go of any of it."

"I just want to be with my friends all the time. I stay up too late, but then I have a hard time getting to sleep."

"I feel empty and don't find my activities to feel as meaningful to me as I'd like...but I don't like to just sit around. I want my life to always be productive."

"I watch TikTok or Netflix every afternoon after class because I'm worn out from class. But they don't really help me feel better."

"I work on homework every Friday and Saturday night. I'm scared I won't get it all done if I ever slow down."

Our 24/7 culture promotes being always on — no more bankers' hours or Sabbath days — and it values the highest productivity, no matter the cost. We focus on multiple screens, rather than nature or other people, which creates sensory overload. The bar for what we perceive to be success is constantly going up, as is our fear of failure (a very strong feeling). We value "busy busy" and view taking time to just be with ourselves as a luxury. Our bodies have become accustomed to being in high-alert, fight-or-flight mode much of the time, which is designed to help us respond quickly in the face of life-threatening dangers, but the resulting stress takes a toll. At times it seems hard to know where we're at on a deeper level.

How can we create some balance in our bodies? How can we shift out of fight-or-flight mode (which is related to the sympathetic nervous system) and into "rest-and-digest" mode (related to the parasympathetic nervous system)? The answer is simple: *Slow down*. Once we slow down and tell our bodies and minds that we are safe, we can replenish and connect with ourselves in a deeper way.

WHY QUIET TIME IS A CHALLENGE

It is no accident that, in general in society, stress and anxiety levels are rising as quiet time is falling. Our society has done a great job of teaching us how to move forward, work hard, and excel, but it hasn't modeled how to recharge our batteries. This is true for our whole culture, not just college students. However, this has sparked a growing interest in all the ways we can slow down and foster mental and emotional wellness. In fact, talk about sustainability for humans mirrors the need for sustainability in our environment.

Students often scoff at the suggestion to slow down. Their schedules are packed — with far too much homework, extracurricular activities, part-time work, and social (or family) plans — and they argue it's impossible to carve out time for daily (or weekly) periods of quiet time or "doing nothing."

Further, students feel the cultural pressure to be productive and accomplished and not be seen as "lazy." Just like everyone, they often struggle to accept the seeming paradox that occasionally slowing down actually enhances our ability to achieve all our goals.

STRATEGIES

Value Quiet Time

If you doubt the value of taking some quiet time for yourself, try it out for a while. Experiment with the strategies in this chapter and see for yourself. Our culture doesn't necessarily support this idea, and people sometimes dismiss seemingly "unproductive" activities, so people sometimes need to discover the benefits for themselves. Once you do, I'm sure you will find that setting aside some quiet time for yourself on a daily basis will help you feel better and meet your goals, too.

Be Curious and Experiment

What qualifies as "quiet time" for one person might not work for someone else. Be curious and explore what works best for you; avoid being judgmental or assuming what you "should" do. As the strategies here make clear, quiet time doesn't necessarily mean doing nothing, though it could. Rather, it is anything and everything that refreshes body, mind, and spirit. Not only is every person different, but so is every day. Take a walk, read a book, practice an instrument, draw, meditate, talk to a friend — make time to do whatever feels good. That will be the right thing for you.

Lose Yourself in Nature

We intuitively know that being outside enjoying nature — either by ourselves or with others — feels good and renews our energy. Connecting to nature just helps us feel more comfortable in our bodies. Scientific studies in ecopsychology, ecotherapy, or green therapy back this up. They show how nature benefits our general well-being and a host of mental health issues.

There are many possibilities for making nature a part of your day while at college. These can vary in intensity — from training with your varsity team outside for a couple of hours to going on a fifteen-minute walk before class. Whatever you choose, enjoying nature is a great way to relieve stress and increase your mental health. Try these:

- Play with an animal; visit a local shelter, or see if your campus has a program where they bring in dogs for students to visit.
- Visit water. This could take many forms: a local fountain, river, pond, or any body of water. Many people say the sound of water is very calming.
- Take a leisurely walk or run outside (but not in a competitive

way). Perhaps treat a slow walk as meditation. Try walking without headphones playing.

- Pull weeds in a garden, walk barefoot in the grass, or otherwise get your hands and feet dirty. Join a campus gardening club. Touching the earth helps us feel grounded, and studies show that soil microbes help us feel better.
- Take a few minutes to look up at the sky and take in the world with a feeling of wonder or awe.
- Study outside when the weather permits, or sit by a window with a view outdoors.
- Plan your route to class so you walk by gardens or through nature, and challenge yourself to use all five senses as you walk.
- Plan a regular weekly or daily walk with a friend.
- Find work in campus groundskeeping.
- Participate in an outdoor intramural sport.
- Sit under a tree, then give the tree a hug.

Engage in a Creative Activity

Creative pursuits that engage our mind and often our body have been shown to lower stress, increase positive feelings, and help activate a "flow state" similar to meditation. Pick any activity that appeals to you; experiment with things you don't usually do. When done in a group, some of these activities also provide social benefits.

- Read a book for pleasure. Yes, college students read a lot, but they rarely read books that *they* have chosen. For twenty minutes at night, read something that interests or engages you.
- Read or write poetry.
- Take up a handiwork project, such as knitting, crocheting, cross stitch, wood carving, or model building. Spending a few minutes a day creating something for yourself or as a gift for someone else can make a precious break from studying.
- Sketch or draw, or color in a coloring book. Art isn't just for art

majors! Visual expression can open up a side of ourselves that is often neglected.

- Model with clay or Play-Doh.
- Solve a puzzle game, like Sudoku, or put together a jigsaw puzzle.
- Sing or play a musical instrument. Quiet time doesn't have to be quiet! Making music can create a sense of calm — but only if you play for enjoyment, not to be "perfect."
- Visit an art museum.
- Listen to calming music.

Get Physical

Doing something kinetic can also be calming and qualify as "quiet time." Many people benefit from activities involving movement. All the activities under "Lose Yourself in Nature," above, are good choices. Or consider taking a yoga class or a slow martial arts, such as tai chi or qigong (which emphasize breathing).

Another idea is to treat an everyday activity like brewing and drinking a cup of herbal tea like a meditative slow movement. As you prepare the drink, use all your senses and savor the entire process, which can be centering and induce contentment.

Practice Your Faith or Spirituality

The practice of faith or spirituality is a traditional way to slow down and connect to something greater than ourselves. This can be a traditional religious faith or simply gratitude for being alive. See "Prayers — Religious and Otherwise" (pages 321–22) for more on this, but here are some possibilities:

- Daily prayers, with yourself or others
- Daily meditations
- Daily study of sacred texts, words of wisdom, or devotional readings
- Writing daily in a gratitude journal

"I was overwhelmed with all my studies, but mostly I felt homesick for my hometown in China. I was also exhausted from talking and learning exclusively in English. I felt I couldn't allow myself time to do anything that wasn't a résumé builder, as my parents had made so many sacrifices to get me to college in the United States. After talking to my adviser, however, I agreed to take twenty minutes before bed to read a Chinese-language magazine or book. This new practice gave me much comfort and peace. What a surprise that something so small could help me get through the day."

— LI

Practice Mindfulness Meditation

Similar to spirituality, mindfulness meditation gives us the chance to "just be" and accept ourselves as we are in each given moment. Doing a sitting meditation provides numerous benefits: stress reduction, improved ability to concentrate, better sleep, slower reactivity to problems, and more self-acceptance, just to name a few. For more advice, including instructions, see "Meditation" (page 318).

Learn "Instant" Calming Techniques

This might sound like a contradiction, but you can practice "quiet time" at any time, even during other activities. When you feel worked up or overwhelmed, learn strategies for finding calm and peace in the moment, wherever you are.

- **Press pause:** Take one slow deep breath, filling your lungs from bottom to top. As you do, feel your ribs expand to the sides and the back. Hold your breath for just a moment before exhaling as slowly as you can.
- **Square breathing:** For instructions of this slow-breathing exercise, see "Calm a Racing Mind" (page 14).
- **5-4-3-2-1:** This technique focuses mainly on the senses. Notice five things you can *see* right now, four things you can *touch* and feel, three things you can *hear* right now, two things you can *smell*, and end with one good thing you can *think* about yourself.
- **Cool or warm:** Hold a bottle of cold water or a cup of warm tea in your hands. Take a drink and feel the coldness or warmth seep into your body. Take your time and experience the cold or warmth in your mouth.

WHEN TO SEEK PROFESSIONAL HELP

If you struggle to find ways to relax, can only relax when you use substances, or you feel you don't deserve to take any downtime, then it would be worthwhile to reach out to a trusted peer, mentor, or campus life staff for help and advice. Quiet time is about taking care of yourself.

"I had been struggling with general anxiety and adjustment when I first got to college. I thought that trying a daily meditation practice might be helpful and decided to join a campus meditation group. I loved the weekly meeting and the sense of calm it offered. It made a difference for my anxiety even though I wasn't able to establish a daily meditation practice."

— MALCOLM

RESOURCES

On Campus

- College wellness center: These will likely have classes on mindfulness meditation or other stress-reducing classes or activities.
- College religious services: Find out what programming is available for religious practice, or ask a chaplain for mentorship on how to develop a personal prayer practice.
- College athletics department: These usually offer courses on yoga or meditative martial arts.
- College counseling center: Counselors can provide support and help for developing calming techniques as part of overall mental wellness.
- College student organizations: Every campus has a wide range of groups that focus on gardening, outdoor adventures, crafting, book clubs, and much more.

Websites

- Do Nothing for 2 Minutes (www.donothingfor2minutes.com): This website is very simple: A clock times out two minutes and asks you to "do nothing." If you touch your keyboard, the clock starts the countdown again. It's a fun and easy way to take a quick break.

Books

- *Rest Is Resistance: A Manifesto* by Tricia Hersey: This book is a political take on why rest is so vital and healing, especially for Black Americans.
- *The Mindful Twenty-Something: Life Skills to Handle Stress ... & Everything Else* by Holly B. Rogers: This book covers mindfulness techniques to help students stay grounded when life is busy.
- *The Nature Fix: Why Nature Makes Us Happier, Healthier, and More Creative* by Florence Williams: This book uncovers the powers of the natural world to improve health, promote reflection and innovation, and strengthen our relationships.
- *Forest Bathing: How Trees Can Help You Find Health and Happiness* by Qing Li: This is a popular guide to the therapeutic Japanese practice of shinrin-yoku, the art and science of how trees can promote health and happiness. It includes beautiful forest photographs.

Chapter 6

Your Personal Body Culture

"I get headaches a couple of times a week. When I slow down and do some yoga moves, it really helps."

"I didn't want to admit that I always feel terrible for a couple of hours after I eat pizza."

"I started to heal from my sexual assault when I realized my numbness was a way for me to protect myself from feeling any sexual feelings."

"I was trying to dress for my partner before. Now I am dressing in thrift store T-shirts and I feel more like myself."

"When my room is tidy, I study and sleep better. I hate to admit it, but a chaotic room leaves me feeling chaotic!"

This chapter addresses our own personal culture around how we treat our body. It's about our awareness of our body in a deeper, more philosophical way. Western culture often ignores the body and heart in order to focus on the head — which is a bit like focusing on productivity without considering ethics or values.

The reality is that we are bodies, and our bodies have a lot to tell us.

WHY BODY CULTURE IS A CHALLENGE

In general, we often avoid tuning in to our bodies. We tell ourselves that we are too busy to slow down and really pay attention, but in fact, it can be painful and even frightening to fully experience how bad some parts of our body are feeling. We are taught to power through and tough out pain or discomfort rather than acknowledge that there might be more serious underlying problems that our pain is trying to show us.

In our culture, accepting our bodies just as they are is an uphill battle. Body awareness and care is a challenge for many reasons:

- Our culture, and especially social media, present an idealized image of how we should look — that is, thin, rich (wearing brand-name clothes), fit or buff, cisgender and hetero, energetic, white, and so on. But media rarely affirms us for being the way we are.
- Our culture seldom values physical awareness. Rather, we are usually taught to put on a good front and hide our pain or feelings of bodily discomfort. This is what happens when a parent tells their child to stop crying when they fall down.
- There are few role models for how to care for our bodies, clothes, or living space.
- Our culture is "anti-rest." We are supposed to be productive all the time or to go hard with socializing. Few teach us how to cope with difficult sensations in a healthy way, such as slowing down and resting or exploring whether physical symptoms are connected to our thoughts or feelings.
- We may have experienced others hurting our bodies, and as a result our bodies have become a space to be avoided.
- We may have been bullied for our looks, and then internalized those horrible messages.

STRATEGIES

Listen to Your Body's Signals

Value bodily awareness, and listen to how your body is feeling. Often tight shoulders, a painful back, a stomachache, or a headache are the first clues that something important needs attention. Many students have told me things like, "I didn't realize my headaches were so tied to my test anxiety!" Conversely, many students have physical issues that impact their academics or social life — such as low iron, allergies, a concussion — and getting the appropriate treatment has been life-changing for them.

Use the ABC Method: Awareness, Being, Choosing

This is one of many methods to help bring yourself into the moment and explore what is going on without judgment. The ABC method stands for "awareness, being, choosing." This three-step process helps us make sense of the times when our experience, thoughts, or emotions seem overwhelming or impossible to cope with. This method guides us to acknowledge and name what is happening, which provides a tiny bit of distance from what we are experiencing. This then allows us to gain some perspective and make a more conscious choice for how we want to respond in the moment. The ABC method is based on years of research and practice in cognitive behavior therapy, mindfulness-based cognitive therapy, and dialectical behavior therapy.

I use this approach for exploring thoughts and emotions in parts 3 and 4. Here is a summary:

Awareness: What are you feeling in your body right now? Run your awareness from the top of your head to the tips of your toes, slowly, to assess what your body is experiencing and where. You can do the same with thoughts and emotions.

Being: Be curious and accepting about what you find, rather than dismissive, harsh, or judgmental, even if the information is hard to accept — such as, "I've had the same backache for a week." Just notice and take in the information, and name the problem without denying it or berating yourself.

Choosing: Once you honestly assess how your body feels (or any difficult thoughts or emotions), you give yourself the freedom to choose what to do about it. Sometimes, the choice is to do nothing and just let the feeling be. Sometimes you might choose to seek help, such as make an appropriate doctor appointment. And sometimes, the best intervention might be simpler — asking for a hug from a friend, snuggling with a pet, having a warm cup of tea, and so on.

Take a Body-Mind Movement Class

Body-mind movement classes, such as dance, yoga, or martial arts, may help you connect your mind to your physical feelings. When looking for a class, it is especially important to find one where the teacher emphasizes listening to the body rather than focusing on moving in a perfect way.

Practice Self-Acceptance

In your journal, write a list of the ways you judge your body. Society presents us with so many "shoulds" about appearance — enough to fill a whole book — that can lead us to negatively judge ourselves. Here are some common examples:

"I have too much fat in my belly."
"I should have thicker biceps."
"My skin is too dark."

Next, try to identify where the judging voice comes from. You might discover that it comes from a TV advertisement, from an Instagram post, or from relatives or friends. This is an important step, as it helps transform the voice in your head from being "the truth" to someone's opinion. We don't have to believe someone's opinion!

Here are some examples:

"My mom told me I should be a size 6."
"The coach says there will be hell to pay if I don't gain at least
      twenty pounds over the summer."
"The bus driver called me shorty."

Next, ask yourself who you think you will be, or what you will gain, if your body fits these expectations. How will you feel to lose ten pounds, or to have six-pack abs, or to get rid of acne or a zit?

The good news is that you can choose to feel that way right now!

Imagine you've been handed a magic wand that allows you to change whatever you want about your body. Choose to feel that way even though you don't have a magic wand.

Here are some examples:

"I will be confident enough to talk to people."
"I will feel good about myself."
"I will focus on the moment instead of worrying about my looks."

Find a way to love and honor where you are right now. It might sound like a paradox, but choosing to accept — and love, if possible — where we are right now, instead of judging ourselves harshly, will lead us to treat our bodies better and to feel better.

What can you do to feel good about yourself right now? Here are some examples:

- Wear clothes that fit.
- Feel proud to work out in the weight room.
- Lavish a favorite oil or lotion all over.
- Only use makeup that brings you joy.

Practice seeing yourself accurately instead of judging yourself harshly. How you talk to yourself is important. (For more on self-talk, see part 3.)

Here are some examples of positive self-talk:

"I choose to love myself just the way I am."
Look in a mirror and say: "I love you just the way you are."
"My body is just right for me."

Shut Down Negative Body Talk

If you have friends who talk negatively about diet, exercise, or body image — such as disparaging dessert or how their own body looks — do what feels appropriate to minimize your exposure to their unhealthy body talk. Sometimes, that might mean spending less time with certain people, but with good friends, simply ask them to stop. This might seem easier said than done, but it is very important. Here are some examples of how to phrase this request:

> "I love having lunch with you, but when you express negative body talk, I get triggered. Can we stop talking about our bodies?"
>
> "When we have these diet discussions, I struggle with my body image stuff, so it would be much healthier for me if we didn't do it anymore."
>
> "When you criticize certain foods, I feel really uncomfortable about what I'm choosing to eat."

You will likely have to make this request more than once, but continue to do so. Behavior patterns take time to change, and everyone is dealing with these toxic body topics.

Another way to greatly increase body acceptance is to shut down negative media. This includes TV shows that portray violence against women, social media feeds or groups that are pro anorexia or thinspo (short for thinspiration), or sites that fetishize certain ethnicities. Trust your gut about what feels good or risky to watch or follow. Be honest with yourself about how you feel after reading certain blogs or sites, and *unfollow what doesn't feel safe and healthy.*

Update Your Personal Hygiene

Personal hygiene refers to how well and often we clean our teeth, hands, and body. Keeping ourselves clean is an important part of physical and mental health. As part of improving your body awareness, reflect on how much attention and care you put into keeping your body clean, and consider how this part of self-care affects how you feel about yourself. If you have unstable housing, explore on-campus resources for where you might be able to shower regularly (such as gyms).

General standards of cleanliness include the following:

- Brushing teeth twice per day and flossing once per day, per ADA guidelines.
- Taking a bath or showering as needed. Some folks shower daily,

while others might shower every few days (if they have sensitive skin).

- Hair washing frequency can also vary, from daily to weekly.
- Keeping finger- and toenails trimmed so they don't harbor germs.

Washing hands is an essential element of keeping ourselves and our community healthy. Here are some CDC guidelines for key times to wash your hands:

- Before, during, and after preparing food
- Before eating food
- Before and after treating a cut or wound
- After using the toilet
- After blowing your nose, coughing, or sneezing
- After touching an animal, animal feed, or animal waste
- After handling pet food or pet treats
- After touching garbage

Visit Your Doctor and Dentist Regularly

For many college students, it's a real challenge to make, keep, and pay for regular medical and dental appointments. There are many reasons for this, such as not wanting or being able to pay the copay, not having adequate insurance, being afraid of doctors, being afraid of pain, being too busy, having low self-esteem, being afraid of judgment, racism, or homophobia by medical personnel, and so on.

If any of this applies to you, here are some ideas:

- Know that your health is important, and you are on a journey to learn how to care for it. Try to be gentle and patient with yourself as you learn how to care for your body in this way.
- Be honest with yourself about what is getting in the way of regular medical and dental checkups. This will likely take time and have many layers.
- Ask a friend, college staff, or family member for help. Ask someone to be with you while you call for a doctor's appointment,

"When I look back on my living situations with different roommates, it really made a difference when I had roommates who were comfortable enough to hang out in the common area at the end of the day. When I didn't feel comfortable in the common spaces, it made everything so hard. When we all had similar ideas about how clean to keep the space and how to share food in the kitchen, that was also incredibly helpful. I learned I also need a bedroom with a window that I can retreat to when I need some quiet time."

— TOM

or ask them to accompany you to the appointment. Getting support can make all the difference.

Wear Clothes You Like

Wear clothes that you like and that reflect your taste. How we dress indicates how we feel about ourselves and is a way to express who we are. Many students say they feel better all day when they take the time to dress in a way that makes them feel good.

Wearing clothes that are clean, comfortable, and appropriate for the elements is another way to care for your body and yourself. There are many opinions on how often to wash clothes, but in general, most people wash their undergarments after one use and launder other clothes when they look soiled or smell bad.

Clothes also reflect our values. Some people choose to spend more money on clothes because they want to be stylish, but clothes don't have to cost a lot of money to be clean, durable, and attractive. To be stylish on a budget, look for college-hosted free clothes swaps and visit secondhand or vintage stores. You can also ethically source new clothes through online sites such as Good On You or Remake.

Clean and Decorate Your Living Space

Plenty of research shows that there is a correlation between having a decent, clean, attractive place to rest our heads and our mental health. So take responsibility for your living space, whatever it is, to keep it clean and to decorate it in ways that you enjoy.

College dorms, typical off-campus housing, and even living at home present challenges. Students often have roommates, or share communal apartments or houses, and they are not in complete control of their shared spaces. Obviously, everyone has different standards for cleanliness and definitely different tastes when it comes to decorating and interior design.

Even so, be aware of how your space affects you. Many students report that they feel better after they declutter their workspace, and some can't focus until they clean up. You show respect for yourself, and those you live with, by caring for your space and keeping it comfortable and clean. Here are some ways to do this:

- Make a weekly plan for cleaning your room that works for you. Create a schedule for vacuuming, dusting, and taking out the trash. Your roommates or housemates will appreciate your tidiness.
- Arrange your space so it supports how you actually use it, not how you think you should use it.
- Only keep the amount of stuff that you actually want and need. More than a few students report feeling overwhelmed by having to take care of their stuff, so be thoughtful about how much stuff you have.
- Use the on-campus free swap or other reuse organizations to outfit your living space. Decorating your physical space doesn't have to cost a lot or sometimes any money at all.
- Keep your bedding clean to promote good sleep.

"I had been struggling with painful physical symptoms and feeling sad and isolated since high school, and those feelings are persisting into my senior year. I was afraid to seek out medical help because they had not given me the right help in the past. I finally decided to visit the college health center, where I was diagnosed with depression and prescribed a medication to try. I also made some changes in my diet, cutting out a couple of foods that I know irritated my system. These actions helped me be kinder to myself and to keep a balance of self-care and working at my academics."

— LATRICE

WHEN TO SEEK PROFESSIONAL HELP

If you struggle to accept yourself just as you are, reach out to one of the student support offices on your campus, such as counseling, residential life, or a chaplain.

If there is something about your body that you know in your heart doesn't match up with the real you, such as your sex or gender identity, seek compassionate support. If you find that your college resources are not supportive, seek help elsewhere.

If you have never been taught how to care for your body — and many people haven't — please make an appointment with a nurse at your student health services to learn about the specific elements of how to have healthy personal hygiene.

Whatever your circumstances, if you need, and aren't getting, appropriate medical and dental appointments, reach out to your student health services to see what they offer. They will likely be able to refer you to an affordable and compassionate resource.

RESOURCES

On Campus

- College counseling center: A counselor can help you understand what is getting in the way of self-acceptance and support your efforts to practice new self-compassion strategies. A counselor can also recommend referrals to off-campus providers.
- College medical center: Medical staff can provide information on personal hygiene and other physical self-care.
- College chaplain: A chaplain can provide support for self-understanding.
- College residence staff: They can help provide support and connection.
- College diversity office: Many campuses have a diversity office dedicated to providing mentorship and connection for people of many ethnicities, cultures, and identities.

Websites

- US Department of Health and Human Services (www.hhs.gov /programs/prevention-and-wellness/index.html): Their "Prevention & Wellness" webpage provides resources on vaccines and immunizations, health screenings, and other health-related issues.

- American Dental Association (www.mouthhealthy.org): The ADA provides resources on how to brush and floss, when to see a dentist, and information related to dental care.
- Centers for Disease Control and Prevention (www.cdc.gov /handwashing/index.html): Their "Handwashing in Communities" webpage has everything you ever wanted to know about handwashing.
- National Center for Transgender Equality (www.transequality. org): This organization advocates for transgender rights and is a clearinghouse for resources of all kinds.
- Remake (www.remake.world): This organization educates about the ills of the global clothing industry. They maintain a list of recommended brands that meet their robust sustainability criteria.

Books

- *Beautiful You: A Daily Guide to Radical Self-Acceptance* by Rosie Molinary: Written for a female audience, this guide provides 365 practical, doable activities designed to inspire loving yourself just as you are.
- *My Grandmother's Hands: Racialized Trauma and the Pathway to Mending Our Hearts and Bodies* by Resmaa Menakem: This book is a call to action for healing the racial trauma that is "deeply embedded" in the bodies of African Americans, as well as the secondary embodied trauma that affects white Americans and police officers.
- *The Body Keeps the Score: Brain, Mind, and Body in the Healing of Trauma* by Bessel van der Kolk: This groundbreaking book details how trauma physically affects the mind and body and how to heal.

Part II

YOUR IDENTITY

Caminante, no hay puentes, se hace puentes al andar.
(Voyager, there are no bridges, one builds them as one walks.)

— GLORIA ANZALDÚA

ike eating and exercising in the way that is right for us as individuals, we should "just be ourselves." However, this is a bit like saying "just be happy." If it were easy to be grounded in ourselves, to be sure of who we are, and to feel safe being our true selves, we'd already be doing it.

Identity work is critically important because lack of knowledge about, expression of, and acceptance around our true self can cause significant pain. College is an ideal time, and some say it is *the* time, of identity development — to investigate how we understand, express, and cope with our identity.

By the time they reach college, many teenagers have an established sense of self based on their family, their upbringing, and their high school experiences. Yet these identities, which may have run on autopilot, can be challenged in college. As students learn to navigate new relationships and new experiences on their own, they can begin to question every aspect of their selves: from their academic interests to their racial, class, social, and religious identities. Students often feel pushed to reevaluate their concept of who they are, and some find college is a time when they can experiment with new identities. In college, some finally feel safe to discover hidden sides of themselves.

Some students have been so busy "toeing the line" that they haven't had time to get to know themselves. They may be successful, but they still don't feel good or authentic, which can be very confusing. They may be getting straight As and have a thousand Instagram followers, but they still aren't happy. College is a perfect time to develop our personal values and a sense for our life's mission and purpose.

This is not without challenges. All societies, including our own, possess racism, sexism, homophobia, xenophobia, and prejudice and bias against those who are "different" (however that is defined). At the same time that students are struggling to "discover themselves" and cultivate self-acceptance and self-compassion, others in society may criticize their particular identity and refuse acceptance. Working to confront the many "isms" of society is unavoidable, but meeting that challenge leads to more justice and possibility for all.

Curiosity about our identity becomes almost a radical act whenever it disrupts the status quo. In college, the status quo tends to be seeking academic success and productivity on the path to career success. Discovering and developing one's identity is often considered secondary or even a distraction. However, *identity work is a healthy and necessary, though often challenging, part of growth and development, and college is an ideal time to do it.*

That said, while the core of identity work ideally begins in our teens and twenties, we are learning about ourselves until we die. Self-knowledge does not have an end point.

This work has three parts: understanding our upbringing, what we were taught, and where we came from; being curious about and investigating who we are right now; and empowering ourselves to change if we want and choose to create the self we would like to be.

Chapter 7

Family: Your Personal History

"I was taught to 'conceal, don't feel,' so it's really hard for me to reach out for help or admit my feelings."

"There is no acknowledged homosexuality where I come from. They think it only exists in other countries. I can never tell my family that I'm gay."

"It's hard to admit my extended family has mental health and addiction issues. I don't know how that will affect me."

"I'm proud of what my family sacrificed to get me to college. I wish they could help me with what it's like here, but they have no idea."

"My big brother and all my cousins have majored in economics or pre-med. Those are the only majors my family values. How can I tell my family I love psychology?"

A deeper investigation of our family and cultural values helps increase self-awareness. This is admittedly a huge and ongoing task! But it's where an understanding of our identity begins.

When we discern and appreciate the forces that have influenced our lives, we can make a conscious decision to live in alignment with those influences or to challenge their role in our lives.

WHY PERSONAL HISTORY IS A CHALLENGE

The values of our family and culture are instilled in us as children, and they run very deep. However, these values can often be hard to see clearly while we are still growing up and living in our family home.

In addition, family and cultural values are a complex web of influences and ideas. They are not a simplistic system we can understand quickly. And identity can get even more challenging to untangle for young adults who are adoptees, foster children, or those with complicated family histories.

For many students, going to college is the first time they have lived away from home for an extended period. As a result, some students need both time and distance away from their family to be able to see and name all the values they have absorbed from their family.

Eventually, students may recognize that certain family values are not healthy, or don't reflect the values they want to embody, and this can be uncomfortable or even painful. Disagreeing with or rejecting certain values might feel like it's being disloyal to the family. We can still love and respect our families, even as we reflect on what we don't agree with. However, the main goal with the strategies in this chapter is to explore your family history simply in order to see it clearly. Increasing awareness is the first step, and the next step, deciding what to do with this knowledge, if anything, is each person's individual choice.

STRATEGIES

Value Understanding Your Family and Upbringing

In order to understand ourselves, we need to know where we come from. So the first strategy is simply to recognize the value of this work. We need to believe it's a worthwhile endeavor — one that will help our growth and development. Exploring our upbringing, and recognizing how we've been influenced by our family and cultural values, can be challenging, difficult, and even painful. Knowing that it's useful and important is half the battle.

That said, be gentle with yourself as you begin. If you start to explore your family history and find you aren't emotionally ready for this work, feel free to set it aside. Your past is not going anywhere; it will still be there when you are ready. Life nudges us at different times and offers opportunities to get or be ready.

Also, know that understanding our upbringing is not a onetime task. This is ongoing work that lasts a lifetime, and it's okay to go slow and do this work gradually. It takes time to understand our past, so take as much time as you need. When you come upon a new realization, welcome it as part of your identity growth, and avoid the impulse to beat yourself up for things you think you should have already known.

Consider the Meaning of Your Name

In a journal, reflect on your name. Our names are an important part of our identity, and they can influence how we feel about ourselves. Answer the following questions:

- Does your first, middle, or last name have a special meaning?
- Does your name have a special significance for your family?
- How does your name connect you to your family?
- Are you named after someone?
- Have you ever been treated with privilege or bias because of your name? If so, how did that affect you?
- How do you feel about the heritage of your surname?

Reflect on Your Cultural and Ethnic Background

In a journal, write about your family's heritage and background. How has this played out over the generations in your family? Dive as deeply as you can into how your ethnicity, gender, location, and other factors from your past have shaped you. Notice how these qualities intersect with one another.

Below are some prompts to help you start thinking about aspects of your background. Don't feel limited by these questions. Write about anything related to your background, culture, or heritage that feels important or relevant. There are really hundreds of questions to ask!

Don't feel you must answer these questions fully in one session; reflect on and write about these issues over time. Take a break and revisit your answers weeks, months, or even years later. For example, you might return to these prompts once a semester and see if you discover new things or if your reactions to them change.

- How has your race and ethnic heritage impacted your upbringing and life experience?
- How did your gender influence your interests and choices? Were different genders treated differently where you grew up?
- How would you describe or characterize your social class? Was your lifestyle notably different from others in your community? How has class shaped you?
- If you grew up with a physical, mental, or learning disability, how did others deal with that? And how did it impact your life and education?
- If anyone in your home has suffered from chronic illness or addiction, how was that managed, and how did that affect the rest of the family?
- Was there divorce or another disruption in your family and how did that impact you?
- How did the region where you grew up influence your upbringing? Did you feel you belonged where you grew up?

Describe Your Family Culture

In a journal, write about what it was like to grow up in your family. You may have already pondered this a lot, and this will no doubt continue your whole life. Focus on where you are right now, and reflect on how your feelings or understandings may have changed since going to college.

As above, use the prompts below to spark reflection, but don't feel limited by them. Discuss your upbringing in whatever terms fit your life, and again, approach this as a topic to reflect on over time. Revisit your answers later and see if you discover new things or have different reactions.

- What are some key positive values in your family?
- Can you identify some family values that don't work for you?
- How have family members treated you in positive ways, and how have they valued you?
- What family behaviors have hurt you, and in what ways?
- What are some cultural activities or traditions that your family is known for? Do you enjoy these activities? Why or why not?
- What are some talents or skills that your family is known for? Do you share these attributes, and how has that impacted your sense of self?

Reflect on Your Community Culture

In a journal, consider the influence of the community you grew up in. That could include your friends, peers, and mentors, your city and neighborhood, your school and teachers, your religion, and your participation in sports and activities. Reflect on any significant aspect of your community.

Again, write about and reflect on these questions over time, and revisit your answers to see how your feelings and understandings may have changed.

- Think about any significant friendships and what you learned from those friendships. What positive values or behaviors have your friends embodied that have been helpful to you? Have there been harmful experiences?
- How have the values of your larger community or town impacted you?
- Think back on your education, from preschool through high school. Are you satisfied with the opportunities that were available to you? Was anything lacking in your educational opportunities? How big a role did education play in your childhood?
- Reflect on any extracurricular activities, such as sports, arts, or scouting. How influential were these to your growth and development? Did you choose activities you loved or for other reasons,

"College is a fresh start, right? I don't want to be thinking about the past. But almost as soon as I got here, things started to get hard, and I realized I do need to be more honest, both with myself and with others, about my background. I have a lot of trauma in my life, my mom is struggling with addiction, and we had food insecurity in my home growing up. The more I can talk about it, the more I am able to make sense of why things can feel hard for me right now. I can admit that at times I can't focus and get work done on time. I've learned that when I am patient with myself, I can get to my work faster and with more motivation."

— MICHAEL

like family expectations? Which activities provided a sense of belonging and which didn't?

- What sort of religious or spiritual upbringing did you have? How important have religious values been for you and your family? What are they, and how did your religious or spiritual upbringing fit within the larger community growing up?
- Growing up, which teachers and mentors influenced you positively and how? Were there teachers or mentors who influenced you negatively and how?
- What books, music, movies, or other arts were influential to you as you were growing up? What do you think attracted you to those things?
- Did you follow any sports teams growing up, and if so, how has being a fan impacted you?
- Did you follow current events or politics, and how has that influenced your development?
- Did you have any particular heroes? If so, how did their values shape you?

Reflect on National or Regional Identity and History

It's important to reflect on the impact of society in general, or how your upbringing has been impacted by national or regional identities and history. The region of your upbringing may not be the same place you are going to school now, so focus on where you lived during childhood.

- Are there negative values or legacies — such as racism, xenophobia, and prejudice — that define a region's history? If so, how have they personally affected you?

- How has society at large valued individualism versus community, and how has this played out in your life?
- How have you felt personally impacted by a sense of national or regional identity — such as the "American dream," or the idea that anyone can make it if they try hard enough?
- In what ways does the national or regional culture foster equality or inequality, and how has that impacted you and influenced your choices?

WHEN TO SEEK PROFESSIONAL HELP

If your past includes family dysfunction or trauma, it is worthwhile to assess your adverse childhood experiences (ACEs) score. This assessment tool can be a reality check and provide validation that your childhood was indeed hard, and thus you deserve extra support. It is important to know that, without intervention of some kind, negative childhood experiences are likely to affect health and development (for more about ACEs, visit www.cdc.gov/violenceprevention/aces/index.html, and see resources below). If reflecting on your past is very difficult and upsetting, seek counseling or mentorship.

"My parents have never put any overt pressure on me, but I feel the pressure because they are professionals with higher education degrees, and my whole family culture supports elite careers, such as law, medicine, and finance. Sometimes it feels crushing, like I can never meet the ideals of my family. They are all passionate about their work, and it is the enthusiasm that drives them more than the elite labels. Once I could think of that culture as based on passion rather than elitism, I started to give myself permission to explore my interests rather than just jump on a certain path. That has made college more meaningful and enjoyable."

— NIKKI

RESOURCES

On Campus

- College counseling center: A counselor can provide confidential support as you explore family dysfunction or trauma. A counselor can recommend referrals to off-campus providers and assess appropriate treatment for long-term issues (such as anxiety, depression, post-traumatic stress disorder, and so on).

- College chaplain: A chaplain can provide mentorship and caring support.
- College residence staff: Residence staff can help provide support and connection.
- College diversity office: A diversity office can often provide mentorship and support that match your culture.
- College medical center: Visit the medical center for assessment and medication or referral to off-campus resources.

Websites

- ACEs Too High (www.acestoohigh.com): Visit this website to learn more about adverse childhood experiences (ACEs) and to take the test to determine your ACEs score.

Books

Here is a short list of revealing, honest memoirs that I recommend. These memoirs provide a window into how family and cultural influences can impact us. Reading about someone else's life and struggles can often inspire deeper understandings of ourselves. This list is just a start; there are countless other excellent memoirs!

- *Between the World and Me* by Ta-Nehisi Coates: This profound book is written from the author to his son to help him prepare for life as a Black man in America.
- *Born a Crime* by Trevor Noah: The heartfelt book recounts the author's experiences growing up in South Africa as a mixed-race person.
- *Dreams from My Father* by Barack Obama: This book explores former president Barack Obama's early life growing up in Chicago and Honolulu.
- *Educated* by Tara Westover: This book chronicles the author's childhood in a survivalist Mormon family and how her subsequent college education changed her life.

- *Fun Home* by Alison Bechdel: This graphic memoir recounts the author's childhood in rural Pennsylvania, focusing on her family relationships.
- *Hunger of Memory: The Education of Richard Rodriguez* by Richard Rodriguez: The son of Mexican immigrants, Rodriguez details his struggles with assimilation and educational success.
- *Men We Reaped* by Jesmyn Ward: The author takes us through her upbringing in Mississippi, focusing on the many losses she experienced.
- *Persepolis* by Marjane Satrapi: This graphic memoir describes the author's childhood in Iran during and after the Islamic Revolution.
- *The Latehomecomer* by Kao Kalia Yang: Yang recounts her childhood in a Hmong refugee camp in Thailand and her subsequent move and adaptation to a new culture in Minnesota.
- *The Liars' Club* by Mary Karr: This book chronicles the author's childhood in a small Texas town, coping with family dysfunction, alcoholism, and mental illness.
- *Thinking in Pictures: and Other Reports from My Life with Autism* by Temple Grandin: The author recounts her childhood struggles with autism before it was widely recognized and her subsequent success as a scientist.

Chapter 8

Self-Knowledge

"I'm usually too hard on myself, so it's been helpful to me to have a roommate who takes things easier and inspires me to chill out at the end of each day."

"I'm not sure what I care about at college. It's hard to figure out what I want to do next."

"It was surprising to me how fun it was to bake cookies and share them with my friends. Sometimes it's the simple things that can bring the greatest joy."

"I love working with the little kids at my church on Sundays. It kind of makes my week."

"I tend to default to being a homebody, which can get lonely, so it's important for me to make some plans for the weekend to inspire me to get out."

In addition to exploring your family's history and your culture's values, you can also explore the present: Who are you right now? What are the parts that make up you? Getting to know yourself better is an essential step toward finding joy and meaning in life and knowing how you belong in the world.

WHY SELF-KNOWLEDGE IS A CHALLENGE

It takes a lot of trial and error to discover what we are drawn to, what we are good at and not so good at, and what we believe. Discovering our true self is tough, particularly in our culture, which presents an impossible standard of an ideal person, with characteristics that are often unrealistic, if not damaging.

Our society is diverse, and there is no one set of values. However, there is always a tension between doing what feels good and provides instant gratification and doing the "right thing," whatever that means in any given situation, or sacrificing our comfort to make the world a better place.

With our busy lives and high productivity standards, it's easy to feel stuck on a treadmill, with no time to contemplate our lives on a deeper level.

For many students, college feels like a pressure cooker filled with "shoulds," whether from family, peers, professors, or society. It can be very hard to unearth the truth of who we are, since the outside voices of others often drown out our inner voice. It can seem impossible to navigate who we are or what we really want.

This sense of overwhelm in college may be a continuation of a similar experience in high school, where students spent all their time focusing on grades, part-time jobs, test scores, and extracurriculars, without ever stopping to figure out who they are, what they really like to do, or who their real friends are. They are "living on the perimeter" by focusing on accomplishments and expectations rather than on who they are independent of those things. Meanwhile, at their core, they don't know who they are or what they stand for, and as a result they can feel empty, numb, or confused.

We live in a materialistic culture that often judges people based on exterior accomplishments and acquisitions — rather than on the quality of their character or their values.

Further, people can feel defined by their roles, which can make finding their authentic self very challenging. In college, the most obvious role is the good student! Obviously, this has a practical side: Earning a college

When we live on the perimeter, we are making
choices to look good or look as expected
(i.e., exterior accomplishments).

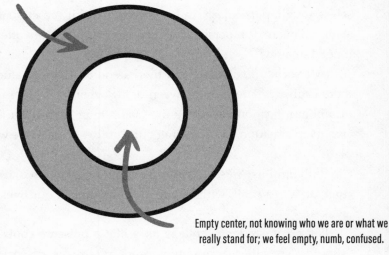

Empty center, not knowing who we are or what we
really stand for; we feel empty, numb, confused.

Living on the perimeter

degree is an important step to getting a decent job in someone's desired field. But they still might not love reading textbooks, writing papers, and taking exams. But another, opposite expectation is that students are supposed to party, and many students say they feel they are missing out if they aren't attending huge parties every weekend. In ways subtle and not-so-subtle, colleges also value different interests over others. For example, many promote business or the sciences as good majors, but they may not value writing poetry or studying philosophy as highly.

STRATEGIES

Value Introspection

It takes determination to carve out time for personal reflection in our busy world. To make that effort, we have to value introspection. Indeed,

college students are in one of the biggest growth phases of identity development, so foster reflection, focus on it, and you may be surprised by
how much you learn about yourself. Plan to do this work on a regular
basis!

Take a Personality Inventory

One quick way to start a journey of self-examination is to take one or
more personality or character surveys. These aren't the be-all and end-
all of knowing yourself, but they are easy to do and can be fun. They
can provide some insights into your tendencies and strengths, which can
generate deeper questions as you explore yourself. Websites for the four
surveys described here are listed under resources below.

- **The VIA Institute on Character survey:** This twenty-four-question
  survey focuses on identifying the character strengths you value
  most. As the website states: "By taking the VIA survey you will
  discover your unique character strengths profile. When you discover your greatest strengths, you learn to use them to handle
  stress and life challenges, become happier, and develop relationships with those who matter most to you."
- **The Myers-Briggs Type Indicator:** This personality inventory
  identifies people as one of sixteen main personality types, based
  on questions about how we perceive others and the world and
  make judgments. As the website states, the goal of the test "is to
  make the theory of psychological types described by C. G. Jung
  understandable and useful in people's lives. The essence of the
  theory is that much seemingly random variation in behavior is
  actually quite orderly and consistent, being due to basic differences in the ways individuals prefer to use their perception and
  judgment."
- **The Life Values Inventory:** This forty-two-question assessment
  helps you clarify your values and determine how those values
  influence your behaviors and decision making in different areas
  of your life. As the website states: "Your values are the lenses
  through which you view yourself and your world. As values

develop, they are crystallized and prioritized to form a values system. In essence, they form your own 'personal truth' from which self-esteem, fulfillment, and resilience develop."

- **The Self-Compassion questionnaire:** Developed by psychologist Kristin Neff, this questionnaire helps you assess your level of self-compassion. As the websites states: "Different than self-esteem or self-indulgence, with self-compassion, we give ourselves the same kindness and care we'd give to a good friend."

Make Your Own Personality Lists

In your journal, make your own personality or character attributes lists. These are quick ways to reflect on what you enjoy and on your strengths and values. Use these prompts or come up with your own.

- **A spark list:** Write down the times when something sparked a good feeling in you, even for a quick moment. Look for surprises. This is important information about what interests you and what you value.
- **A favorite things list:** Jot down an array of your favorite things, such as songs, colors, foods, and books.
- **"In the zone" moments:** Make a list of the times when you felt "in the zone" or in a "flow state." This refers to feeling fully immersed and energized by an activity. Describe what you were doing and try to identify patterns. Keep adding to this list whenever you experience the flow!
- **An inner truth list:** Make a list of "inner truths," or what, according to your inner barometer, you feel is inherently right or wrong. We can often ignore our inner voice, so this is a way to listen more closely to our inner barometer.
- **A special talents or gifts list:** Make a list of what you consider your special or unique talents. If this is hard, consider what family, friends, and mentors have said about you; sometimes others can see our gifts more clearly than we can. Add to this list whenever you get a compliment or have your own insight.

Meditate

Mindfulness meditation practice is a way to get in touch with our deeper self. When we are sitting alone with our thoughts and feelings, less noise clouds what we are really thinking and feeling. College is full of constant busyness or distractions, so it can be really hard to be quiet and just be alone. However, many studies confirm that meditation helps promote calm and focus, as well as boosting self-knowledge and self-acceptance. See appendix A for advice and instructions for meditating.

Reflect on Your Race

It is important to acknowledge your own race and increase awareness of how it impacts you. In a journal, explore the questions below. Make your feelings and thoughts about your race explicit.

- How do you name and feel about your race?
- How are you treated because of your race?
- In what ways do you experience privilege or discrimination because of your race?
- In what ways do you have any biases about races different from your own?

Reflect on Your Gender

Similarly, it is important to acknowledge your gender (or your sense of gender fluidity) and increase awareness of how it impacts you. In a journal, explore these questions.

- How do you name and feel about your gender?
- How are you treated because of your gender?
- In what ways do you experience privilege or discrimination because of your gender?
- In what ways do you have any biases about genders different from your own?

"I came to an American college from China, seeking a career in finance, and that's why I chose to major in economics and business. I began to struggle with mental health issues after experiencing a sexual assault. Previously, I always thought I should seek the highest prestige job I could find after graduation, but my beliefs about the ultimate job have begun to change. I am now allowing myself to consider other factors in my job search, such as community mental health resources, a jobsite that is supportive, not competitive, a place that I can work with some other recent grads, and a location that has a population of young Chinese immigrants."

— APRIL

Reflect on Your Sexual Orientation

As above, in a journal, explore these questions about your sexual orientation.

- How do you name and feel about your sexual orientation?
- How are you treated because of your sexual orientation?
- In what ways do you experience privilege or discrimination because of your sexual orientation?
- In what ways do you have any biases about orientations different from your own?

Reflect on Your Physical Abilities

Our sense of self is also impacted by our physical self: the state of our health and whether we have any ongoing or permanent physical issues or disabilities. We often downplay or deny health issues and their impacts, but in a journal, be explicit about the state of your physical health and abilities.

- How do you characterize and feel about your physical abilities?
- How are you treated because of your physical abilities?
- In what ways do you experience privilege or discrimination because of the state of your physical abilities?
- In what ways do you have any biases about the physical abilities of others?

Try New Things

Learn more about yourself through trying new things. Give yourself permission to have different experiences, and take careful note of the ones you enjoy. It is crucial to let yourself explore different aspects of your identity.

- **Self-care:** Try a new hairstyle, wear clothing that isn't your usual style, eat food you've never had before, cook or bake something new, rearrange your room, and so on.
- **Creativity:** Visit an art museum, listen to new music, explore a new art or craft, write a poem, attend theater or dance performances, and so on.
- **Nature:** Visit a zoo, have a picnic in a local park, hike in a place you've never been, get up early to watch the sunrise, and so on.
- **Movement:** Play a new sport, try a different style of workout, watch an unfamiliar sport for you, dance at a club, and so on.
- **Socializing:** Play new games with friends, invite new friends to play a favorite game, hang out in a park and people-watch, and so on.
- **Culture:** Take a college class outside your normal interests or comfort zone, attend a religious service other than your own faith, read a type of book or author you usually don't, eat at a restaurant of a different culture, and so on.

"My relationship wasn't going so well, and I was taking care of my boyfriend on every level. I needed to confront my fear of being single, the belief that I would only be okay if I had a boyfriend. Once I got the courage to break up with him, and left behind that caretaking version of myself, I was able to make a group of supportive friends who share my interests and was able to get a meaningful internship that led to a job after graduation."

— JAMAL

WHEN TO SEEK PROFESSIONAL HELP

If you feel you are living your life on autopilot, if you are taking classes that you don't find meaningful, if you are unable to identify activities that feel good, if you feel numb or like there is a "hole in your soul," it may be helpful to seek counseling or assistance from a trusted mentor. If you struggle to "be yourself" for any reason, know that you don't have to struggle alone, and you deserve support.

RESOURCES

On Campus

- College counseling center: A counselor can provide confidential support while you talk through what doesn't work in your life. Counselors can also recommend referrals to off-campus providers.
- College chaplain: A chaplain can provide mentorship and caring support.
- College residence staff: Residence staff can help provide support and connection.
- College diversity office: A diversity office can offer support that matches your culture.

Websites

- VIA Institute on Character (www.viacharacter.org): The VIA character strengths survey is free.
- Myers-Briggs Type Indicator (www.mbtionline.com/en-US): The Myers-Briggs Foundation charges a fee for its official Type Indicator survey, but free versions can be found online.
- Life Values Inventory (www.lifevaluesinventory.org): The Life Values Inventory is free online.
- Self-Compassion (www.self-compassion.org): This free self-compassion test was created by Dr. Kristin Neff.

Books

- *Flow: The Psychology of Optimal Experience* by Mihaly Csikszentmihalyi: This classic book explains the flow state and gives strategies for intentionally encouraging flow experiences.
- *The Artist's Way* by Julia Cameron: Though written primarily for an audience of "creatives," this book is encouraging for anyone and offers robust strategies for connecting to our voice and fostering self-knowledge and growth.
- *Me and White Supremacy: Combat Racism, Change the World, and Become a Good Ancestor* by Layla F. Saad: This workbook is for white or white-passing people of color to "help you explore and unpack your relationship with white supremacy."

Chapter 9

Living Your Own Life

"At first I looked down on myself because I love painting and arts. I care a lot about social justice and worried about how I am helping the world. It took a while for me to accept that I'm a creative person and my work has an important place in society."

"It's hard to be Black on this campus. I'm often the only person of color in my classes and it feels very lonely. Finding the courage to attend the Black Student Union made college sustainable for me."

"I thought I had to be a big partier in college. But I really like smaller gatherings where I can connect more closely to people."

"At the end of my college career I define my success as being a kind friend. When I started college, I defined success by my academic achievement."

"Getting bad grades in the hard sciences opened up a door to a public health career, which is something that is more meaningful to me than pure biology or chemistry."

We are born with many parts of our lives already in place, such as our family history, our current circumstances, and our body. Yet we have the ability to grow and change and make choices about what we value and believe and how we want to be in this world.

College is a great time to consider your values and how you want to live life, what you believe is worth working and living for. It is an act of bravery to take time to reflect and strive to discover what your heart and intuition have to say. If you don't take the time to do this, you risk living the life or the values of someone or something else — instead of living your life intentionally with full consciousness.

WHY LIVING OUR *OWN* LIFE IS A CHALLENGE

It can be difficult to find the strength to name our own beliefs. It's much easier to go with what is handed to us, especially when beliefs or values may conflict with those of others.

College includes a long list of huge stressors, and it can feel like there is no time to contemplate "why." Sometimes, it's easier to just do things the way we've always done them or the way everyone else is doing them. Living intentionally takes courage and work.

STRATEGIES

Value Yourself

Prioritize taking the time to dive deeply into your vision for yourself and your future. Without conscious commitment, the act of examining our life mission and values won't happen. This does not happen automatically.

All the exercises in this chapter are meant to help you live your own life. Choose the ones that jump out to you, and try new ones regularly. There is no time limit or schedule you must follow, but take time to do this regularly. August, right before the start of a new school year, is an ideal time for college students to reassess their values, goals, and sense of self.

A helpful metaphor is to imagine your values as your North Star. They guide you on and help you navigate your life journey. This helps us stay on course when life inevitably hands us losses, hardships, and challenges.

Your ship navigating according to its North Star

Write a Mission Statement

A mission statement defines our big-picture values, beliefs, and goals. It provides clarity and direction that helps us make choices as we live our life. The act of writing this down turns vague wisps of thought into a road map that can be used when things get tough, confusing, or tedious.

Mission statements can seem intimidating, but treat yours as a work in progress. A mission statement can be as long or short as you want, even a single sentence, and it's not set in stone. Revisit and revise yours regularly.

Here are some prompts to get you started thinking:

- How do I want to be in the world?
- What is meaningful to me?
- How do I want to connect to others?
- What am I striving for?

- What do I want to become?
- What is my life asking of me?
- Where do the world's needs match up with my talents?
- What is my life purpose?

Here are some examples of short mission statements:

- My mission is to nurture children as they grow and develop.
- My mission is to solve problems that haven't been solved before.
- My mission is to be a good parent and heal the past dysfunction of my family.
- My mission is to heal injustice in our world.
- My mission is to reverse environmental degradation in our world.
- My mission is to be kind to all and to be a good friend.
- My mission is to work hard and to create a good life for my family.

Imagine Your Life Highlights

Start by pretending you have made it to a ripe old age. You have lived a life that reflects your dreams and values. Use your imagination and explore what you truly care about by writing the highlights of the life you hope to have lived. Include your work and volunteer accomplishments, name your closest family members and friends, and describe your favorite hobbies. Include how people saw you and related to you. Include the people, places, events and other things that were the most important to you.

Identify Your Heroes

The people we admire reveal a lot about what we value and respect. Make a list of your personal heroes and the qualities you admire. These people can be alive or dead, real or imaginary, folks you know personally or have never met.

Here are some examples:

- Michelle Obama, who is strong and gracious in the face of criticism and rudeness
- Thomas Edison, who persisted despite failing thousands of times before succeeding
- James Baldwin, who was poetically insightful
- Ida B. Wells, who fought for justice and equality
- Mrs. Maguire, my children's (real-life) third-grade teacher, who treated all children as special and precious
- Thich Nhat Hanh, who taught peace, loving-kindness, and delight

Name the Codes You Aspire To

"Codes" are the concepts that guide our behavior. They represent our values, character strengths, morals, ethics, and positive principles. In chapter 8, the strategy "Take a Personality Inventory" (pages 87–88) encourages you to list your current values, but this is a chance to be aspirational. Which values would you like to have more of in your life? Which values do you hope will form the core for your future self?

Adaptability: the ability to cope with changes and surprises
Authenticity: living our true self, wherever we are
Awe: sublime wonder at the natural world, the arts, and spiritual connection
Compassion: heartfelt kindness for self and others
Courage: acting despite our fears
Creativity: having and expressing new ideas
Curiosity: being continually interested to know more about the world
Discipline: behaving in a way that is ordered even when it's not easy
Empathy: heartfelt understanding for self and others
Energy: rising to the occasion as best we can
Equality: valuing the innate equality of all human beings
Equanimity: staying calm and responding thoughtfully

"It took me a couple of years to get the courage to acknowledge to myself that I am queer. It took even more time to get the courage to come out to some of my friends. I'm still working on telling my family. Every time I come out a bit more, I've noticed that I feel more and more happy with my life and just more enthusiastic in general."

— DINAH

Faith: assuming that things will work out rather than endlessly worrying; faith can also be spiritual

Generosity: seeking to give emotionally and materially to self and others

Gratitude: being conscious of the good things we have in life

Honor: acting in a way that aligns with our beliefs

Hope: having a positive vision for the future

Humility: knowing our ideas might not always be right; not always taking the spotlight

Joyfulness: finding the good in each day and enjoying it

Love: heartfelt feeling and care for self, others, community, and the natural world

Love of learning: enjoying the act of acquiring new skills or knowledge

Moderation: keeping balance in all the important parts of our life

Open-mindedness: being open to new ideas and the viewpoints of others

Patience: trust and tolerance around life's challenges

Responsibility: acting appropriately according to our role and re-lationships and our position in the world

Self-awareness: cultivating awareness of thoughts, feelings, and physical self

Service: working on behalf of others and community, seeking good solutions for all

WHEN TO SEEK PROFESSIONAL HELP

Do you feel unable to be connected to yourself? Is something blocking the message of your heart or your intuition? Half the battle is admitting this to ourselves, so if this is true for you, pat yourself on the back. When you are on a journey to be more connected to yourself, it is helpful to have a trusted mentor, perhaps but not necessarily a counselor, who can empathetically listen and actively encourage you to listen to and trust yourself.

"I had never thought about being disciplined in my life as a particular value. However, I found more success with my schoolwork and enjoyment of my friendships when I learned how to take an ordered approach to my day, developing both morning and evening routines that I enjoy."

— JOHN

RESOURCES

On Campus

- College counseling center: A counselor is an excellent resource for discussing your values and life purpose.
- College chaplain: Chaplains often specialize in helping students define meaning and purpose.
- College diversity office: This office can offer support that is culture specific.

Websites

- This I Believe (www.thisibelieve.org): This nonprofit organization gathers personal essays from everyday people about their personal beliefs and core values. It's inspiring and enlightening to explore what motivates others.

Books

- *Becoming Wise: An Inquiry into the Mystery and Art of Living* by Krista Tippett: Thoughtful writing on finding meaning in today's world.
- *The Power of Purpose: Find Meaning, Live Longer, Better* by Richard Leider: This is about why having a purpose in life significantly improves satisfaction, and it includes ways to assess your life purpose.

Part III

YOUR THOUGHTS

I know but one freedom, and that is the freedom of the mind.
— Antoine de Saint-Exupéry

The need to take care of our thoughts might not seem as obvious as the need to take care of our body. This is partly because our thoughts exist in our head, with no tangible evidence. However, the health of our mind and thoughts greatly impacts our lives. Our thoughts are connected to our body and our emotions in complex ways, but they are the driving force behind whatever is happening with us in any given moment.

Why is it so hard to know, let alone control, what is going on in our mind?

Well, because our brains are exceedingly complicated organs. There are billions of neural connections in our brains, and more than a hundred trillion synapses — an unimaginably large number.

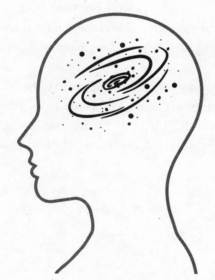

- 100 trillion synaptic connections in your brain
- 2 trillion galaxies in the universe
- 100 billion neurons in your brain
- 100 billion stars in the Milky Way

The universe in your head

The complex nature of our brains helps explain why we often find it so challenging to identify what we are thinking and feeling. Scientists are still trying to understand the intricate workings of the brain. If we can appreciate this complexity, it is easier to understand why something that sounds easy — such as identifying a thought — usually isn't and why it takes consistent practice to master.

Most students hesitate to accept the notion that they can gain awareness of and have an impact on their thoughts. Many say things like, "I'm just negative and always have been"; "It comes out of nowhere"; or "This is so intense, I don't believe there is a way to change this." Students frequently believe their mind "just is" and we can have no effect on it. However, the truth is that we can have just as big an influence on our mind as we can on our body.

Modern science has given us lots of hope in regard to the trainability, or plasticity, of the brain. It turns out our brains can grow and change where we lead them (to a point, of course). Sports, music, and language are helpful metaphors when trying to understand how the mind learns new thought patterns. For example, it takes years of practice to run a five-minute mile, play a Mozart piano concerto, or become fluent in another language, but it can be done. The same is true for changing habits of the mind.

The paradigm that this book uses to gain more composure with our thoughts and emotions is ABC: awareness, being, choosing. I describe this three-step process in "Use the ABC Method: Awareness, Being, Choosing" (pages 61–62), and this approach informs many of the strategies in parts 3 and 4.

Chapter 10

Awareness 101: Noticing Your Thoughts

"I'm not even sure where my head is at."

"My mind is like an echo chamber of thoughts that I can't stop."

"My binge eating comes out of nowhere."

"There are constant thoughts in my head that I can't get out."

"I always check my phone the minute I don't have something else to pay attention to."

Self-awareness is being aware of thoughts that are happening in the present moment. It's as simple and challenging as that.

Without self-awareness, we can go about life on autopilot or have automatic thoughts that lead to reactive, rather than thoughtful, behaviors.

This chapter is focused specifically on present-moment awareness. That is, it's about "waking up" to our thoughts in each moment, whatever they are, and no matter what we do about them. Present-moment awareness is essential. Without it, we can get trapped in unthinking reactivity; with it, we give ourselves the opportunity to make conscious choices.

WHY SELF-AWARENESS IS A CHALLENGE

Self-awareness is challenging because life happens fast, our brains are capable of taking us far away from the present moment, and we simply forget to practice it or we don't value doing so.

This is part of the human condition. Everyone finds it hard to stay in the moment and not fantasize about what might happen, not get lost in memories of the past, or not anticipate the future. Great philosophers have been grappling with these issues for thousands of years.

This is certainly true of college students. You might be familiar with the experience of sitting in class listening to a chemistry lecture, but your mind wanders to a conversation with friends or you fret over a mistake you made on a test. At first, you aren't even consciously aware that you are no longer listening, but then you "wake up" to realize you missed part of the lecture and have no idea what the professor is talking. about.

College students can find cultivating self-awareness particularly challenging for several reasons. For the most part, they are grappling with many new, challenging life issues — pursuing their calling, insecurities about their identity, new relationships — that raise challenging feelings.

But also, our culture supports avoidance behaviors, such as being overly busy and focusing on entertainment, personal comfort, and distractions. Many students grow up never learning the value of self-awareness, and so they must learn that in college, too.

STRATEGIES

Value Self-Awareness

Some students don't see the need to develop present-moment awareness, thinking, *Our minds are just thinking, what's the big deal?* When we never learn to examine our thoughts we can be overwhelmed when our thoughts are challenging ones.

Pause to Get in Touch with Your Thoughts

Our thoughts can seem like a blur or a fog. When you notice this happening, learn to pause and pay attention. This is like an aha moment where you realize that your mind is somewhere else and not in the present. This pause doesn't have to be long, but just enough to "wake up," slow down, and allow for self-awareness. Being aware of the movements of our own mind is a hard-won skill, and it takes much practice. It's particularly hard in our media-saturated modern world, but over time, it gets easier.

Listen to Your Body

Often our bodies alert us to agitation, such as tight shoulders, a stomachache, or a headache. If you notice physical signs like this, take that as a cue to pay attention to your state of mind.

Develop Habits That Encourage Awareness

It's possible to build habits that remind us to practice present-moment awareness. After all, remembering to be aware is half the challenge. For example, at certain times of day, or before certain activities, make it a habit to take a deep breath and check in with yourself. Here are some possibilities:

- Whenever you feel the urge to check your phone
- Walking to class
- When you first sit down in class
- As you start to study
- When you sit down to a meal

Write about Your Thoughts

Journaling is an intentional time to express your inner thoughts, and writing helps build self-awareness. This applies to any of the journaling prompts in this book, and also see "Journaling" (pages 328–30).

"I feel like I live at the extremes of either being swamped with thoughts or zoning out. I was looking for a way to stay current with my thoughts but not get overwhelmed. I had a couple of friends using a bullet journal, so I thought I'd give it a try. By having a specific space to check in with my thoughts and jotting them down in a calendar, I was able to feel more present in a short amount of time."

— TAMIKA

Talk about Your Thoughts

We discuss our thoughts with friends all the time. However, consider having an intentional conversation with a trusted friend or family member about your efforts to increase self-awareness. Discuss your struggles and experiences with others.

Meditate

Mindfulness meditation practice is the ideal training to build the muscle of self-awareness. See appendix A for meditation advice and instructions.

WHEN TO SEEK PROFESSIONAL HELP

Are you struggling to know your thoughts, even after you've tried journaling or deeper discussion? If so, reach out to a trusted adult or counselor and start a conversation.

RESOURCES

On Campus

- College counseling center: Counseling is itself a way to help become more aware of what we are thinking. A counselor can help you develop good mental habits even if there is no larger issue.

Books

- *The Power of Now: A Guide to Spiritual Enlightenment* by Eckhart Tolle: This book is a bestseller for a reason — it gives practical techniques for living in the present in an easy-to-read format.

- *Wherever You Go, There You Are: Mindfulness Meditation in Everyday Life* by Jon Kabat-Zinn: This book presents the science of mindfulness in an enjoyable and engaging way.
- *You Are Here: Discovering the Magic of the Present Moment* by Thich Nhat Hanh: Written by a Vietnamese Zen Buddhist monk, this book focuses on how to cultivate mindfulness in daily life and has a slightly more religious bent.

"I was finding myself not doing well, but not sure how I got there. I was able to identify some signs that are my particular tells that indicate I need to be more honest with myself about what I am thinking. I've noticed that when I don't text back right away — which I usually do — or begin using emojis instead of words — I hate emojis — it means I may not be doing well and would benefit from taking some time to get clear on where my head is at."

— BRUCE

Chapter 11

Being 101: Naming Your Thoughts Without Judgment

"I shouldn't be so down on myself this often. I'm lucky to be in college."

"I'm a loser if I don't ace this test."

"I hate having intense thoughts."

"I don't want to admit I need help with my problem set. I used to be the one helping others."

"I should be able to handle this right now."

As we gain awareness of our state of mind, we obviously become aware of the *content* of our thoughts. When we catch ourselves lost in thought, and then "wake up" to the present moment, what were we thinking? Was it a worry, memory, fantasy, or something else?

The goal is to name the thought with curiosity rather than judgment. This is a hard step for anyone, but especially students. Yet it is essential not to negatively judge our thoughts or ourselves. This is like adding insult to injury. *Learning to recognize our thoughts without negative judgment can make all the difference.*

WHY OBSERVING WITHOUT JUDGMENT IS A CHALLENGE

Another part of the human condition is having difficulty being brave enough and wise enough to see "what is" without judgment. Everyone struggles with this.

It is pretty easy to name an optimistic or positive thought, but it can be more difficult to name a more challenging thought. The truth is, negative, unhelpful, fearful, and alarming thoughts are part of the human experience. Humans evolved to respond immediately to threats, while delaying or devaluing pleasure, in order to survive. Thus, it makes sense that we are very good at anticipating or seeing "threats" even when what we are reacting to is only our fear or the possibility of threat. We can't control negative thoughts. The challenge is to recognize them when they arise and not react to them if they are unfounded.

College students are in a situation where they are being asked to develop their critical thinking, while also being constantly evaluated and judged themselves for their efforts. Being asked to suspend judgment can seem unfamiliar and even alarming! This paradox makes it extra challenging to simply notice thoughts without judgment.

STRATEGIES

Value Nonjudgmental Curiosity

While suspending judgment is hard, we can only do so if we value that approach and see the benefit. In essence, this boils down to recognizing that thoughts are just thoughts and we can notice them without reacting to them.

This means respecting whatever we are thinking without trying to change our thoughts. The point is to notice with curiosity and just see what is. There is no wrong answer, no bad thought.

Here are some examples of how to use the language of nonjudgmental curiosity:

"I notice that I'm thinking XYZ."

"I'm curious that I'm thinking XYZ."

"I'm having a lot of anxious thoughts today."

"I'm having some frustrating thoughts about my homework right now."

"I'm thinking about what's for lunch."

"This is just a thought and I don't have to do anything about it."

Meditate

Mindfulness meditation is perfect training for nonjudgmental observation. See appendix A for advice and instructions on meditation.

Regard Thoughts as Thoughts, Not Facts

We don't have to believe everything we think. Indeed, one goal of nonjudgmental curiosity is to take a moment to distinguish our thoughts from "reality." Our thoughts are real reactions, but they reflect our subjective reality, not necessarily objective, external reality. When an upsetting thought arises, there are times when it can be good to think, *Thoughts aren't facts. There is no data to support this thought.*

Identify Thought Patterns

Our thoughts often reflect certain patterns or types, and identifying the specific types of patterns as they arise can provide the distance to know they are "just thoughts" and not necessarily true reality. Psychiatrist David Burns calls these thought patterns "cognitive distortions" (for more, see the resources). Here is a list of the most common ones (from Burns's book):

- **All-or-nothing thinking** (seeing things in polar extremes):

  "If I don't study as much as I can, I'll fail."

  "No one thinks I'm interesting."

- *Should* statements (motivating yourself with punishing guilt):

  "I should be studying all the time."
  "I should be able to handle a full course load like everyone else."

- **Mental filter** (focusing only on the negative and failing to see the whole picture):

  "I'm too introverted to make friends."
  "I'm not great at organizing, so I'm going to fail at college."

- **Discounting the positive** (denying positive judgments):

  "That professor says nice things to everyone."
  "Everyone has as many friends as I have."

- **Emotional reasoning** (believing feelings and ignoring evidence):

  "I feel so awkward, so I'm bad friend material."
  "I'm afraid of this class, so I don't belong in it."

- **Overgeneralization or labeling** (seeing a single event as a fixed pattern):

  "He cheated on me. All guys are cheaters."
  "I messed up on the exam. I'm a horrible student."

- **Catastrophizing/minimizing** (exaggerating or shrinking the importance of things):

  "If I get a B, I'll be homeless."
  "I'm not involved in enough extracurriculars, so I'm failing at college."

- **Mind reading, or jumping to conclusions** (making assumptions without proof):

  "My professor will be disappointed in me if I don't get an A."
  "That person must not like me because they didn't smile at me."

"When I practice mindfulness meditation, I've noticed that as thoughts come up, I am very judgmental of any thoughts that are critical of myself. I noticed that I often think, *I shouldn't think that*, which makes me feel even worse. It took much practice, but in time I have been able to see a self-critical thought as just a thought and be curious about it rather than 'shoulding' myself."

— AISA

- **Mind reading, or fortune telling** (making predictions that prejudge outcomes):

  "I didn't do the reading, so this class will turn out badly."
  "I won't make any friends at this party."

- **Personalization** (making yourself the cause of larger problems):

  "I'm the reason I always feel anxious."
  "The class went badly because I didn't speak up enough."

Whenever you recognize a thought pattern, just name it. Don't beat yourself up for faulty thinking, but simply recognize where your mind went. Here are some examples of what to say to yourself:

"I'm having a cognitive distortion right now."
"I'm having a lot of all-or-nothing thoughts today."
"I am having some catastrophizing thoughts about my homework right now."
"I'm jumping to conclusions about what that guy is thinking about me, but I don't really know."

Of course, not all our thoughts or thought patterns are negative, and you shouldn't focus only on identifying negative thoughts. Be open and curious and name what you see. If thoughts are neutral or positive, it's important to not only name them but embrace them:

"I'm having a lot of creative thoughts today."
"My mind is focused on fun plans for the weekend."
"All I can think about is that cute person I met at the party last weekend."

WHEN TO SEEK PROFESSIONAL HELP

Are you struggling with judging your thoughts or with being hard on yourself for not controlling your thoughts? If so, reach out to a trusted adult or counselor and start a conversation.

RESOURCES

On Campus

- College counseling center: A counselor can help you acknowledge negative thoughts and thought patterns without judgment, and develop healthier mental habits, even if there aren't other issues.

Books

- *The Feeling Good Handbook* by David Burns: One of the most-used self-help books by mental health therapists, this book helps make cognitive distortions easy to understand and recognize.

"I was isolated and lonely when I first came to college. I identified that I held myself back from reaching out because I thought I was being a bother to my friends. When I allowed myself to observe my thoughts of being a burden, I was able to consider changing my behaviors."

— ROWAN

Chapter 12

Choosing 101: Coping with Your Thoughts

"I've often thought that I'm not smart enough to make it here, but as I label that as 'impostor syndrome,' I feel like I belong more."

"I need help to cope with the 'doubt voices'!"

"I'm really hard on myself about everything. I know if I could change that, I'd feel better."

"When I remind myself that I'm here to learn, not to already know everything perfectly, I can focus on my homework."

"Learning to take a step back and not jump to conclusions has changed my life."

Once we become aware of a thought, and accept that it arose, we can choose how to respond to it: to listen to it or let it go. This is the ABC method: awareness, being, choosing.

Choosing is not easy, and in some cases, coping with our thoughts, deciding whether to listen to them and what to do about them, takes extra support. But it is doable, just the way learning a new language or a musical instrument is doable — with lots of practice.

We have agency and can choose what we let stay in our head.

We can't control the thoughts that pop into our head. We can't control the messages we receive from others and the world or the situations we find ourselves in. But we *can* learn to manage what we do about our thoughts.

Note: Since this book focuses on mental health strategies, it mostly addresses coping with negative thoughts and difficult emotions and avoiding unhelpful reactivity. It doesn't take a deep dive into all the many types of positive thoughts that are wonderful and interesting and make us feel great. Keep in mind that not all thoughts are troublesome, and remember to notice and acknowledge healthy, positive, good thoughts when they arise.

WHY COPING WITH THOUGHTS IS A CHALLENGE

Developing the self-awareness to continually notice the thoughts that arise and then to consciously choose which ones to listen to takes a lot of work and attention. Our minds can get so overwhelmed with everything that's happening in our lives that we forget to pay attention to our thought patterns.

It's easy to become passive and simply accept our thoughts as reality or facts. If a thought arises, we feel we must listen to it and act on it.

As I've described in chapters 10 and 11, this is not true. Thoughts embody our personal reactions, but they do not *necessarily* represent other people or issues accurately. Paradoxically, the harder we work at being aware of our thoughts, the easier it gets to handle difficult emotions and challenging situations.

Coping with thoughts can be extra challenging for college students, who are still exploring their sense of self. Meanwhile, they must deal with all the very real experiences of bias and microaggressions that exist in the world, whether related to racism, sexism, homophobia, transphobia, classism, and so on. When these experiences cause lots of rumination and anxiety, it becomes even harder to step back and observe our own mind.

STRATEGIES

Believe in Your Own Inner Knowing

Believe that you have the power to know your mind, and that you also have the power, no matter what you feel and think, to choose how to act.

Value the subtle but persistent work it takes to check in with your thoughts and then take the appropriate action. Be patient!

Choose the Best Response to a Thought

Once you have named a thought with nonjudgmental awareness (as described in the previous two chapters), decide the best way to respond to that thought. While there are potentially many options, choices fall into three main categories:

1. **Take no action:** Simply acknowledging a thought might be enough. This informs you about where your head and heart are at, and no further action is needed.
2. **Take thoughtful action:** After naming the thought, you can decide to act on it. Choosing the best or most helpful action still requires thoughtfulness, but in itself, making the effort to be self-aware of thoughts and then choosing what to do about them helps avoid reactivity.
3. **Replace "unhelpful" thoughts with healthier ones:** If you recognize a negative thought pattern, or a cognitive distortion, label that thought as "unhelpful." Then replace that thought with a healthier option.

Take No Action

Sometimes the best strategy is just to stay with nonjudgmental awareness of your thoughts. No action is needed. In such instances, it can be very helpful to label the category of thoughts that you are having.

For example, if you are sitting in class but constantly lost in thought about the professor's polka-dot bow tie, you might simply acknowledge that: *Wow, I'm really distracted by that bow tie right now.* That might be enough to get you back to your bigger goal of paying attention to the lecture.

Here are some other examples for how to talk to yourself with nonjudgmental awareness:

"I'm thinking a lot about XYZ right now."
"I'm aware that my mind is getting pulled back to XYZ as the morning goes on."

"I'm in the zone right now. My mind is very focused on my
    work."

"My mind is being tugged to think about spring break."

Take Thoughtful Action

If a thought arises that contains important information, then we can decide to act on it. Part of human nature is denying or ignoring important
but difficult thoughts because they are … difficult. So at times, choosing
to act can also be hard.

If we ignore difficult thoughts and they keep arising, then we need to
do something to resolve the situation. Sometimes, we know exactly what
to do and just need to gather the courage to do it. Other times, we are
confused and uncertain about the best action. Either way, it can help to
get advice and support from a friend, counselor, or trusted adviser. Here
are some examples:

- You become aware that you keep having thoughts about how
  uncomfortable you are in your living situation. You label that as
  "I am having issues with my roommates." While you know what
  those issues are, you seek advice from your residence hall assistant about the most productive solutions and how to have that
  conversation.

- You become aware that a professor is criticizing you in class much
  more frequently and forcefully than others. You know your participation in class is respectful and appropriate, so you suspect
  that this isn't about academics or behavior. You label that as "I
  believe I am experiencing microaggressions from my professor
  because I am Black, and my classmates are white." You talk this
  over with a trusted mentor and decide to bring the issue up pri-
  vately with the professor during their office hours.

How do you know if you should take action? It isn't always easy to
discern. The main goal is to take time to contemplate your thoughts and
feelings, while perhaps seeking advice from others, and to respond in a
thoughtful way. That avoids thoughtless reactivity, which is never a good
response.

Replace "Unhelpful" Thoughts with Healthier Ones

As I describe in chapter 11 (see "Identify Thought Patterns," pages 112–14), some thoughts represent negative thought patterns or what psychologist David Burns calls "cognitive distortions." These are ways we distort reality in usually negative, unhelpful ways. When you recognize a thought pattern, label it as "unhelpful," and then replace it with a neutral or positive characterization. Here are examples using the same categories and thoughts that are listed in chapter 11:

- **All-or-nothing thinking** (seeing things in polar extremes):

  "I've never failed anything, so I think I'm studying enough" (versus "If I don't study as much as I can, I'll fail").

  "Some people think I'm interesting" (versus "No one thinks I'm interesting").

- *Should* **statements** (motivating yourself with punishing guilt):

  "I already study a decent amount" (versus "I should be studying all the time").

  "I do much better when I take a slightly lighter course load and that's okay" (versus "I should be able to handle a full course load like everyone else").

- **Mental filter** (focusing only on the negative and failing to see the whole picture):

  "I've made friends in the past despite being an introvert" (versus "I'm too introverted to make friends").

  "I'm talented in many ways, and I can learn how to make a schedule so I can succeed in college" (versus "I'm not great at organizing, so I'm going to fail at college").

- **Discounting the positive** (denying positive judgments):

  "It feels good to get positive words from that professor because I really respect her" (versus "That professor says nice things to everyone").

"I have a special group of friends" (versus "Everyone has as many friends as I have").

- **Emotional reasoning** (believing feelings and ignoring evidence):

"I have close friends, so I must be a good friend despite my awkwardness" (versus "I feel so awkward, so I'm bad friend material").

"I belong in this class even though it is intimidating" (versus "I'm afraid of this class, so I don't belong in it").

- **Overgeneralization or labeling** (seeing a single event as a fixed pattern):

"I'm hurt that he cheated on me" (versus "He cheated on me. All guys are cheaters").

"Everyone messes up exams from time to time" (versus "I messed up on the exam. I'm a horrible student").

- **Catastrophizing/minimizing** (exaggerating or shrinking the importance of things):

"If I get a B, I'll be disappointed, but it isn't the end of the world" (versus "If I get a B, I'll be homeless").

"One good extracurricular activity is enough for me" (versus "I'm not involved in enough extracurriculars, so I'm failing at college").

- **Mind reading, or jumping to conclusions** (making assumptions without proof):

"My professor will be understanding and wants to help me learn and grow" (versus "My professor will be disappointed in me if I don't get an A").

"That person could be sad for a million reasons that have nothing to do with me" (versus "That person must not like me because they didn't smile at me").

> "I have been shocked by how helpful it is to allow myself to talk about my thoughts out loud, instead of ignoring them and just soldiering on. I've learned that speaking about what is on my mind allows me to make decisions that are healthier for me. Instead of scrolling mindlessly on my phone to numb myself, I now consciously choose an activity that is more connecting or meaningful, such as getting coffee with a friend or reading some pressing homework."
>
> — KOFI

- **Mind reading, or fortune telling** (making predictions that prejudge outcomes):

  "I didn't do the reading, but I can still get something out of listening to the class discussion" (versus "I didn't do the reading, so this class will turn out badly").

  "I really have no idea what will happen at this party because some parties are fun and some aren't" (versus "I won't make any friends at this party").

- **Personalization** (making yourself the cause of larger problems):

  "Certain situations trigger my anxiety, and I need help figuring out how to handle them differently" (versus "I'm the reason I always feel anxious").

"The professor and all the students were just off today, so the class didn't go as well as usual" (versus "The class went badly because I didn't speak up enough").

Distract Yourself from Unhelpful Thoughts

Another strategy for dealing with unhelpful thoughts is to simply think about or do something else. Focus your mind on another topic. Give yourself a break by calling a friend, watching a favorite show, or reading a favorite book. Distraction can make all the difference to get our minds off the wrong track.

WHEN TO SEEK PROFESSIONAL HELP

Are your unhelpful thoughts in charge of your life? Because you are listening to those unhelpful thoughts, do you find yourself staying with unhelpful behaviors, such as avoiding situations, isolating from friends, or choosing quick fixes that aren't what you really want? If so, then consider seeking counseling to help cope with negative thought patterns.

Here are some other signs that indicate counseling might be needed:

- You would never talk to a friend the way you talk to yourself.
- You can't turn off your thoughts.
- Your thoughts cause regular negative moods.
- You feel hopeless about ever feeling good about yourself.
- You haven't been able to change negative thoughts on your own.

"I have developed a practice for myself in the morning and at night that helps me be more intentional with my response to my thoughts. I now take a few moments at the beginning and end of my day to reflect on what I am thinking, where my head is at in general. Then I explicitly work to show myself the same grace that I show to others in my life. I feel so much better since I started this practice — it has prevented negative spirals and generated much more empathy for myself."

— MORGAN

NEED TO TALK NOW?

If you or someone you know is thinking about suicide — whether in crisis or not — **call or text 988** to chat with a counselor for free confidential support.

Get help right away if you notice any of the following:

- You don't want to be alive right now, or you wish you could go back to a happier time or be in the future when the pain might be over.

- You think about death or are preoccupied with the idea of death.
- You worry you are a burden on others.
- You question whether life is worth living.
- At times you have visualized ways you can end your life.

If any of this applies to you, *you deserve to get counseling as soon as possible, if not immediately.* See the resources below and review the "Suicide Prevention Checklist" (pages 330–32).

RESOURCES

On Campus

- College counseling center: A counselor can help you learn to recognize your unhelpful thoughts, create ways to replace them, and support your efforts to practice new coping strategies. A counselor can also recommend referrals to off-campus providers to treat other underlying issues (such as anxiety, depression, bipolar disorder, and so on).
- College chaplain: Chaplains can provide mentorship and support.
- College residence staff: Staff can help provide support and connect you to other resources.
- College diversity office: This office may be able to offer support that matches your culture.
- College medical center: Visit the medical center for assessment and medication, as well as referrals to off-campus resources.

Websites

- ULifeline (text HOME to 741-741; www.ulifeline.org): ULifeline offers a text and phone line for immediate help. Resources include general information and a "self-evaluator," which is a screening tool for most major mental health issues.

- The Jed Foundation (www.jedfoundation.org): Jed is a nonprofit that protects emotional health and prevents suicide for our nation's teens and young adults. Visit their Mental Health Resource Center.
- 988 Suicide & Crisis Lifeline (988; www.988lifeline.org): If you or someone you know is thinking about suicide — whether in crisis or not — call or text 988, or visit the website, to chat with a counselor. Previously known as the National Suicide Prevention Lifeline, this national network of crisis centers provides 24/7, free, and confidential support to people in suicidal crisis or emotional distress.

Books

- *10% Happier: How I Tamed the Voice in My Head, Reduced Stress Without Losing My Edge, and Found Self-Help That Actually Works* by Dan Harris: This book follows the author's journey to discover how mindfulness meditation helps lower stress and brings more self-acceptance and equanimity.

Chapter 13

Comparing Yourself to Others

"If that person can do it, then there's no reason I shouldn't be able to do it. So why can't I?"

"Her post got 187 likes but mine only got 143."

"I felt fine about my old computer until I saw that everyone in class seems to have a brand-new MacBook."

"Everyone has a girlfriend or boyfriend but me."

"So many people here have married parents. I feel really different because I've never even met my dad."

Since our eyes face out, it's only natural that humans watch the world and what other humans are doing. Evolutionary psychologists tell us that humans actually evolved to be acutely aware of other members of our group, as our very survival depended on staying with the group. In short, comparing ourselves to others is part of the human condition. What we need to pay attention to is *how* we compare ourselves to others. This tendency can either uplift and motivate us or bring us down, with all kinds of detrimental effects.

Negative comparisons, when we perceive others as better and/or ourselves as worse, can feel like a blow to the soul, since we usually negatively compare ourselves to others in the very areas where we already feel vulnerable or lacking. Thus, it can be easy to globalize reactions and feel someone who's more successful in one way is better in all ways. Negative comparison is such a pervasive issue in college that it warrants its own chapter. Indeed, this issue causes a huge amount of pain for so many students and is only getting worse, largely due to social media.

Meanwhile, positive comparisons, when we see ourselves as better and/or others as worse, can be helpful if this inspires gratitude and appreciation for ourselves. It's good to feel we are doing fine — and maybe much better than we had feared. However, positive comparisons can have a negative impact if they lead us to feel smug and superior. In essence, comparisons can cultivate a "me versus them" mindset, and the challenge is to cultivate a "we're all on this planet together" mindset.

WHY COMPARISON IS A CHALLENGE

The opportunities to compare ourselves to others have exploded with the rise of our 24/7, social media culture.

It's easy to forget that, on social media, what we see about others is a surface presentation — only the headline, a visual snapshot, which is often carefully crafted, a highlight reel. What we know about ourselves, on the other hand, is a vast trove of information. We know every detail of our own experience and keenly understand all the ways we're imperfect. This makes for an unfair comparison. We aren't comparing apples to apples because we don't have all the data about the other person. It's more like comparing an enticing movie poster to the full documentary.

For most students, college is a time of enormous personal change, and students are extremely vulnerable to the effects of negative social comparison. They are struggling to negotiate a complex stew of expectations, desires, and obligations, and when they notice how others are doing, they can find many reasons to think they are not good enough.

Further, students are being regularly "judged" (given grades), which can create a competitive atmosphere and provide quantitative "proof" for negative comparisons. Invariably, someone is always getting better grades, participating in more clubs, or receiving more accolades than we are. Taken together, it's a hazardous combination. I have almost never had a client who didn't negatively compare themselves to others as one of their main presenting concerns.

Most people will never again live in a situation where all their work is reduced to a letter grade, multiple times per month, and in front of hundreds of peers and friends. Students are also usually living in close quarters, which can leave them feeling exposed, their choices and behaviors on display for all to see.

However, negative comparisons related to academic success don't hold a candle to those related to social life. Many college students think, *Everyone is having more fun than me.* It is a classic but statistically impossible observation. Social norming data tells us that perceptions of behavior are usually very inflated. Only those who make the most noise — the person who partied so hard they made a fool of themselves, or who announced their sexual exploits on social media — are known to all the next day. The quiet folks who stayed in and played Cards Against Humanity or watched a *Star Wars* marathon are not on the general social radar.

Social media puts the ability to compare at our fingertips. The feedback is immediate and often overwhelming. Recent studies have shown that frequent users of social media perceive themselves to be less happy than others. The reason? Too much time in the virtual world and not enough with in-person friends. Students talk about feeling "left out" when they see their friends having fun without them, which can lead to anxiety-producing FOMO (fear of missing out), especially on weekends. Students compare everything: how many "likes" their posts get, whether their musical tastes are considered cool, how many friends they have on Instagram, followers on Twitter, and pins on Pinterest…. Don't even get me started on dating sites.

Perhaps most destructive, our perfectionist culture invites negative comparison. Being average or good enough is not okay. College culture celebrates getting a 4.0, sculpting a perfect body, excelling at sports or music, being awarded the best scholarship, winning a coveted internship, and even volunteering at the most notable nonprofit.

To a degree, all these things can be true at any age, but many college students don't have the life experience yet to put these comparisons in perspective. Simply put, it's hard to realize that perceived failures and successes are temporary, ephemeral moments in a long journey. Whatever happens today rarely makes or breaks anyone's life from that moment on.

STRATEGIES

Be Prepared for Social Comparison

One of the best ways to deal with "compare and despair" is to know that comparisons will inevitably come up. Like all thoughts, we can't control or stop comparisons, but we can control our reactions to them. If we develop coping strategies ahead of time, negative comparisons become much less hurtful.

Be Self-Aware of Negative Thought Patterns

Negative comparisons are another negative thought pattern. So follow the ABC advice I describe in chapters 10, 11, and 12: be aware when such judgments arise, gently accept and name them — "Oh, I'm comparing myself here" — and choose how to react. Most of the time, you don't have to do anything else; just recognizing and naming the negative comparison often stops the process in its tracks. Labeling the negative comparison can help lessen or even stop the residual negative vibrations.

"I notice that I'm doing a lot of comparing related to XYZ."
"I'm really judging myself against my classmate/friend today."
"Oh, I'm comparing and despairing again."

Avoid Negative Self-Criticisms

When you engage in negative comparisons, do not exacerbate the situation by saying something like, "I'm such an idiot for comparing myself all the time." Don't pile on with more negative comparisons! Just recognize your negative thoughts and be kind to yourself.

"When I first got the test handed back, I was happy with the grade I had received. That good feeling lasted until I glanced over to my neighbor and saw that person scored a few points higher. Instead of sticking with *I did fine on this test*, my thoughts changed to *I'm not as good as...* and *I wish I had what they had*. Those bad feelings hit me with a thunk and like a slow burn that lasted for hours. It started to get better when I realized that I am obsessively focused on grades and worrying about where I stand in college as a first-year student."

— FINN

Feel Your Feelings for a Little Bit

In the awareness and being steps of the ABC process, it's okay and even helpful to allow yourself to feel your feelings, at least for a little bit. Give yourself a moment to be jealous, if that's how you feel, but then choose what to do about it: take no action, do something productive, or replace the thought.

Replace Negative Comparisons with Empathy

What positive thoughts can you use to replace negative comparisons? Usually, a negative comparison indicates a need for kindness and gentle attention, not criticism. So say something kind to yourself. What would you say to a friend who needed some kindness?

"You are being awfully hard on yourself today. You don't need to do that."
"You deserve some support today."
"I like you just the way you are."

Be Curious about a Negative Comparison

Be curious and brave and look directly at what you are comparing. Thoroughly assess the issue. Then ask yourself, is this issue something you actually, really care about, or is it an expectation you feel others or the culture have placed on you? Will you remember it in ten years?

Don't Confuse Exterior Portraits with Internal Reality

This relates to social media, but it can be true at any time. We only see people from the outside and the portrait they present; we can't know their struggles, history, or how they feel inside. Remind yourself that, if you knew their whole story and any pain they have dealt with, your comparison might be different.

Reduce Time on Social Media

If social media use is triggering lots of negative comparisons, reduce your exposure to social media. See chapters 34 and 35 for more on this.

WHEN TO SEEK PROFESSIONAL HELP

If you are constantly disabled by negative comparisons to others, and struggle with self-esteem, consider seeking outside help. Visit your campus counseling center or get a referral to an off-campus therapist.

"I have been comparing myself to my boyfriend's ex-girlfriends, and I'm really afraid of not measuring up. I want to appear effortlessly cool, as they seem to be. I think my comparisons are driven by my fears of losing him. I now realize that I don't want to be so down on myself over whether or not I hold on to a guy."

— DAE

RESOURCES

On Campus

- College counseling center: A counselor can help you identify any underlying issues behind negative comparisons and help you develop coping strategies. They can also make referrals to off-campus providers.
- College residence staff: Residence staff are often connected to students and can offer reassurance. Trust your gut and reach out to someone who appeals to you and seems understanding.
- College chaplain: Chaplains, and the chapel itself, can offer support and validation.

Books

- *The Comparison Cure: How to Be Less "Them" and More You* by Lucy Sheridan: This book offers detailed assessments and strategies for coping with many types of comparisons.

Chapter 14

Perfectionism

"Things are all-or-nothing with me — if it's not perfect, it doesn't exist."

"I keep studying, no matter how much sleep I am missing, until I am sure I know it beyond well enough."

"I think that I've failed if I get an A-. I'm always going for an A."

"Everything is something I *have* to do."

"I'm so worried about getting things wrong."

Perfectionism is one of the defining mental health issues of our era. Perfectionism isn't about striving to do well or aiming for excellence. Perfectionism is the belief that how well we do is a measure of our value as a person. Thus, if we want to judge ourselves well, we must do well every time and all the time. This belief leads to a cycle of negative thoughts and patterns: We work hard but it never feels like enough, since we feel we could always have done more. Thus, we almost never feel satisfied. We may earn an A+ on one paper, but the proud feeling vanishes as the next task looms. Perfectionism is often driven by the fear of failure, since failure is not an option, as it means we are worthless as a person. That makes the stakes of almost everything we do very high. Our sense of self depends on how well we do in class, how good we look, how much we earn, how smart we are (compared to others), how many friends we have, and so on. Then, if something doesn't go well, it is not just disappointing; it's devastating.

Striving for excellence is wholly different. It pushes us to work hard for achievement and feel satisfied when we've done the best job we can. It pushes us to have high standards, but to value the process as well as the outcome. Striving for excellence means being highly motivated to achieve a meaningful goal without failure being seen as a reflection of our personal worth. Indeed, it includes the recognition that our effort is the main thing that defines us, not outcomes, since every undertaking involves risk and is ultimately out of our control. When we strive for excellence, failure *is* an option, but that is not a failure of the self.

WHY AVOIDING PERFECTIONISM IS A CHALLENGE

Our culture celebrates exterior accomplishments. As a culture, we value who makes the most money, who went to the most prestigious school, who is the most fit and beautiful, and so on. Thoughtful people of high moral principle might be acknowledged but not valued to the same degree. Being kind is sometimes praised, but more often it is attacked or belittled.

Students often feel hounded by a fear of failure, since failure is a continual threat grade-wise. That makes it quite easy to falsely equate their level of success in college as a reflection of their relative worth as a person.

Being judged on every assignment in every class can lead to constant comparison, both with other students and with the ideal of the "best student." This can lead to the following problems:

- Overworking, especially on weekend nights when everyone else is playing
- Being overscheduled, by taking every possible class, joining multiple student organizations, doing an internship, doing volunteer work, working jobs for money, and attending to family responsibilities
- Feeling overwhelmed and miserable, since it is never possible to keep up with and do well at everything every day

Trying to meet an idealized standard can lead to paralysis. This can show up in a few different ways:

- A high rate of procrastination as people get stuck by fear of not being good enough
- Not spending time doing activities that are pleasurable or meaningful if the person can't be "the best" at them or if the activity doesn't serve a practical purpose, like looking good on a résumé

At college, since there is always the potential to learn more — because there is an infinite amount of knowledge — there is rarely a break from perfectionism. This can lead to a lack of boundaries between work and play.

- Even when the appropriate work is completed, worry remains; there is no off switch to feeling stressed.
- When doing something fun, it's hard to let go and truly enjoy it, since we feel we should be studying or doing something productive.
- Decision making becomes debilitating because there are so many right answers and an intense fear of making the wrong choice.

STRATEGIES

Admit That Perfectionism Is a Problem

We live in a productivity culture, so it is a radical act to admit that trying to be perfect every day is a problem.

To combat and undo the harm that perfectionism causes, the first step is acknowledging that perfectionism causes harm. This is harder than it sounds. The insidious nature of perfectionism is that it uses the language of excellence to mask the fear of failure underneath: *Isn't it commendable to read every word of every article assigned? Isn't it right to skip some sleep in college to get all your work done?* Not necessarily. Choosing to do those things isn't necessarily a problem, but if they are driven by a fear of failure, then they won't help. That fear will remain no matter how hard you work. It may take a concerted effort to recognize and name what is really going on.

Assess Your Particular Brand of Perfectionism

Every person has a slightly different way of telling themselves they have to "do more" in order to "be okay," so it can be very challenging to identify and name your version of perfectionism. It may be helpful to make a list of your personal perfectionism messages. Here are some examples:

> "Since I can't write a flawless paper, I'm not going to even start."
> "I have to be there for everyone, all the time. Otherwise, I'm not a great friend."
> "I study every Friday and Saturday night because that's what the best students do."

Recognize Perfectionistic Messages

Remember, simply recognizing negative thought patterns and labeling them as they happen is half the battle to healing. Consider these perfectionist messages as red flags:

> "I have to get all As; an A- is not good enough."
> "I have to get the top score in the class."
> "I'll only be happy if I fit in a size 6 dress."
> "I need to read all the classics of literature."
> "I'll have more friends if I'm always chill and in a good mood."

Choose to Replace Perfectionist Messages

As I describe in chapter 12, we can choose to label negative thoughts as "unhelpful" and replace them with healthier ones. Replacing negative messages with positive ones is like creating a road map for where you want to be. Here are some examples of healthier, nonperfectionist messages:

> "I am learning so much in this class."
> "I love how I feel in this dress."

> "I was working on my honors thesis and found myself crippled by the overwhelming scope and expectation of this research paper. I started to use the astrophysics metaphor of the Hohmann transfer orbit, where a space launch must wait for the required planetary alignment to occur, to help remind myself that certain things can't be rushed, and I can put the work in step by step and still meet my goal."
>
> — REMY

"I am really enjoying this novel."

"I am a good person no matter what my grades."

"I'm doing well when I've studied as hard as I can and sought out help from professors and tutors."

"I deserve to love my body just as it is."

"It's okay to make mistakes. No one is perfect. It is impossible to *not* make mistakes."

"I have done enough today."

"I deserve to hang out with my friends on Friday and Saturday nights."

"I deserve to get enough sleep every night."

"I deserve some downtime every day."

"I am enough."

"I'm learning and growing; I don't have to know it all now."

Set Specific, Achievable Goals

This is where thoughts and behaviors intersect. Once you recognize the areas where you are particularly hard on yourself, set some boundaries, which help both over- and underachievers. Changing some behaviors will set the stage for being able to change thoughts.

For example, having a firm cutoff point for homework of 10 p.m., knowing you want to get to sleep before midnight, works for both overachievers and underachievers. Overworked students can practice saying, "I've done enough for one day," and procrastinators can practice saying, "I don't have to get everything done, but I commit to working from seven to ten at night."

Adopt a Growth Mindset

Many students struggle with feeling that they should look smart rather than be fallible and in learning mode. The question is, how do you deal with that? As the psychologist Carol S. Dweck describes it (in her book *Mindset*; see resources below), people with a "fixed mindset" avoid challenges, give up in the face of obstacles, believe that effort is fruitless, ignore criticism, and are threatened by the success of others. Meanwhile, people with a "growth mindset" take the opposite approach:

- They embrace challenges.
- They persist when faced with obstacles.
- They believe that effort is what leads to mastery.
- They learn from criticism.
- They are inspired by the success of others.

"I usually overstudy to such an extent that there is little chance that I could not get a great grade. I have been hounded by fears of imperfection as long as I can remember, as my mom has been critical of both my academic success and my looks. I have been journaling about the ways that I demand the impossible of myself, and I've started to be able to choose how I want to see myself and the worth of the work I am already doing."

— ASAMA

Consider Family and Cultural Sources of Perfectionism

In some families, parents do everything to a high level of achievement or excellence, and they expect a high level of achievement or excellence from their children. On the other hand, in some families, children have a hard time feeling worthy of love and belonging. This can trigger a reaction to try to use exterior achievements (being perfect) to "earn" the deep, interior state of feeling loved with no expectations. In some cultures, perfection is expected at the cost of everything else. Some cultures also have a history of enduring hardships, and children can believe they must work as hard as possible to match their family legacy. Finally, students from marginalized cultures may feel they are representing their whole culture, and as a result they feel great pressure to be perfect.

WHEN TO SEEK PROFESSIONAL HELP

Does perfectionism cause you to lose joy in your studies, stop enjoying the present moment with friends, or devalue your self-care (such as sleeping, eating, and so on)? Have you recognized a family or cultural pattern that leads you to believe you must be doing it all, all the time? Do you regularly feel you don't measure up, that you aren't enough just as you are, or that you should be doing better at everything you try? If this speaks to you, consider reaching out to a trusted resource or counselor for help confronting your inner perfectionist.

RESOURCES

On Campus

- College counseling center: A counselor can help you identify any harmful perfectionist beliefs and help you develop kinder beliefs and coping skills. They can also recommend referrals to off-campus providers.
- College study skills center: If your work habits are suffering, the study center can help you make a realistic plan.
- College career center: A career counselor can help you determine how to meet your career goals, either offering reassurance that you are doing enough or advice for what exactly will help.
- College chaplain: Chaplains, or the chapel itself, can offer radical acceptance of who you are, the ultimate antidote to perfectionism.

Books

- *The Gifts of Imperfection: Let Go of Who You Think You're Supposed to Be and Embrace Who You Are* by Brené Brown: This is one of the best resources for students (of all ages) on how to learn to be themselves, not perfect.
- *Mindset: The New Psychology of Success* by Carol S. Dweck: This book introduces the concept of growth and fixed mindsets, which is crucial to understanding what gets in the way of motivation and helps you rediscover the joy of learning.
- *Radical Acceptance: Embracing Your Life with the Heart of a Buddha* by Tara Brach: This book offers Buddhist and mindfulness teaching about how to be our authentic self instead of suffering with perfectionism or self-judgment.

Chapter 15

Negativity

"I'm an idiot."

"I'll never make it."

"I'm the dumbest person at my college."

"I'm so fat and ugly."

"I hate myself."

Negativity refers to the pessimistic inner messages we tell ourselves no matter what happens. When negative thoughts become our daily soundtrack, they can diminish our ability to learn and grow, to perform as we know we can, and to bounce back from difficult events (including physical healing).

Negativity is different than being realistic or honest. When bad things happen, it's wise to acknowledge that, along with any disappointment, fear, and pain we feel. Life can be hard, and we can become frustrated, discouraged, depressed, overwhelmed, hopeless, and angry over the challenges we face. By definition, these are negative thoughts, and at times, there is no avoiding them.

Negativity, on the other hand, does not need a source; it is an ongoing or perpetual mindset, a continual expectation that things will not work out or go our way. This might seem obvious, but ongoing negativity makes maintaining a positive outlook impossible, and having a positive outlook is critical to our health. Like negativity, positivity is an ongoing mindset, and it is key to our resilience. Positivity helps us cope with the daily ups and downs that are part of life, so that negative feelings and thoughts don't become a permanent state of mind.

This is not false optimism, or the belief that things will always work out no matter what (which is sometimes called toxic positivity). Research shows that being hopeful *and* realistic is the healthiest outlook.

WHY AVOIDING NEGATIVITY IS A CHALLENGE

Why do we have negative thoughts in the first place, and why is it so hard to change them? Our minds have a negativity bias — that's how humans have survived for hundreds of thousands of years. In order to survive, we learned to be constantly alert to danger, not knowing if a rustle in the leaves was the wind or a saber-toothed tiger. Our ancestors may also have appreciated the beauty of a sunset, but getting lost in positive feelings was sometimes a good way to get killed.

So humans developed a knee-jerk, almost automatic negative reaction to anything. We remain wired with this negativity bias today, and unless we interrupt it, it can run rampant. That is, one negative thought can lead to another, each one worse than the last. For example, the negative thought "That guy just ignored me" might trigger the thought "People don't like me," which leads to another, "I must be worthless."

This is how negative thoughts turn into negativity, which is often signaled by rumination. That is, the more we think negative thoughts, the stronger they become. This is the process of all learning: We get better at whatever we practice.

Further, our upbringing can influence our temperament. If we are raised by more optimistic or more pessimistic parents, caregivers, and family, those tendencies have a way of rubbing off on us.

Given the intensity of college — and the perception that college is a make-or-break time, both career-wise and socially — it is easy for students to feel overwhelmed and fall into negativity.

Students certainly want, and often expect, to be successful in classes, extracurriculars, and with friends. But falling short in any of these areas can lead to a negativity spiral. Sometimes students develop "impostor syndrome," so that even when they are successful, they feel like frauds who are only fooling everyone. Students can be very hard on themselves. When they assess their self-talk, they find they aren't being kind and encouraging. They admit: "I'd never, ever talk to one of my friends the way I talk to myself."

Negativity can also be contagious. That is, if students are hanging out with friends who are themselves full of negativity, they can be easily adopt the same mindset.

STRATEGIES

Examine Your Self-Talk

If you aren't sure whether or not you are being too negative in your self-talk, try jotting down your inner dialogue for a few days. This doesn't have to be formal or fancy; write down whatever you notice in a running list over a period of time. Catch your mind at regular intervals, such as when you sit down to class.

Then evaluate what you find and acknowledge the overall tone and content of your thoughts. Name this or characterize it, to make this evaluation concrete.

Just acknowledging the quality of our thoughts is a huge step, and it's vital for recognizing negativity and letting it go. You might be surprised at how negative your running inner dialogue is, since it is easy to get used to hearing a negative soundtrack and accepting it as "normal."

Recognition alone can be enough to shake up and release negativity. If we don't pay attention to our self-talk, or don't believe it matters how negative we are, then negativity will undoubtedly continue to adversely affect our state of mind.

Practice More Positive Self-Talk

As you learn to recognize negative self-talk, interrupt and replace it with more positive but still honest self-talk. When you think something negative about yourself, reframe it into a positive statement or say something kind about yourself. Here are some examples:

> If you think, "I'm a loser," replace this with, "I am kind and care about others."
>
> If you think, "I'm such a f@#kup," replace this with, "Making mistakes is how we learn."
>
> If you think, "No one cares about me," replace this with, "The people who know me best love me."
>
> If you think, "I hate myself," replace this with, "I'm learning to love myself."

Tell Others Positive Things

Tell others positive things on a daily basis, if possible. This creates more positivity for everyone: you, the person you are complimenting, and anyone who hears you. Do this in all communications: via text, email, and face-to-face. Here are some examples:

> "You're an awesome friend."
>
> "Your hair looks nice today."
>
> "Thanks for your support. I really appreciate it."

Give Negative Thoughts a Persona or Label

Personifying negative thoughts, or creating a shorthand label for them, can help identify and diffuse them quickly. For instance, some people might repeat a mantra, like "Thoughts aren't facts," whenever they recognize a negative thought. Others might embody their negative thoughts as Eeyore (the sad donkey from Winnie-the-Pooh) or a green gremlin on their shoulder. Others will tie a colored string around their wrist or wear a necklace that they can touch to help remind them to think more positively.

Some students relate to the acronym ANT, which stands for "automatic negative thoughts." Notice a negative thought? Start singing or humming, "The ants come marching one by one." Poking fun at ourselves is a good way to undermine negativity.

Notice When Good Things Happen

Our "negativity bias" makes us prone to noticing when things go wrong. To counteract this, practice noticing when things go right, or when you simply feel good, even for no reason. Take the time to name moments, thoughts, and events as "good," or even "neutral," which is at least not bad. Too often we only remember to label the "I don't feel good" moments.

Keep a Gratitude Journal

Gratitude journaling has helped many students improve their outlook and perception of events. When you practice paying attention to the good things in life — things you might otherwise just let slip by — you feel them more. This is amplified by writing them down, rather than just noticing them in our minds. A gratitude journal doesn't need to be fancy or something that's dedicated to only this purpose. You can use any type of notebook, an existing journal, a bullet journal, a daily planner, or a phone app.

It doesn't have to take much time, but every few days or daily, write down one or two things you are grateful for. Here are some topics you might write about:

- What moments have you enjoyed today? These can be small things. For example, if you appreciated the free hot tea in the library, write about why you liked it.
- What professor, staff member, or friend has been helpful this week? Noticing caring people can have a great impact on our state of mind.
- What parts of your day would you be sad to go without? This can be everyday stuff. For example, do you really appreciate a morning hot shower or having fruit for breakfast? Taking the time to notice what we'd miss if it was gone helps us appreciate what we have.
- What aspects of your life are working well, or what would cause distress if it wasn't going well? Appreciate things like your health,

"My panic and anxiety symptoms were getting worse and had recently interfered with my ability to concentrate in class. I was ready to challenge my beliefs that *I need to tough it out* and *I don't need time for myself.* To start, I worked on catching my negative self-talk and giving myself permission to take some deep breaths and make time in my day to relax."

— NICHELLE

your relationships, or any aspect of life that is easy to overlook or take for granted. For example, how much did you enjoy not having a toothache today?

- What positive things happened that you didn't expect? As humans, we delight in pleasant surprises. Recording them in a journal will help strengthen that feeling and make it last.

WHEN TO SEEK PROFESSIONAL HELP

We all have negative thoughts. These are normal reactions to life's rough moments. However, when negative thoughts are persistent and don't resolve on their own, or when they interfere with daily life — such as causing feelings of isolation or disinterest in studies — they could be a part of depression or another mental health issue. When in doubt, seek advice and help.

However, if persistent negativity has led to suicidal thoughts, get counseling help as soon as possible, *if not immediately*. Here are some examples:

- You wish you could go back to a happier time.
- You wish you could be in the future when the pain might be over.
- You often think about death or are preoccupied with the idea of death.
- You feel you are a burden on others.
- You think life isn't worth living.
- You think about ways you can end your life.

See the resources below and the "Suicide Prevention Checklist" (pages 330–32).

> ### NEED TO TALK NOW?
>
> If you or someone you know is thinking about suicide — whether in crisis or not — **call or text 988** to chat with a counselor for free confidential support.

RESOURCES

On Campus

- College counseling center: A counselor can help you recognize and shift negative thoughts, as well as develop ongoing coping strategies. A counselor can also help recommend referrals to off-campus providers for mental health issues that need long-term treatment.
- College residence staff: Part of the job for residence staff is to provide a resource for students struggling with campus life, including negative thinking. They can also connect you to other campus resources.
- College student organizations: One way to counteract negativity is to get involved with other students outside of academics. Student-run groups can be a source of joy, meaning, and companionship. Explore what's available and try something new or that appeals to you.
- College study skills center: If negativity is arising because of academic struggles, reach out to the study center for support and guidance. They can help you create a better study plan.
- College career center: Having a vision for your college path and future career can be an important aspect of coping with negativity.

"I am finally able to understand how a negative thought — *I shouldn't be feeling bad since I've started to take medication* — caused a recent downward spiral. I was able to connect that thought to other 'shoulds' I have about how I am supposed to be in my life. I have been able to start practicing more supportive and understanding self-talk, such as *I don't have to be productive all the time*, which led to practicing behaviors that helped me enjoy my life like reading for pleasure and solving puzzles."

— PARKER

- College chaplain: Chaplains, or the chapel itself, can offer a place of refuge or peace, which can be a positive antidote to negativity.
- College athletics: Movement and exercise improve mood and can help counteract negativity. Join a club sport or take a movement class like yoga, dance, or martial arts.

Books

- *Self-Compassion: The Proven Power of Being Kind to Yourself* by Kristin Neff: This book makes the best case for stopping self-judgment and treating yourself with the same kindness that you give to others.

Apps

- MindShift: This free app includes a "Thought Journal" and "Coping Cards," which help develop more effective ways of thinking.
- ThinkUp (www.thinkup.me): This free, easy-to-use app provides positive affirmations on many different topics.
- Happify (www.happify.com): This free app takes a gaming approach to help train the brain to overcome negative thoughts.

Chapter 16

Impostor Syndrome

"I'm not smart enough to be here. They just needed to make a quota."

"The professors must feel sorry for me to give me these good grades. I'm not sure my work's that good."

"I work harder than everyone else, so I do okay, but I'm actually not smart enough to be at this school."

"I fear the day when my professor calls me out and finds out that I actually don't know what I'm doing."

"I think I'm fooling everyone and any day now they will discover I don't belong here."

Impostor syndrome is not the same as low self-esteem. Rather, it's the sense that we are fooling others, that we are undeserving of success, and that we will be found out as not as talented, smart, or high-achieving as people think. Instead of owning our success, we explain it away, attributing it to something besides ourselves, such as a college meeting a quota, good luck, a friendly teacher, being at the right place at the right time, or working hard (but lacking talent).

When it was first studied, impostor syndrome was thought to apply only to women. Recent studies show it affects many people, regardless of gender, ethnicity, social status, and so on. In college, it affects many people of color, first-generation students, and people with marginalized identities.

Some researchers and therapists think that impostor syndrome damages Black women the most. In a 2021 essay titled "Black Women: You Are Not Defective," author Resmaa Menakem writes, "In America, Black women often experience themselves as fraudulent, substandard, or not good enough." Even Black celebrities like Oprah Winfrey and Michelle Obama have admitted to experiencing impostor syndrome.

WHY IMPOSTOR SYNDROME IS A CHALLENGE

Impostor syndrome is common in academia and the business world, since these are arenas that emphasize high achievement and where people are often judged by subjective standards. Impostor syndrome can lower a person's belief that they can achieve their goals or succeed, and lack of self-belief can affect engagement, motivation, mental health, and a sense of belonging.

Impostor syndrome can greatly impact college students. Every class discussion, every quiz, paper, or exam, involves being evaluated by teachers and other students. Each is an opportunity for impostor syndrome to spark feelings of self-doubt, anxiety, and even depression. Even when students are doing well, they can experience impostor syndrome multiple times a day.

In general, students will respond to impostor syndrome in one of three ways:

1. They overprepare, causing stress and exhaustion, and then attribute their success solely to their effort, not their abilities.
2. They procrastinate, causing stress and anguish, and then attribute their success to luck or their failure to lack of organization.
3. They try to be invisible or unobtrusive, which leads to less attention or affirmation.

STRATEGIES

Remember That Impostor Syndrome Is Common

Roughly 70 percent of high achievers have experienced impostor syndrome at one time or another, but unless someone tells you, there is no way to know if someone is experiencing it, since it is invisible! When you feel it, remind yourself that this is a common condition, which can help take the edge off.

Recognize Impostor Syndrome Self-Talk

Don't forget to use the ABC approach (awareness, being, choosing) to tackle this issue. Start with awareness, and learn to recognize when impostor syndrome tends to show up and what it sounds like. Here are some examples:

"I can never fail; I have to be perfect."
"I'm a fake, so I should just give up."
"I can't ask for help or people will know how dumb I really am."
"I should be able to do it all, but I can't, so I suck."
"I have to hide my struggles and look like I've got it all together."

Acknowledge Impostor Syndrome When It Occurs

Once you become aware of impostor syndrome, identify it in the moment and just be with it. Call out impostor syndrome self-talk: "That's my impostor syndrome talking"; "Welcome back, impostor syndrome. I see you."

Choose Positive Self-Talk

What should you do once you recognize impostor syndrome? First, you can label it as "unhelpful" and ignore it. Choose not to believe it. In *The Secret Thoughts of Successful Women* (see resources below), Valerie Young advises, "The important thing is not to take the discomfort of feeling out

> "One of the hardest things for me to learn was that I could say no and not try to do it all. When I came to college, I thought I should say yes to everything, but now I know that isn't sustainable for me. Now I'm starting to give myself time to refill my well, and this has helped me be able to stay positive and remember the good I have done and am doing, rather than defaulting to my impostor syndrome thinking."
>
> — ENRIQUE

of your element to mean you are somehow less intelligent, capable, or worthy than others. You are where you are because you deserve to be. Period."

At the same time, you can choose to replace negative thoughts with more positive and empowering thoughts. Choose self-talk that builds self-confidence, rather than tears it down. These could be mantras you use to start each day or that you say before class. Here are some examples of positive self-talk:

"I'm qualified to be here, but I'm here to learn. I'm not supposed to already know everything."

"I'm proud of what I've accomplished even though I don't excel at everything."

"It's wise to seek help and feedback. That's how smart people succeed."

"The more I study and learn, the better I will get."

"I will graduate and find a job in my field."

Keep Track of Your Successes

Impostor syndrome minimizes what is good, which creates self-doubt and can lead to anxiety and depression. Instead, write down a list of your talents, gifts, and successes (see the instructions under "Make Your Own Personality Lists," page 88), and then add to it whenever something good happens, big or small. This list is just for you, not for anyone else (or for your résumé). Then reread this list whenever impostor syndrome rears its head. Here are some examples of what to write down:

"My professor liked what I said in class today."

"I enjoyed writing that essay."

"The study group I started has been a game changer, and all the group members love it."

"I was invited to speak on a panel, and I feel proud to be included."

WHEN TO SEEK PROFESSIONAL HELP

Are you unable to overcome feeling like a phony? Are you unable to give yourself credit for your intelligence or qualifications? Have you been feeling down on yourself, unable to be as productive as you know you could be? If so, reach out for help from a trusted mentor or counselor. Since impostor syndrome is invisible, it is an amazing feeling to hear that teachers, professionals, and other adults have also struggled with impostor syndrome.

"Learning to notice when I get into my impostor syndrome thinking has made a big impact for me. Once I stopped blaming myself for having impostor syndrome thinking, I was able to take the next step and switch my thinking from negative to positive self-talk. I use my journal to look up the positive affirmations that I want to practice."

— ZENI

RESOURCES

On Campus

- College counseling center: A counselor can help you identify impostor syndrome and provide support. They can also recommend referrals to off-campus providers.
- College diversity office: A diversity office can often offer support that matches your culture. Minority students who are the first in their family or community to attend college frequently experience impostor syndrome.
- College chaplain: A chaplain can provide mentorship and support and help you practice positive affirmations.
- College residence staff: Staff can provide support and connection.

Books

- *The Impostor Phenomenon: Overcoming the Fear That Haunts Your Success* by Pauline Rose Clance: Dr. Clance, along with Suzanne

Imes, coined the term *impostor syndrome* in 1974. This book is a thorough explanation of impostor syndrome, what it feels like to live with it, the consequences, and how to overcome it.

- *The Secret Thoughts of Successful Women: And Men: Why Capable People Suffer from Impostor Syndrome and How to Thrive in Spite of It* by Valerie Young: This book is another comprehensive overview by a major researcher in the field.
- *Imposter Syndrome Remedy: A 30-Day Action Plan to Stop Feeling like a Fraud* by Emee Vida Estacio: This book breaks down the aspects of impostor syndrome, gives many practical strategies for challenging it, and includes a workbook.
- *Shifting: The Double Lives of Black Women in America* by Charisse Jones and Kumea Shorter-Gooden: This book looks at the daily reality of how Black women have needed to shift away from their real selves to cope and survive in white America, and how this phenomenon might begin to change.

Part IV

YOUR EMOTIONS

Many of us spend our whole lives running from feelings
with the mistaken belief that you cannot bear the pain.
But you have already borne the pain. What you have not done
is feel all you are, beyond that pain.

— KAHLIL GIBRAN

Emotions make us human. Emotions are hardwired into every cell. They serve important functions; for example, fear helps us react to danger, love helps us form lifesaving social bonds, joy keeps us going, anger motivates us to make change. However, those same emotions can become maladaptive and get in the way of us living our lives as we want. Fear of making a mistake keeps us from trying something, loving without boundaries can lead us to forget ourselves, pleasure without boundaries can lead us to forget our responsibilities, unchecked anger can prompt us to act in destructive ways.

The result of maladaptive emotions is often that our emotions take over running our lives, rather than serving us. Or the effort it takes to hide strong but uncomfortable emotions, such as grief or fear, can turn into something much worse.

I placed the "Your Thoughts" section before the "Your Emotions" section on purpose. In general, college students are more aware of their thoughts than their emotions. Usually it takes some conversation and exploration for students to discern what they are feeling. Students may know something is wrong, they feel bad, but they struggle to name the specific emotions they're experiencing.

As in part 3, "Your Thoughts," the paradigm I use to help you understand and cope with emotions is the ABC approach: awareness, being, choosing. This easy-to-remember three-step process helps us make sense of the times when emotions seem overwhelming or impossible to cope with. This method helps us name what is happening, gain a tiny bit of distance and perspective on our emotions, and make conscious choices for how we want to respond in the moment. For a review of this process, see "Use the ABC Method: Awareness, Being, Choosing" (pages 61–62).

Note: This book offers advice for working with current emotions, or emotional reactions in the present moment. This is *not* focused on processing emotions from the past, especially traumatic experiences. If you are struggling with trauma, seek help from a professional counselor or therapist; see appendix B, "Counseling," for more advice.

Chapter 17

Awareness 102: Recognizing Your Feelings

"I don't know how I'm feeling."

"My unwanted behavior comes out of nowhere. I'm not sure if I was feeling something before I acted."

"My feelings are all over the place."

"All I know is I'm overwhelmed. I can't define my specific emotions."

"I'm confused about how I feel."

Self-awareness of our feelings means being aware of emotions that are happening in the present moment. It's as simple and challenging as that.

It sounds like it should be easy, but often our emotions are simmering below our consciousness. Just acknowledging that there is an emotion at work can be very difficult.

It's like being in the middle of a storm. Emotions can be overwhelming, and it's hard to know what is happening. If you can recognize that you are in a storm of feelings, it gives you a chance to see what is going on. When you observe the workings of your own mind, it gives you just enough space from the emotions to be able to cope with them most effectively.

Being in the storm of feelings (left) vs. observing the storm

WHY RECOGNIZING EMOTIONS IS A CHALLENGE

Many cultures, especially Western culture, devalue emotions. Instead, they value rationality and stoicism, which leads to denial and dampening of emotions. When so-called negative emotions such as sadness or grief occur, we're supposed to act tough and not let those emotions show. Meanwhile, positive emotions are acceptable so long as they don't get out of hand.

Even when we accept and embrace our emotions, certain feelings are painful to experience, such as fear, sadness, and anger. In many cases, we can believe it's easier to bury those difficult feelings.

Many people don't have a lot of practice naming or talking about their feelings. They can find it hard to define their emotions, much less admit to themselves and others any painful emotions they are feeling. While some people have an easier time with this than others, most people need help developing the communication skills to discuss emotions.

This leads to another difficulty: It can be very hard to find someone who is open to talking about someone else's emotions and knows how to listen empathetically. These skills are rarely taught in any context, and it's obviously much harder to express our emotions if we don't have someone to share them with.

For students, emotional awareness is a particular challenge for these main reasons:

- Students are working hard and tend to avoid difficult emotions that get in the way of their studies.
- Social media presents an unrealistic, idealized portrait of "how to be" (usually happy), but it almost never affirms people for being the way they are. So students often don't want to "let in" any feelings that don't seem acceptable.
- Our culture supports avoidance behaviors, such as streaming entertainment, internet browsing, eating, shopping, and partying. This makes it very easy for students to escape their emotions.
- Students are rarely taught to value emotional awareness; they are usually taught to value "smarts" and to hide their feelings.
- Students are rarely taught to cope with difficult emotions in healthy ways. Since they, like most people, have experienced others being emotional in unhealthy ways, it can seem safer to avoid difficult emotions as much as possible.
- Students may want to avoid strong feelings that have been stereotypically connected to their identities, out of fear of prejudice and outside judgment.

STRATEGIES

Value Emotional Awareness

It is much harder to develop awareness of our emotions if we don't value this awareness. So make a commitment to yourself to develop your emotional awareness — knowing that you are rebelling against cultural norms to do so!

Listen to Your Body

Our bodies often signal when we have important feelings that need attention. Some indications are tight shoulders, a painful back, a stomachache, or a headache. Feeling overwhelmed or disoriented are also signs that big, challenging emotions are present. Here are some physical signs of the main emotions:

Happy: smiling face, relaxed body

Sad: crying, low energy, slumped shoulders

Disgusted: scrunched-up face, turning away

Angry: a red face, increased heart rate, feeling overheated, tense body

Fearful: wide eyes, tense body, increased heart rate

Surprised: gasping, mouth open, tense body, increased heart rate

Develop Habits That Foster Emotional Awareness

Remembering to be aware of our feelings is half the challenge. So develop the habit of checking in on your emotions regularly and often. You can do this in a variety of ways, for example:

- Whenever you think of it, pause, take a deep breath (or three), and ask yourself, "Where am I at? What am I feeling?"
- In between activities, slow down and check in with yourself. Consider how you feel about what just happened and about what you are doing next. Key points could be walking to class, before meals, going to the restroom, commuting to and from work, and so on.
- Use a feelings tracker app.
- Journal about your feelings, either in the morning or the evening. Use a bullet journal to track your daily mood.

Expand Your Emotional Vocabulary

In addition to paying more attention to your emotions, become more exact and specific about what you are feeling. There are many kinds of happiness and many kinds of sadness. For help, consult the feelings vocabulary list:

Feelings Vocabulary

Happy

Mild: amused, cheerful, content, genial, glad, pleased, satisfied

Moderate: delighted, enthusiastic, gleeful, inspired, jolly, joyful, up

Strong: ecstatic, elated, euphoric, exhilarated, overjoyed, rapturous, thrilled

Sad

Mild: blah, disappointed, displeased, down, fragile, glum, low, somber, unhappy

Moderate: blue, discouraged, downcast, gloomy, hurt, melancholic, rejected, sorrowful, upset

Strong: anguished, dejected, desolate, despairing, dismal, grief, grim, hopeless, woeful

Disgusted

Mild: annoyed, disappointed, dismayed, dissatisfied, irritated

Moderate: appalled, grossed out, offended, repelled

Strong: horrified, nauseated, revolted, sickened, violated

Angry

Mild: annoyed, bugged, frustrated, irked, irritated, let down

Moderate: aggravated, crabby, disrespected, exasperated, fuming, irritated, resentful, scornful

Strong: betrayed, furious, incensed, infuriated, outraged, vengeful, wrathful

Fearful

Mild: cautious, disquieted, shy, tense, timid, uneasy, worried

Moderate: afraid, anxious, apprehensive, belittled, distressed, fretful, nervous, overwhelmed, scared, threatened

Strong: alarmed, desperate, dread, frightened, horrified, incompetent, panicky, petrified, terrified

Surprised

Mild: bewildered, curious, excited, perplexed, startled, wondering

Moderate: amazed, confused, jolted, shocked

Strong: astonished, astounded, awed, dumfounded, stupefied

"I wasn't reaching out to my friends as much as I needed to, so I wasn't having as many fun social connections as I wanted. I journaled about my feelings, and I realized that I was feeling scared of rejection and feeling fear that people didn't want to hear from me. When I was able to be clear about that, I could make a rational argument to myself that my friends adore me and would love to hear from me. I could avoid letting those lingering feelings from the past rule my present behaviors."

— GWENDOLINE

Then practice using the feeling words in a sentence; either say it to yourself or write in your journal. Here are some examples:

- **Happy**

    "I feel joyful when I'm dancing in a big crowd."
    "I feel inspired after I connect with my roommates."

- **Sad**

    "I feel despair when I read about gun violence in our country."
    "I usually feel fragile on Sunday nights."

- **Disgusted**

    "I feel disappointed that the professor assigned a last-minute paper."
    "I feel repelled when I see classmates cheating on a test."

- **Angry**

    "I felt betrayed when my boyfriend said he had cheated on me."
    "I feel disrespected that my roommate never picks up her clothes."

- **Fearful**

    "I feel nervous about choosing a major."
    "I feel overwhelmed in my first-year seminar."

- **Surprised**

    "I feel astonished when people yell at each other in public."
    "I feel shocked when I see homeless people camping on the street."

Treat Numbness Like a Red Flag

Numbness isn't itself a feeling. Rather, when we feel numb, we are usually holding off very strong emotions we aren't ready to feel or are afraid we can't handle. If you feel numb, that isn't a lack of feeling, but a sign of perhaps too much feeling. Treat it as a sign that you need to find a safe way to explore what's going on, such as through journaling or talking to a friend or counselor.

Use Spiritual Practices for Self-Reflection

Spiritual practices can be a great entry to self-awareness. This doesn't require being a member of a specific faith or organized religion. For example, taking time out to pray (in your own way) or read spiritual writings can allow moments of self-reflection.

"I've been struggling with procrastination, specifically on writing papers. I would sit and stare at the computer and be unable to start. I decided to brainstorm what I was feeling at the computer the next time I sat down to write. I discovered I was experiencing feelings of worry and fear. I felt worried about not expressing anything special in my writing; my fear was that my professors would think I'm a mediocre student. Once I identified exactly what I was feeling, I was able to build kinder self-talk and this helped me move forward."

— BEN

WHEN TO SEEK PROFESSIONAL HELP

As you become more self-aware of your feelings, you may find your feelings are too much to handle alone. You might feel overwhelmed with too many emotions, unable to figure out what you are feeling, or notice that you feel numb most of the time. If this is the case, see a counselor or reach out to a trusted friend or family member.

RESOURCES

On Campus

- College counseling center: A counselor can help you learn to recognize your feelings and offer coping strategies. They can also recommend off-campus providers.
- College chaplain: Chaplains can provide mentorship and support.

- College residence staff: Staff can help provide support and connection.

Websites

- Verywell Mind (www.verywellmind.com): This mental health website has published an excellent article, "The 6 Types of Basic Emotions and Their Effect on Human Behavior," that provides a straightforward description of emotions and their role and importance in our lives (www.verywellmind.com/an-overview-of-the-types-of-emotions-4163976).

Chapter 18

Being 102: Naming Your Feelings Without Judgment

"I shouldn't be sad. I'm lucky to be in college."

"I hate being anxious!!"

"I thought I'd be done feeling sad about this breakup after a month."

"I don't want to have these feelings."

"These feelings aren't legitimate."

Following the ABC model, once we are aware of our feelings, the next step is naming and accepting those feelings without judgment.

Pushing feelings away, or freaking out about being freaked out, is never helpful; it always makes things worse. How we talk to ourselves is really the critical step here. Name feelings without judging whether they are "easy" or "challenging" or "confusing."

WHY NOT JUDGING FEELINGS IS A CHALLENGE

Once we recognize that we're having difficult feelings related to a specific event, we often jump right into judgment mode. We criticize our feelings or deny our feelings and try to bury them. It takes bravery to be curious and allow "what is" without judgment. There are so many cultural rules about feelings, and people rarely model this kind of nonjudgmental acknowledgment.

There are many reasons for this. Consumer culture associates feelings with consumerism itself, as if we are and feel what we buy. Sexist culture considers feelings to be female, and thus devalued. Racist culture considers anger to be inappropriate in people of color. Individual families develop their own norms: Some encourage suppressing feelings in order to keep the peace, while others value expressiveness, but usually only some emotions are okay, while others are not.

In college, while curiosity is encouraged, being nonjudgmental is not. Students are constantly being judged by their teachers, and they are being asked to evaluate every topic and everything they read and to engage in critical thinking. This central academic skill is all about discernment and judging.

STRATEGIES

Know That Accepting Emotions Takes Courage

It can feel like swimming against the tide to say, "Just acknowledge your emotions without judgment." It takes a lot of bravery to be real and honest about our feelings, since we so often get the message not to — from our culture, our family, and our friends. However, bravery is contagious, and as we learn to fear our emotions less, we help others do the same.

Recognize Your Own Resistance

It can be hard to accept difficult emotions without pushing those feelings away, dismissing them, or belittling ourselves. Be patient if this happens and try to let go of any judgmental thoughts. Keep observing what you feel without acting or resisting. Value the ability to notice and be curious about your feelings. Here are some examples of what that might look like:

> "I'm feeling sad about Grandpa's death," without also saying, "I should be over this by now."

"I'm really scared to start this paper," without also saying, "I
don't belong at this school if I can't write a paper."

"I'm anxious about winning this basketball game," without also
saying, "I'm such a loser for feeling this way after having
played thousands of games."

Understand That Feelings Are Temporary and Go Up and Down

Feelings are like the weather — they never last for long. They ebb and
flow, go up and down. Know that you are not your feelings; you remain
while feelings just pass through. See for yourself: Keep track of your
mood for one day or one week and see how often your feelings change,
sometimes on a dime.

Our culture promotes the idea that we should be happy all the time,
which is impossible and misleading. There is no way to be happy all the
time. It is normal and healthy for feelings to go up and down naturally,
our reactions changing with the events of the day. This is actually more
"logical": It makes sense to be sad over a loss, angry about injustice, and
lonely when we miss close friends and family, sometimes all in the space
of an hour.

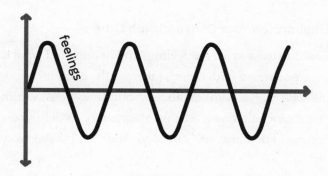

It's normal for feelings to go up and down.

Accept Painful Emotions as They Are

This is difficult. We don't want to feel hurt, so it is natural to reject, deny,
dismiss, or "hate" painful feelings. We sometimes try to talk ourselves

"My dad had always encouraged me to 'get over my feelings,' and so I haven't wanted to feel or accept where I'm at. It seems radical to get permission to feel and not repress what I am feeling. After practicing this for a while, it can be hard and exhausting to know I'm having sad or hurt feelings, but it doesn't last, and I end up feeling better."

— RIVER

out of them, as if we are wrong for feeling sad or disappointed. But that is the challenge of being nonjudgmental. The goal is to accept whatever we are feeling in the moment, whether we like it or not, rather than dismiss it because it doesn't match what we think we *should* be feeling. Allow yourself to see the truth of the moment.

Here are some examples of what it might look like to acknowledge feelings without judgment:

"I am feeling so sad today, and it is natural to be sad right now."
"I feel angry, even though my friend didn't mean to make me angry."
"Of course I am feeling guilty for what happened."
"I notice I'm heartbroken right now, and that's okay, even if I don't know all the reasons why."

Explore Emotions on Your Own and with Others

It is really hard to tease apart our feelings and understand what is driving them. On your own and with others, embrace the complexity!

On the one hand, journal about your emotions. Writing helps make feelings concrete. Use a feelings vocabulary to help you correctly name emotions. For help, see "Expand Your Emotional Vocabulary" (pages 160–62).

On the other hand, seek out trusted friends and mentors you feel safe talking about your feelings with (which can be a challenge to find but is worth the effort). Often, the best way to name and understand a feeling is to talk it out.

WHEN TO SEEK PROFESSIONAL HELP

It takes a lot of practice and persistence to work our nonjudgmental muscles. If you find that you are struggling to do that on your own, which is understandable, reach out to a counselor or any supportive person in your life and talk about ways to be more kind to and accepting of yourself.

RESOURCES

On Campus

- College counseling center: A counselor can help you learn to recognize your feelings and provide nonjudgmental support. A counselor can also recommend off-campus providers.
- College chaplain: Chaplains can provide mentorship and support for self-understanding.

Books

- *Rising Strong* by Brené Brown: This book helps us understand why we might want to avoid our feelings, and how to find the strength to face them bravely.

"I always wanted to understand and make sense of why I felt anxious at times. At first I didn't like the concept of nonjudgmental observance. I wanted to control it! However, as I started the practice of 'just noticing' my feelings rather than being so mad at myself that I wasn't perfectly calm — or however I thought I should be that day — I found that it made all my challenging feelings less overwhelming to me."

— MILDRED

Chapter 19

Choosing 102: Coping with Your Feelings

"My life started to get better when I realized my numbness was a way for me to protect myself from feeling sad about missing my mom."

"When I can allow myself to see my worry is a feeling that doesn't have to rule me, I can let myself take action on my problem set."

"I feel so fearful that I'll let down the team when I step up to bat, but I know that's just a feeling, and I let myself focus on the moment where I know I have the skills to hit the ball."

"I was so upset when my car got hit. When my friend said, 'Car stuff is the worst,' and took me out for a cup of tea, I was able to put it in perspective."

"It's okay to let myself just be sad today. I have a lot to be sad about. I'll go on a long nature walk and that will feel soothing."

We can't control a feeling; it "fires" in our brain before we are aware of it. How feelings are connected to thoughts and experiences is still cutting-edge science, but suffice it to say, emotions are part of being human, and they happen outside of conscious thought. However, once we become aware of our feelings, we can consciously decide what to do about them or how to cope with them. With practice, we can temper our reactions to our feelings.

Using the ABC model, once we acknowledge a feeling (awareness), and name it without judgment (being), we can decide how to respond (choosing). We can't control emotions, but we can choose how to act upon our feelings.

As with thoughts, we have essentially three choices for what to do (see "Choose the Best Response to a Thought," pages 118–22):

1. We can take no action; just acknowledging the emotion might be enough, and we can let it be without doing anything else.
2. We can take thoughtful action; the feeling might be valid and important and indicate something that needs to be addressed, fixed, or changed.
3. Or we can take actions that help to calm us or shift our focus away from the feeling.

WHY COPING WITH EMOTIONS IS A CHALLENGE

Our culture does not usually support or teach the healthy paradigm described above. Instead, people tend to do one of the following: repress or deny strong feelings, acknowledge painful emotions while suffering with them in silence, or react to uncomfortable feelings in inappropriate or harmful ways.

A good way to visualize the tendency to repress or deny strong feelings, and their consequences, is to imagine a "feelings trash compactor": When we push down feelings to avoid them, they become "compacted," (which can be important in certain extreme situations) but they don't go away. Instead, that repressed energy can come out "sideways" — it can manifest as physical symptoms like headaches and stomachaches or generalized feelings of anger, anxiety, or depression. A healthier way to deal with feelings is to "uncompact" them by letting ourselves feel and express them. This isn't always easy, but we end up feeling better.

Coping with emotions is especially tough when they are intense and painful. Sometimes emotions can feel bigger than us; they overwhelm us so that we feel unable to stop our reaction. For example, grief over the loss of a loved one can feel all-encompassing. We don't know what to do with all the hurt we feel. In those times, sometimes the best, most appropriate response is to do nothing and just allow grief and loss to wash over us. It can also help to remember that feelings are ephemeral; they pass and change. In the moment, they can seem like they will last forever, but they won't.

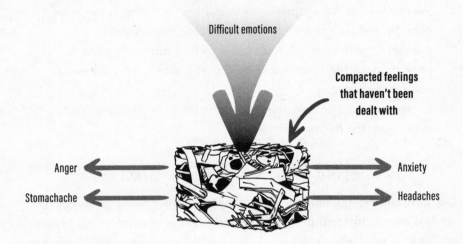

Feelings trash compactor. Pushing down or "compacting" feelings can make them easier to avoid, but their energy can then come out "sideways" as physical symptoms or anxiety, anger, or depression.

It's an art to know when to take action and what to do about our feelings. There is no perfect solution or approach that works the same way every time, and that is part of what makes coping with emotions challenging. The "best" solution might change from day to day.

Finally, it also takes patience to deal with feelings. It requires time and attention. And patience and attention are often in short supply in our modern world. Dealing with the unavoidable roller coaster of human emotions isn't easy, but with practice, as we learn what makes our own hearts tick, we get more skillful.

STRATEGIES

Remember to Feel First, Act Second

Recognizing and naming a feeling is not synonymous with following a feeling! We get to choose what to do about our feelings, but only if we remember not to immediately react to our emotions. In fact, understanding exactly what we feel and why can take time. We might know instantly, in a nanosecond, or it might take weeks, months, or even years to fully understand complex feelings that have been buried for a long time. Our initial knee-jerk reaction to strong emotions is rarely the best course of action, so remember to take the time to experience and understand what you feel before deciding what to do.

Take Care of Yourself and Explore Emotions in Safe Ways

Whenever you are examining or exploring strong emotions, be compassionate and gentle with yourself. Coping with emotions can be exhausting and even dehydrating. You might need to get some extra sleep, drink plenty of water or herbal tea, and eat foods that are gentle on your system.

Just as importantly, find safe ways or safe spaces to do this work. What qualifies as "safe" depends entirely on what you're feeling and your circumstances. Almost always, journaling about feelings is a wonderful approach, since writing is private, and there isn't any time limit.

Talking to others can also be vital and even necessary, but consider carefully who the "safest" people are in your situation. Talking about difficult, intense emotions takes courage and vulnerability, so consider who you will feel okay being vulnerable with. That might be a trusted friend or family member. Or that might be a counselor, therapist, or other mentor outside of your personal life. Keep a list in your journal of safe people to talk with so it will be easy to access the next time you need it.

Manage Strong Emotions Safely in the Moment

When strong, overwhelming emotions arise, the immediate main goal is to experience them in a safe way until the intensity subsides. With strong feelings, we need to deescalate our emotions before we can evaluate them and choose what to do. This is what it means to feel first and act second.

Here are some options for coping with strong emotions as you are experiencing them:

- If you are with people and it would be better to be alone, go to a private place, such as a bathroom, or walk away from the group.
- If you are alone and it would be better to be with people, reach out in any way you can — via text, phone, or email, or by leaving your room and joining others in a common area, residence hall, restaurant, or other place.
- To help calm emotions, use a focused breathing technique, such as square breathing or counting breaths (see "Breathing to Bring Calm," pages 313–15). Slowing our breath signals to our body that we are safe, and our emotions usually settle.
- Touch your toes, lie on your back with your legs up the wall, or move physically in any way to "shake out" and release your feelings.
- Get something cold on your face: Put a cold drink on your face, put your face in front of a fan, take a cool shower, or splash cold water on your face.
- If you fear you are about to act in a way that you might regret, do anything safe that buys you enough time to calm down. Be creative and do whatever works in your situation that isn't harmful.

Use Kind Self-Talk

Use self-talk to name emotions in a nonjudgmental way and accept them. Sometimes, the only things we need to do with emotions is recognize them and let them pass on their own. It's good to feel sad when we're sad, or angry when we're angry. If it helps, talk to yourself out loud — some people find that calming. However, use a gentle voice and focus on acceptance. Here are some examples:

> "I'm feeling neutral today. I'm going to go through my day and see how it goes."
> "I'm a little down. I'm glad all I have to do today is some reading."

"This, too, shall pass. Emotions are like the weather — they don't
   last."

"I feel terrible right now, and I don't know what to do, so I will
   deal with the issue when I feel better."

"Strong feelings are part of being human."

"I can tolerate this emotion. I've done so before."

"I'm angry and feel like punching a wall. But just because I feel
   like punching a wall doesn't mean I have to do it."

Diagnose Strong Emotions with HALT

HALT is an acronym that stands for "hungry, angry, lonely, tired." When
you are experiencing a strong, out-of-control emotion, use HALT as an
assessment tool. Could any of these four states be the cause of your reaction? Often, we discover that we are simply too tired to deal and need to
rest. Or we're hungry, and after getting something to eat, our emotions
resolve themselves.

Take Appropriate, Thoughtful Action

Choosing what to do about a feeling tends to fall into two categories:
either doing something that helps address the emotion itself or doing
something that addresses whatever caused the emotion. Often, we choose
to take several actions that do both things.

   The most important thing, though, is to act in accordance with our
values. For instance, when we're angry, we might feel an urge to lash out
violently (either verbally or physically), but we can choose not to act that
way. We can take a walk or a run instead of smashing the project we're
working on (which isn't turning out the way we want), or after calming
down, we can speak respectfully to a person we disagree with.

   Here are some other examples:

"I'm sad today and need some comforting. I think I'll ask a friend
   to get some hot chocolate."

"I'm devastated that I got a C on a test. It makes me want to quit
   college. But I know I just need better study habits. I'll make
   an appointment with a tutor at the study center."

"When I walked out of class I became aware that I was feeling down and doubtful of my ability to succeed as a college student. I took a moment to think about where that feeling came from. I realized that a classmate had been really judgmental of what many students, including myself, were saying in class and it felt icky. After taking a moment to roll my eyes at Joe Cool and how he always has to have the last word, I was able to feel much less down on myself, and I was able to enjoy lunch with my friends."

— GLORIA

"I'm upset about a social injustice. I'm going to join the student organization that works on that issue."

"I freaked out when I realized I have four less credits than I thought. After taking a walk, I realized, *This is fixable*. I'm going to visit the registrar to make a plan for how to fill those credits."

"I'm overwhelmed and feel like shutting down. I'm going to have lunch with my friend and talk it through."

"I don't feel good about myself, which is something I struggle with. In the past, I've practiced cutting, but I know self-harm doesn't fix anything. I don't want to burden my friends with this, so I'm going to see a counselor."

WHEN TO SEEK PROFESSIONAL HELP

If your emotions seem to be running your life, if you feel regularly anxious and scattered, if you feel depressed and lack motivation, if you feel isolated from others, or if there are certain overwhelming emotions or situations you can't seem to cope with on your own, consider seeing a counselor. Reaching out for help can be a huge challenge. We sometimes feel it's a form of defeat, or that it means years of therapy or even medication. None of that is true. Speaking to a professional simply means you take yourself and your need for change seriously. How that journey unfolds is up to you to decide. Nothing is more important than getting help to regain a feeling of control over your life.

That said, if you are overwhelmed with despair, questioning whether life is worth living, preoccupied with death, or having suicidal thoughts, *you deserve to get counseling as soon as possible, if not immediately*. See the resources below and the "Suicide Prevention Checklist" (pages 330–32).

NEED TO TALK NOW?

If you or someone you know is thinking about suicide — whether in crisis or not — **call or text 988** to chat with a counselor for free confidential support.

"I was sitting at my computer in the lounge on my floor trying to start a challenging paper. I noticed that my breathing was getting shallower, I felt warm and uncomfortable, and I started feeling jumpy. Instead of trying to tough it out, I decided to take a break. I went to my room, lay on my back in bed, and practiced some positive self-talk and slow breathing. I could feel myself calm down and reenergize. I was so happy that I could take a step to take care of myself that I was able to get back to starting the paper with a more positive attitude."

— RILEY

RESOURCES

On Campus

- College counseling center: A counselor can help you recognize your feelings, brainstorm ways to manage them, and support your efforts to practice new coping strategies. A counselor can also recommend referrals to off-campus providers, especially for issues that may need longer-term treatment (such as anxiety, depression, bipolar disorder, and so on).
- College chaplain: Chaplains can provide mentorship and support for self-understanding.
- College residence staff: Staff can help provide support and connection.
- College diversity office: A diversity office may be able to offer support that matches your culture.
- College medical center: The medical center can assess issues and provide medication, as well as referrals to off-campus resources.

Books

- *Don't Let Your Emotions Run Your Life: How Dialectical Behavior Therapy Can Put You in Control* by Scott E. Spradlin: This easy-to-use workbook leads you through how to better understand your emotions and develop step-by-step skills to live with more equanimity.

Websites

- The Jed Foundation (www.jedfoundation.org): Jed is a nonprofit that protects emotional health and prevents suicide for our nation's teens and young adults. Visit their Mental Health Resource Center.
- 988 Suicide & Crisis Lifeline (988; www.988lifeline.org): If you or someone you know is thinking about suicide — whether in crisis or not — call or text 988, or visit the website, to chat with a counselor. Previously known as the National Suicide Prevention Lifeline, this national network of crisis centers provides 24/7, free, and confidential support to people in suicidal crisis or emotional distress.

Chapter 20

Stress

"I'm stressed because I've got a lot of work due this week."

"I feel I must succeed at the highest level because my parents and my community sacrificed so much to get me here. That burden is a huge stressor for me."

"There's just so much riding on college, and I'm always stressed about paying for it."

"I can't get anything done until I feel the stress of it the night before it's due."

"I'm the only Black woman in my computer science class. It's so stressful."

As a physical/emotional phenomenon, stress is defined as the body's way of responding to challenging demands. Our system is designed to cope with the moderate stressors that come and go through the day as well as to survive an intense but brief stressor (such as running from a predator). We all need to "power up" to meet the challenge of taking an exam, running a race, or performing in a concert. It's important to remember that some stress is good — it helps motivate us.

However, our system isn't meant to endure long-term stress, whether physical or psychological. Metaphorically, long-term stress is like flooring the gas pedal all the time. We would never do that to our vehicles. We press moderately on the gas, use the brakes frequently, and only floor the gas pedal for brief moments, like getting up to speed on the highway. Why would we ask anything different from our body's stress system? High, long-term stress has negative impacts on our physical and mental health, such as by elevating our heart rates, keeping our muscles too tense, and preventing our digestion from working correctly. Stress can increase depression, anxiety, and a host of physical diseases.

It is important to note that there is a difference between stress and anxiety. Stress occurs in response to a certain event (or a series of events) or thoughts about an event. Anxiety is a constant condition that isn't necessarily related to specific events (any real or imaginary ones will do). However, they both look similar and include tension, worry, concern, physical tightness, and pressure.

Note that this chapter discusses academic and performance stress. Social stress is covered in part 5, "Your Relationships."

WHY STRESS IS A CHALLENGE

Our whole society struggles with feeling "stressed out," and there are many reasons for this. For example, economic uncertainty, economic inequity, painful and sometimes deadly "isms" (such as racism, sexism, classism), our 24/7 technological culture, global climate change, and an increase in national and global disasters (such as the Coronavirus pandemic).

As for college students, handling stress is the most frequently cited mental health issue. Many factors are at play here. Expectations are sky high to achieve brilliantly in classes, internships, extracurriculars, and social life, and the resulting emotions can be intense and hard to manage. Our 24/7 social media culture has created expectations that work against students. It's easy to get trapped in a narrative that things are only supposed to be one way or we have to conform to the expectations of others. Plus, college students are nothing if not *busy*. So much activity is packed into a day, it's almost like dog years — seven days are lived out each day. Students rarely allow themselves the luxury of truly relaxing or engaging in self-care. The resulting intensity plays out in their emotional lives.

The academic stressors are huge: Classes are more difficult than in high school, keeping to a schedule takes discipline, deciding on a major is a life decision with many ramifications, and there is pressure to stand out within our field.

The rampant glorification of the "stressed out" culture is another reason that stress is a problem on college campuses. Students can often take a grim pride in being stressed out, like feeling stressed means that they are working harder than others — as if being stressed out is a competition and a way to prove that they are taking college seriously. Given that, what student would want to admit they weren't stressed?

STRATEGIES

Practice Physical and Emotional Self-Care

Attend to your basic self-care as much as possible. Students are quick to write this off during stressful times, but it is usually true that time spent in basic self-care will pay off by doubling your efficiency in completing schoolwork. Basic self-care won't eliminate all your stress, but it is the foundation for managing stress.

Students tend to reach for coffee when stressed, but caffeine can put our body into hyperarousal, a state that will make stress feel worse.

Students tend to think they have to stay up later to get work done, and so they skimp on sleep when stressed, but sleep literally recharges the brain. This means cutting back on sleep actually removes the most important way to recharge our battery. Also, sleep deprivation alone causes stress!

Students tend to let go of their movement or workout when stressed, but even ten minutes of moving will release the soothing neurotransmitter GABA, which reduces stress.

When we are stressed, our muscles tighten up, and that prevents us from getting a deep breath. Consciously taking slow, deep breaths gives us more oxygen, which is energizing. This also tells our body that we are safe and triggers the parasympathetic nervous system that facilitates re-laxation (the opposite of the fight-or-flight, sympathetic nervous system). See "Breathing to Bring Calm" (pages 313–15).

Give yourself a little time, even just fifteen to twenty minutes a day, to do something creative and fun that is just for yourself. Taking time for yourself can turn your day or your night around and allow you to get a refreshing night's sleep, to use another side of your brain, to get far away from the worries of the day, and to do something that helps your brain slow down. I also highly recommend that this be time disconnected from electronic devices! For more ideas, see the chapter 5 "Strategies" section (pages 53–56).

Protect Your Time

Many students haven't yet developed a wise approach for using their time during busy or stressful times. So make a plan for how to use your time, so you know you can get everything done. If you haven't made a plan before, seek help from either an academic adviser or the study center. Just knowing you have a plan for how to get things done can be a great stress reliever. For more detail, see chapter 34, "Time Management for Mental Health."

An essential part of the plan is sticking to it. That means *saying no* to what doesn't fit in the plan. Every time you say no to something that is extra, even if fun, you are saying yes to your highest priorities. For more, see "Learn to Say No" (pages 235–36).

Prioritize what has to get done first. This often involves hard choices. So talk to others, like professors, to get clear on what is due when. Some students are great list makers; other students use an electronic system, such as their Google calendar. The method you use matters less than sim-ply doing it.

Finally, when it's time to study or write, practice turning off distrac-tions, like electronic devices. This creates a less-stressful environment so you can get work done and thereby decrease your stress level. For more, see chapter 35, "Healthy Media Use."

Ask for Help

Students often say that the best stress reliever is seeing their friends, even for a little bit. Laughter is the best medicine. So let your friends know you need to connect, even if that feels hard to ask for.

Also seek support from trusted staff members, such as an adviser, professor, hall director, or mental health counselor. A meaningful place to talk about stress can make a huge difference for stress relief.

Adopt a Positive Mindset

It's all too easy to fall into a negative, defeatist attitude, especially when things aren't going your way or seem too much to handle. But of course, a negative attitude only makes stress that much worse and sucks productive energy. For more about the damaging effects of negativity and how to challenge it, see chapter 15, "Negativity."

Accept That Things Will Be Hard

A positive attitude also helps reframe hard work so that it is accepted and expected and causes less stress. Here are some examples:

> "Everyone talks about how hard organic chemistry is, so I know
> it is normal that I am struggling to learn all the material and
> keep up."
> "I am trying to do something very difficult, so I want to honor
> how hard I am working."
> "This class is kicking my ass, but it's my favorite class because
> I'm really learning something useful I didn't know before."

Focus on Gratitude, Not Stress

If stress is taking over, change your focus for a moment. Instead, think of all the good things in your life that you feel grateful about. For two minutes, journal a gratitude list. An attitude of gratitude will decrease the stress hormone cortisol.

"I had always taken pride in never needing to ask for help, but I was noticing that I couldn't let go of the negative thoughts that left me stressed out, such as thinking, *I'm already screwing up so I might as well continue screwing up*, and *I don't deserve any better than this*. After a really terrible week, I decided to do something about my self-sabotage and reached out to the counseling center. I knew that stress was a trigger, so I decided to try some of the prevention strategies the counselor suggested: going on a run more regularly, making a schedule and keeping to it as much as possible, and most importantly, creating positive messages, such as 'I deserve to be at college,' 'I actually enjoy doing this homework when I let myself,' and 'I appreciate that I'm working hard.' I have to work at it every day but I am now able to prevent my stressors from becoming negative spirals."

— QUINN

Change Perspective and See the Big Picture

Students are often so focused on what's in front of them, they miss the forest for the trees. If you can step back and see the big picture of your life, you may feel much better. Ask yourself, is what you're stressing over going to affect the totality of your life? Usually the answer is no. Of course, that doesn't solve the particular problem, but it puts the outcome, whatever it is, in the right context: Something that matters for today, but probably not for next month, next year, or ten years from now.

Identify Patterns of Stress

Stress can follow patterns or become a habit, so notice if that's the case for you. Do you always feel down in the late afternoon? Maybe that's because you're tired and hungry. Do you always feel anxious before a certain class? Seek help or find new strategies to deal with that course. Do you always feel stress at night? Maybe you need a better nighttime routine (see "Include a Buffer Zone," pages 13–14).

Explore the Reasons for Stress

This whole book encourages self-reflection to develop self-awareness, so apply that to stress. How we frame situations, the narrative we tell ourselves, will affect how stressed we feel (or not). Most of the time, we focus on outcomes, on "shoulds," or on comparisons, and all these make us much more stressed than the work itself. When you notice intense stress, stop and follow the trail to the beginning. See if you can get to the root of the matter, which can create a little more distance from the stress.

WHEN TO SEEK PROFESSIONAL HELP

Developing personal strategies for how you deal with stress is one of the most important skills to learn in college, but it is not easy, nor does it always provide immediate results. Many students feel overwhelmed with stress, which can get in the way of life and academics. Here's a partial list of symptoms that often indicate you might benefit from outside help:

- Sleep issues, like trouble falling asleep or getting a restful night's sleep
- Not feeling energized or excited
- Trouble remembering important things, or being unable to keep your usual schedule
- Having a hard time focusing on work, or paying attention in class
- Feeling irritable, frustrated, or easily annoyed over little things
- Getting down on yourself, such as wanting to quit college
- Increased use of alcohol, cannabis, study drugs, sleeping pills, and so on, or using these for the first time
- Making risky decisions, such as overspending, driving too fast, practicing unsafe sex, or doing things that go against your values
- Physical illness, such as frequent colds, indigestion or diarrhea, backaches, and headaches
- Isolating from friends, or changing friendships often
- Family or friends telling you that you seem stressed out (trust them!)

"When I remember that baby steps matter, I can let myself focus on the work right in front of me, instead of obsessing about all I have left to do and getting into a negative stress space. I have to work pretty hard to remember baby steps matter, so I have it written everywhere, in notebooks, sticky notes, and including as my screen background at times."

— NOAM

RESOURCES

On Campus

- College counseling center: A counselor can help you identify the painful stressors in your life and help you learn new strategies and skills to cope. They can also recommend referrals to off-campus providers.

- Academic adviser or professors: Most students hesitate to discuss stress related to academics with advisers and professors. But if you have a sense of trust with someone, they may have insights that help reduce stress. If a professor dismisses your concerns, seek help elsewhere.
- College study center: If you are overwhelmed with too much coursework, or struggling with a particular assignment, see if the study center can help you make a plan.
- College career center: If stress is related to your career path, a career counselor might be able to help. They can make sure you are doing what you need to get where you want to be.
- College chaplain: Multifaith chaplains, or the chapel itself, can offer a place of refuge or peace, which can help with stress.
- College athletics department: Exercise reduces stress, so seek out movement classes, such as yoga, dance, or martial arts. Staff can help you create a conditioning plan.

Websites

- Substance Abuse and Mental Health Services Administration (SAMHSA; 800-662-4357; www.samhsa.gov): This federal organization runs a confidential, free, 24/7 hotline for anyone dealing with mental health or substance use issues. They provide referrals to local treatment facilities, support groups, and community-based organizations.

Books

- *The Stress Management Workbook: De-stress in 10 Minutes or Less* by Ruth C. White: This book's easy-to-follow, concrete steps identify sources of stress and set goals, with plenty of interactive exercises and strategies to help manage stress.
- *Why Zebras Don't Get Ulcers: The Acclaimed Guide to Stress, Stress-Related Diseases, and Coping* by Robert M. Sapolsky: The

author provides a scientific, yet humorous, explanation of how psychological stress impacts our health. Understanding our evolutionary response to stress is an essential part of combating stress in the modern world.

- *Burnout: The Secret to Unlocking the Stress Cycle* by Emily Nagoski and Amelia Nagoski: This book is mainly written for women on the topic of burnout, perfectionism, and body image. However, their wisdom on completing the stress cycle is incredibly helpful for all genders.

Chapter 21

Grief and Loss

"My grandpa was the only person who had time to really listen to me. I know I was special to him. Now I miss him so much."

"My dad has never been there for me. He struggles with bipolar and has to spend all his energy taking care of himself."

"My little sister has an eating disorder and has been suicidal in the past. I can't cause my parents any more problems because they've already been through so much."

"It's so lonely and exhausting to be the only Latina in most of my classes."

"I thought for sure I would major in political science. Now that I realize politics isn't what I love, I feel really lost."

We feel grief for many types of losses. The death of a loved one is the most obvious, but we may need to grieve giving up on a dream, not being able to fulfill a dream, living in a culture that seems broken, not getting the care we deserve, having to care for others in inappropriate ways, and so on. Losses can range from subtle to severe; all can cause pain.

WHY GRIEF AND LOSS ARE A CHALLENGE

It is profoundly painful to let ourselves feel loss. The pain is like an unhealed wound, and it can seem easier to ignore the wound and just carry on with our day-to-day activities. However, it's healthier to face loss and "clean out the wound" in the same spirit that we'd clean out a physical wound. This can also hurt, and there will be a scar, a lasting reminder of the loss, but only then can we restore ourselves to full health and actually continue with our lives.

College is usually portrayed as a time of learning and growth, so it can be unexpected and even shocking that a hefty part of the college experience is loss. During these years, as students grow and change, they generally "lose" a closely held image of their identity or a dream of who they might become. Some experience the loss of friendships and romantic partners. At all times, we might experience a loved one's death. It can be hard to admit or accept that, at this point in life, we need to make room for grief.

The private nature of loss makes grief a real challenge; many times, students experience feelings of loss alone. Even the death of a loved one can feel isolating because it is so hard to talk about, particularly with others who have not yet experienced a death in their lives. Then there's the loss of dreams. When others seem to be fulfilling theirs, it can be hard to admit we have lost ours.

STRATEGIES

Name the Loss

Allow yourself to name your loss. Some are clear and definitive, like the loss of a person or a pet. Others can be confusing or hard to name, such as "losing" a particular sense of self, but naming your loss allows you to then grieve for it.

Memorialize People who Have Died

When someone dies, find ways to honor them that bring you comfort. This can be an ongoing process, such as visiting their grave site regularly or playing music that reminds you of them. Acting on what you learned from that person is another way to remember the relationship as well as the person. This can involve onetime gestures, such as creating a memory collage or putting together a book of their letters.

> "I felt such a loss of belonging when I first came to college. I had been living under the impression that no one cared about that hardship because I was just supposed to be glad I was in college. But I was enduring a lot by leaving my family in another country. I was afraid to vocalize my pain to others. I didn't think I would be heard. After I talked about this in counseling, I decided to tell the truth to a close group of friends, and they cared and understood. This helped me see that I could trust the people who are already in my corner, and that soothed my feelings of loss."
>
> — MICHELE

Allow Yourself Time to Grieve

Many of us want to get over loss quickly; others might also encourage us to do that. We often internalize the message that we should "get over it" and "move on" as quickly as possible. This is false. Grieving takes the time it takes, so take as much time as you need. This is different for every person and every loss.

Grieve in Whatever Way Works for You

Sometimes, we need time to cry and feel sad, either alone or with a trusted person (or animal). Other ways to grieve include journaling about feelings and loss, writing poetry or an essay, writing a letter to someone (that you don't intend to send), or performing rituals, whether personally created or related to our faith.

Know That Grief Comes and Goes

Grief is not a linear process; it's cyclical. You will likely have days when you don't think about loss at all, and days when it hits you like a ton of bricks.

Follow Your Regular Routines

While grieving, stick to your daily routine of classes and activities as much as possible. Dropping out of regular life can cause a sense of isolation. It's possible to grieve and live your life at the same time. However, don't hold yourself to the usual standards. Be gentle with yourself, both in actions and words, or how you talk to yourself.

Practice Self-Care

Grief is exhausting. Get more sleep than usual, stay hydrated, eat regularly, take walks, and do whatever feels healing.

Allow Yourself to Dream Again

Loss and grief can undermine our motivation and desire. We know we can't ever fully replace what is lost. But eventually, we have to dream again. This is an essential step, though it is often a process that develops slowly and shifts over time.

Accept the Scars of Loss

Physical scars do best with tender care; it is the same with emotional scars. Treat them gently. When scars ache, give them time and attention, and accept them as they are.

"I decided to join a grief group for young adults who have lost a parent, after reading about it in the campus newsletter. When I began attending, I quickly found that there is no substitute for being with people who really get it. The group members described losing a parent as 'feeling like we are speaking a different language that only we can understand.' I was able to grieve freely there and feel understood. I will be forever grateful for that group."

— ZANE

WHEN TO SEEK PROFESSIONAL HELP

If you have experienced a loss of any kind, I recommend seeking help if you are having painful symptoms related to the following:

- physical symptoms, like insomnia or appetite changes
- emotional issues, like overwhelming sadness or guilt
- cognitive problems, like trouble focusing or feeling stuck
- behavioral problems, like isolating from friends or an inability to get out of bed
- spiritual issues, like trouble finding meaning in life

RESOURCES

On Campus

- College counseling center: A counselor can help provide the space and time for you to talk about your loss and give it the attention it needs. A counselor can also recommend referrals to off-campus providers.

- College chaplain: Chaplains are well-trained in coping with grief and loss.

Websites

- *Psychology Today*, "Find a Therapist" (www.psychologytoday.com /us/therapists): *Psychology Today* offers a searchable database to find a local therapist who specializes in grief and loss anywhere in the United States. Photos and descriptions help you find someone you can connect with.
- What's Your Grief (www.whatsyourgrief.com): This website address all types of loss and grief through articles, blogs, an online community, and more.

Books

- *The Myth of Closure: Ambiguous Loss in a Time of Pandemic and Change* by Pauline Boss: This book addresses the range of loss and distress as amplified by the pandemic, including social justice and climate issues. It explains how to find hope and resilience.
- *This Thing Called Grief: New Understandings of Loss* by Thomas Ellis: This book offers examples and creative poetry to explore the reality and complexity of grief and how to find a way to hope and healing.

Chapter 22

Procrastination

"I'll do anything else than start the paper. My room is spotless and organized right now."

"I sat and stared at the page but just felt like an idiot."

"Netflix is hard to stop. It feels too easy to ignore my homework."

"I need that motivation of an impending deadline. Otherwise I am not motivated."

"Nothing I can say is good enough. So I never let myself even try."

Procrastination is not delaying or postponing work for a practical reason, such as when you are sick or when something genuinely more important needs to be done. Procrastination has nothing to do with reprioritizing tasks or dealing with unforeseen circumstances. Procrastination is not doing what needs to get done when you know you need to do it. Procrastination is not a rare behavior: According to the American College Health Association, in their 2022 National College Health Assessment, 75 percent of college students cited problems or challenges with procrastination in the last twelve months.

Procrastination has such a profound impact on college emotional wellness that I cover it twice in this book. This chapter looks at emotion-related procrastination, and chapter 34 explores lack of organization.

Procrastination is usually related to emotions. Study skills are usually pretty simple and easy to develop, but understanding the emotions that cause procrastination is always more difficult.

WHY PROCRASTINATION IS A CHALLENGE

To oversimplify, procrastination is basically about avoiding pain — something we are programmed to do as human beings. In a way, we work against our nature when we try to get hard stuff done straightaway. We're designed to prefer immediate gratification over making the effort to achieve long-term gratification.

When faced with a dreaded task, people often overestimate how hard it is, so they put it off. For example, unloading the dishwasher only takes a few minutes, but many people consider it time-consuming. Really, they just don't like it, and they'd prefer a reward now (such as watching a video) than to postpone the reward to do a relatively simple if boring task (putting all the plates, cups, and bowls away).

Full-time students are often overwhelmed by the sheer volume of classwork facing them — on top of working at a paid job, participating in student organizations, athletics, volunteering, interning, and so on. Procrastination probably wouldn't be a problem if students only had to write one essay a month, but who knows?

Separate from their workload, students are also figuring out who they are and what they want to do with their lives. Their sense of self and priorities can be in flux, not to mention the burden of self-doubt. Further, in college as in life, there are so many more enjoyable alternatives readily available, such as seeing friends, going out, and 24/7 media entertainment. It's all too easy to put off work.

STRATEGIES

Be Honest with Yourself

If you have serious issues with procrastination, admit it. This is harder than it sounds because most people don't want to admit it is a real problem. Since it's something "everyone" deals with, people might laugh it off as something that can't be helped. But change requires recognizing and naming what's happening.

Identify the Reasons for Procrastination

Remember, procrastination can have more than one reason, and we can struggle to see ourselves clearly. Here is a list of common reasons that students put off doing classwork or fulfilling responsibilities.

- **They are overwhelmed by challenging work:** For most students, college-level coursework is much more demanding than what they encountered in high school. Especially for math and science students, who were often the smartest in their class in high school, it can be very ego bruising to "hit a wall" or become average in college classes.
- **They fear not living up to their own standards of excellence:** Some fear failing, so rather than do the work and find out their limits, it is *almost* easier *not* to know about the truth or how much they need to learn. They can believe they are a noble failure since the professor never saw their best work.
- **They fear not living up to the expectations of others:** This fear can be intense, even when it's unfounded. Many students idolize their professors, or feel pressured to perform, and they don't want to be less than the best and brightest.
- **They suffer from impostor syndrome:** This is self-doubt that we can't really do anything well, and our only hope is to "fake" our way through college. For more on this, see chapter 16.
- **They feel guilty for not working hard enough:** Many students stop themselves from taking action because they "should have taken better class notes" or "should have taken the intro class first." Rather than do their best, whatever happened before, they let "shoulds" undermine their efforts.
- **They feel unable to seek help when needed:** Our culture's admiration for self-reliance often makes seeking help seem like admitting weakness. Lots of people would prefer to suffer in silence than appear vulnerable.

- **They feel they should already know how to do everything:** In fact, college is all about learning, but many students judge themselves for not already being brilliant and accomplished. Embracing the learning process can be hard — since that includes making mistakes and learning from failure.
- **They don't trust anyone to really help:** If students have been betrayed in the past, it can feel unsafe to ask for help. Trusting others can be hard if we have been shot down or belittled or refused help in the past.
- **They feel they work better and are more creative under pressure,** so it's okay to wait until the last minute.

Use Positive Affirmations

One way to counteract negative messaging is to use positive affirmations. This can make it easier to face difficult work or get necessary help. Below are some positive affirmations that counteract each of the procrastination reasons above.

Affirmations work best when you write them down and use them frequently. Write them on an index card and prop them on your computer as you work, or jot them down in your journal or notebooks — anywhere you will see them often. Practice these new positive messages regularly to fight against the "old" messages that fire automatically in your brain.

- **To counteract being overwhelmed by challenging work:** I am being brave by challenging myself with extra hard work. When I struggle to learn, it means I am pushing myself beyond my limits. It is a sign of strength that I am willing to go outside my comfort zone. I choose to rise to the occasion and seek extra help so I can learn new, challenging material.
- **To counteract the fear of not living up to one's standards of excellence:** I trust the process that working hard today will help me become who I'm meant to be. I deserve to let myself work. No matter what my grades look like, I am a strong, capable student. I am growing and making progress.

- **To counteract the fear of not living up to the expectations of others:** Others will be understanding and accepting of me. Others might not support me in the way I need, but I still deserve to succeed on my own terms.

- **To counteract impostor syndrome:** I am a whole person and can sit and work right now. I have all that I need inside of me.

- **To counteract the guilt of not working hard enough:** I don't have to do my work perfectly. I can do whatever work I am capable of right now. I trust that the work I do right now is good enough and that my effort is worthwhile. Impossible expectations always hurt me.

- **To counteract feeling unable to seek necessary help:** I deserve to seek help when I need it. Help seeking is a sign of strength, not weakness. Getting the help I need will improve my schoolwork and learning.

- **To counteract feeling that one should already know everything:** I am growing and learning. Learning is a process, and I am working hard at it. Many people believe we learn more from failure than success.

- **To counteract not trusting others to help:** It is frustrating that at times I haven't been able to get the help I need, but I am strong enough to keep trying until I find the right person or place that can help me. Help is out there if I persist in seeking it.

- **To counteract pushing off work to the last minute:** College asks students to work on long-term projects, so waiting really isn't an option. I can motivate myself and give myself the appropriate time to finish a project. My creativity will flow whenever I allow it to.

Get Started Now

The hardest part can be getting started. One thing that helps is breaking tasks into little pieces or smaller steps. It's easy to get very overwhelmed by a blank page or the thought of writing a twenty-page paper. Take the first step. Set small, specific goals, such as writing a first paragraph or tackling one problem. Even opening up a file and naming it can get you going. Take one small step at a time.

Setting a smaller goal or a reasonable target also helps with perfectionism, which is often linked with procrastination. If you only have to do a little chunk of work, you stand a better chance of being less hard on yourself and shutting yourself down.

Reward yourself when you accomplish a small goal. Some positive self-talk goes a long way! It's certainly more motivating than negative put-downs. Positive feedback gives our brains a little hit of dopamine, a natural chemical that makes us feel good.

> "I got one sentence written. That is a good start. I can get two
>   more done."
> "I am proud of myself for sticking with this hard problem."
> "Future me is going to thank present me!"

Set the Stage for Success

Decide what you need to work on before you go to work. Perhaps write out a to-do list the night before. Try these strategies, too:

- Pick a workspace that is conducive to staying focused (that is, not a place where you naturally socialize).
- Block social media on your phone, tablet, and computer when you sit down to work.
- Consider using the buddy system. Being accountable to another person can be more motivating than answering only to yourself.

Work in Half-Hour Bursts

Use a power half hour (or PHH), also called the Pomodoro Method. Instead of having a concrete work goal (such as writing the first paragraph or doing one problem), *create a goal over how you use time.* Many students help themselves by putting all phones and distractions away for twenty-five minutes and just powering up for that amount of time. Set an alarm on your phone or computer, and commit to working as hard as possible for twenty-five minutes. Then reward yourself with a five- to ten-minute break. Repeat.

Get up and stretch every half hour or every hour. Swing your arms around, reach your arms up, roll your shoulders (see appendix A for more stretches).

Check Your Attitude

Accept that you may not have fun for an hour or two. Working and studying isn't always enjoyable. Be okay with that. This won't always be the case. Avoiding hard work won't make it go away, but any pain or unpleasantness is *impermanent*. You can tolerate it.

What you believe matters. If you believe that your determination is unlimited, you will be able to work harder and accomplish more. If you believe that you can't do it, you will procrastinate more. Use positive self-talk:

"I know I can power up and get this done today."
"I deserve to start this project right now."
"I have everything I need to put some ideas on paper."

Develop a Long-Term Vision

Visualize what you are working for. Is it becoming knowledgeable about a subject, or even just being consistent with getting work done? Write out positive messages that remind you of what you want for yourself. Look at those messages regularly as you work.

"I deserve to see how hard I am already working."
"I am learning and becoming more knowledgeable."
"I am proud of how much I am doing."

Remind yourself of how good it feels to finish your classwork and turn it in on time. Know that whatever is hard right now will feel much better later.

WHEN TO SEEK PROFESSIONAL HELP

"I originally thought getting a tutor was just for dumb people. Once I scheduled a regular Tuesday night one-on-one tutoring session for my bio-chem class, I had a place to get my questions answered and to review the problem set. I started to feel more confident overall, not just about that one class. I couldn't have been more wrong about the purpose of tutoring in college."

— JOE

If procrastination is an ongoing issue, for any reason, consider talking with a trusted mentor, academic adviser, or mental health counselor. Those who come from impoverished, uncertain circumstances can find it harder to trust that what they do today will matter tomorrow; this affects work habits.

If focus and concentration are regular issues, seek a professional who can assess whether you suffer from attention-deficit disorder, a learning disability, anxiety, depression, or a sleep disorder. These conditions can be hard to tease apart, and an ADHD diagnosis requires a comprehensive evaluation by a licensed clinician. Talk to your college health center or your home doctor for more information.

RESOURCES

On Campus

- College counseling center: A counselor can help you recognize and articulate the deeper issues that might be causing procrastination, brainstorm ways to cope, and support your efforts to change.
- College health center: Most health centers provide testing services or can refer you to off-campus resources to help with assessment of ADD/ADHD, learning disabilities, or other issues.
- College study center: Staff can provide advice and resources to improve study habits.

Websites

- Wait But Why (www.waitbutwhy.com): This blog has two great articles, "Why Procrastinators Procrastinate" (www.wait butwhy.com/2013/10/why-procras tinators-procrastinate.html) and "How to Beat Procrastination" (www.waitbutwhy .com/2013/11/how-to-beat-procrastina tion.html). These provide a visceral portrait of what goes on when we procrastinate and how to get out of it.

- National Institute of Mental Health, "Attention-Deficit/Hyperactivity Disorder" (www.nimh.nih.gov/health/topics /attention-deficit-hyperactivity-disorder-adhd): This is a thorough overview of ADHD and the variety of treatments available.

> "I have spent a lot of time feeling sad about experiencing racism for being multiracial. Now that I am talking about it more with friends and in counseling, making an effort to express myself instead of ignoring or repressing my feelings, I have discovered I am able to focus and study more effectively."
>
> — MIRA

Books

- *The Procrastination Equation: How to Stop Putting Things Off and Start Getting Stuff Done* by Piers Steel: This author's research reveals the universality of procrastination, and he talks through many strategies to conquer procrastination using fun anecdotes about famous people.

Part V

YOUR RELATIONSHIPS

Don't believe the lie of individual trees, each a monument to its own self-made success. A forest is an interdependent community. Resources are shared, and life in isolation is a death sentence.

— BECKY CHAMBERS

Relationship issues tie with stress/anxiety as the most discussed issue at college counseling centers. Students who don't feel close to their friends or don't feel loved or supported express a palpable amount of pain.

Relationship issues come in a wide variety — from finding friends to eat meals with to recovering from a breakup to sheer confusion about what is going on with others.

You don't need a PhD in psychology to know that good relationships are important, but there is a ton of research that shows how essential good relationships are to mental health and even to physical health and longevity. Studies show that life feels more meaningful when we are connected and feel we belong. We are hardwired for bonding, yet it can be hard to bond in healthy ways, which is something most students struggle with in college.

Occasionally, just understanding the dynamics of what is happening can be enough to make changes in our relationships. Shining a light on an issue and thinking it through can often change it. However, in most cases, relationship changes occur over time and with much practice. It is important to take the long view.

The goal of this part is to give you a framework for how to think about relationships. Relationships don't just happen or sustain themselves. We can learn how to create the relationships we want and improve the ones we have.

Chapter 23

Friendship 101

"I know everyone on campus, but I don't feel really close to anyone."

"I have two best friends, but I don't know who to hang out with on weekends."

"I have a great group to hang out with on my floor, but no one knows the real me."

"I thought my boyfriend is all I would need socially. But now I realize that I am lonely a lot because he is busy."

"I and all my friends are so busy as seniors. How are we going to stay connected this year?"

We all need friends, but we don't always have a clear picture of what type of friends we want and how many. What exactly are we working toward with friendships? Does everyone need a best friend? Does having a tight friend group mean eating three meals a day together and studying as a group every night?

College students are in the process of learning about themselves and their style — and about the types of relationships that work best for them. There is not one right type of friendship. It's also important to recognize that needs and friendships tend to change over time.

Of course, everyone is different. A social butterfly and a quiet bookworm will have different relationship goals and desires. Yet we can think of friendships in three categories or three "layers" in the Friend Cake, plus a doily layer underneath.

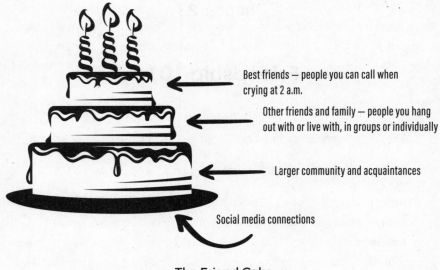

Best friends — people you can call when crying at 2 a.m.

Other friends and family — people you hang out with or live with, in groups or individually

Larger community and acquaintances

Social media connections

The Friend Cake

The top layer is for "best friends," the two or three, or more, friends you can call crying at 2 a.m. These are the soul friends with whom you can be truly honest about yourself, people you know will be there in good times and bad. This group may include a significant other, parents, and siblings, but it's important to have at least one peer as a close friend. For college students away from home, it's also important to develop a college friend who qualifies for this layer, in addition to any friends from home. Most of all, *one person in this category is not enough*. It's the "don't put all your eggs in one basket" strategy.

The middle layer includes the friends you socialize with and the groups you are affiliated with. These are the people you attend parties with and call to make weekend plans. This layer could be your family, if you live with them. This layer can vary in size and be comprised of many types of friendships. Some are people you see regularly in all sorts of contexts, and some might be friends specific to one context. College students often have different friend groups related to their residence hall floor, sports team, religious or cultural identity, music group, academic major, extracurricular activity, or student organization.

This layer represents those people who bring joy and meaning to your life even if they are not "best friends." These may be friends who have connected around a shared identity. It's healthy for everyone, but *especially for those from marginalized groups*, to spend time with people who help us feel seen, accepted, and safe for being our true selves. This can be any kind of shared group identity, and some people have several such groups, including virtual groups that exist only online.

The bottom layer is for acquaintances, our larger community, and the people we know but don't necessarily know well. This layer can form naturally at college and be quite big, as there are loads of people living and working together in a defined space, but that's not always the case. For some, it can be hard to feel part of the college community for many reasons; for example, commuter students may only be on campus when they attend classes. Many students benefit from finding value in seemingly unimportant daily interactions with strangers, such as the barista or the postal clerk, and these micro-encounters end up providing valuable social connections.

The doily layer, beneath the cake, is for social media "friends." For some, these relationships are important and vital; for others, these friendships are "thin" with many holes in them.

WHY FRIENDSHIPS ARE A CHALLENGE

Making meaningful friendships and being a part of a meaningful community takes intention and consistency over time. Many people are so busy with work and family demands that developing friendships and community is something they put on the back burner. Many struggle to find folks they can really relate to and with whom they feel safe to be themselves.

College students often assume they will easily find "their people" the minute they get to college, since everyone lives in close proximity and a high percentage of people are likely to share the same interests. But

"My varsity team has great camaraderie, so I thought that is all I'd need for my friend group in college. However, it ended up making my college career richer when I found a couple of close friends in my major who didn't play sports. I was able to connect with these friends in a different way from the party atmosphere on my team."

— HUNTLEY

making new friends is not always that easy. For transfer, commuter, and remote-learning students, all this becomes even more difficult.

Feelings of loneliness, homesickness, or self-doubt can cause students to withdraw just when they need to be reaching out.

Identity exploration also impacts student friendships. As identities change, the need for different types of friends varies. Meanwhile, uncertainty over identity can lead students to feel like an outsider at times.

Social media can also impact someone's ability to maintain or build new friendships. Some find it easier to keep high school friends via social media or through gaming than to meet new folks in person. For all these reasons, making new friends can present challenges.

STRATEGIES

Define Your Friend Cake

Think about your current friendships. Who is in your life now? Break friendships into the existing "layers of your cake" and jot it down in your journal:

Top layer: "best friends" you can call crying at 2 a.m.
Middle layer: everyday friends you socialize with and groups you enjoy and identify with
Bottom layer: communities you affiliate with and acquaintances
Doily layer: social media or online-only friends

Are some layers of your Friend Cake more robust than others? Are there types of friendships you struggle with and some that come "naturally"? Identify what sort of cake you want and make a plan to work on what you need.

Consider Your Comfort Zone

When looking to make new friends, consider how you like to spend time with people. Then find people who also like those types of experiences and friendships. Do you prefer one-on-one time or big parties or both? Take time to write about these in your journal, especially to check back and add to when you discover new things you like to do with friends.

What experiences do you like?

- All-campus dance parties
- Rowdy house parties
- Quiet, small parties
- Game night
- Movie night
- Chatting over a cup of tea or coffee

How do you like to connect?

- One-on-one
- Small groups
- Large groups
- Quiet groups
- Rowdy groups

"I have been able to make some good friends I can hang out with and connect on a deeper level. I had to learn the hard way that if I don't make time to connect with them every week, I end up feeling way more anxious and down on myself. It is a paradox that I thought I was giving up friend time to study harder, but it ended up making me too anxious to study if I didn't have enough time with my friends."

— DORI

Make Plans

As you become more aware of the friendships you have and the types of friendships you prefer, make plans for improving your current friendships and making new ones. Make specific goals based on your current Friend Cake. Create a vision for what categories of friendships you want.

For instance, do you want to build quantity or quality? Do you want to be part of groups that share your identity? Do you want to explore or develop new aspects of your identity? Journaling about these questions may help you gain clarity.

WHEN TO SEEK PROFESSIONAL HELP

Friend issues pop up across the whole college experience, from first to final semester. If there is any element of relationships that feels overwhelming, unsatisfying, or problematic, reach out for support. Start with a mentor who feels the most comfortable to you, but colleges have a wide range of resources depending on what you need.

RESOURCES

On Campus

- College activities: To build friendships, consider all the activities you're already involved in: your major or minor, dance or language classes, study groups, and so on. There are many opportunities.
- College student organizations: Another great way to find "your people" is to join social groups and student organizations. Remember, your goal is to build your friendships, not your résumé, so join groups that fit your interests and sense of self.
- College residence staff: Residence staff can be a great starting point if you want more input on where to make connections on campus.
- College diversity office: If you have an underrepresented identity, this office can help you make connections on campus that match your culture or identity.
- College counseling center: A counselor can provide support as you build your friendships. They can also recommend referrals to off-campus providers.
- College chaplain: A chaplain can help you make connections that match your religion or spirituality.

Books

- *Belong: Find Your People, Create Community, and Live a More Connected Life* by Radha Agrawal: This book is especially good at discussing the power of community and includes great graphics and worksheets.

Chapter 24

Healthy Friendships

"I'm not sure what a healthy friendship is. My parents don't have many friends besides each other."

"I'm always there for her but she really never asks me how I am."

"A real friend would be there for me when I need them, so if they aren't, then they aren't a real friend. Right?"

"I party with them and love them like brothers, but I want to drink less, and it is impossible to tell them."

"Once I start to feel a close friendship with someone, I feel attracted to them. How can I make nonromantic close friendships?"

Philosophers and artists through the ages have defined friendship in profound and poetic ways. Friendship is both simple and complex. It is easy to recognize, but a lot goes into a good friendship.

Friends enjoy each other's company, share values and interests, and have fun together. Friends trust each other, are honest with each other, respect each other, care and support each other's best interests, and show long-term commitment to the friendship in good times and in bad. Friends "get" each other: They acquire this deep knowledge through deep listening, empathy, and perhaps a certain "chemistry" that just seems to make some friendships work.

WHY HEALTHY FRIENDSHIPS ARE A CHALLENGE

The single biggest block to healthy friendships is an unhealthy relationship with ourselves. When we aren't honest with ourselves, and don't take responsibility for our own happiness, how can we expect to engage with others in honest and happy ways? Many people hope that their friends will fill the gap that they haven't filled themselves, or they believe they can't have a friend if they are their authentic selves.

There are many other blocks to healthy friendships: withdrawal or isolation due to fear of rejection or judgment; misunderstanding how much intention, time, and energy it takes to form and maintain friendships; and false beliefs about what it means to be a friend. The impact of social media and the pervasiveness of screens can also interfere with face-to-face connections.

Students have a lot of expectations about friendships in college. Many feel pressure to make college "the best four years of your life," and this ends up feeling overwhelming and can get in the way of just getting to know people in a real way.

College is a time to explore and learn about ourselves, and what we discover has a very good chance of changing us. Someone might enter college thinking about themselves in one way — that they will party every weekend or pursue pre-med — and a year later have a completely different viewpoint: They prefer dinner and a movie to big parties or they have passion for international relations. It stands to reason that the friends people first make in college might not stay the same as they grow and change. What we value in friendships can grow and change.

Many students come to college with baggage from unhealthy or abusive relationships. These can profoundly affect how students see themselves and cause a negative self-image. Relationships from the formative years of childhood and adolescence can cause students to believe they deserve less than a healthy relationship.

Many college students assume it will be easy to find "their people." This is often harder than they are led to believe, and until students make the effort to develop close, healthy friendships, they can feel very lonely in the crowd.

STRATEGIES

Focus on Yourself First

How well do you know your own thoughts and emotions? Do you know how to have fun by yourself and fulfill your own needs? How clear is your sense of self? If you're unsure, review the topics in parts 1 through 4. Building healthy friendships involves giving ourselves genuinely to others, listening to and helping them, even making them the priority at times. It can seem counterintuitive, but feeling secure and independent in our own self can help us foster strong friendships.

Assess Your Current Friendships

Reflect on the following questions in your journal.

Do you genuinely like your current friends? Do you enjoy them most of the time? No friendship is perfect, and all are a work in progress, but consider whether, in general, you look forward to seeing them. If not, and dreading or avoiding certain friends is ongoing, there is something wrong. Assess who you consider to be a good friend right now.

For instance, are your friends reliable? Do they have your back, or do some friends just show up when it is easy for them? Are your friends respectful, to you and to one another? Do you feel safe with them, and safe to be your true self? Can you be honest with them? Do your friendships feel equitable? All friendships involve give-and-take, giving and receiving, talking and listening, but do you feel, overall, that your friendships are balanced?

It's okay to decide that some friendships need changing. Lasting friendships don't emerge fully formed. They take time, care, and intention, and friendships require maintenance to stay healthy. Further, both parties need to put in the work to maintain the friendship. As you identify issues with particular friends, talk to them. And if you are unable to be honest with someone, or feel disregarded by them, it might be time to distance yourself from the friendship.

"I was putting in a lot of time and energy chasing the so-called cool people. I was ignoring the people on my residence hall floor with whom I had a lot in common. Once I understood that dynamic and started hanging out with the students on my floor, I started to be happier and less worried. I started to have more meals with people and have more plans on weekends, and I found I could let myself enjoy life more when I wasn't always anxious about being seen at the next so-called cool event."

— CHARLIE

Assess Your Values and Needs

Consider what values you have regarding friendships. What needs do you have when it comes to your friends? Be aware of who you really enjoy spending time with and why. Give yourself permission to think about your friendships on an ongoing basis, perhaps through writing in your journal.

WHEN TO SEEK PROFESSIONAL HELP

If you have been trying to make new friends but have found this very challenging, I recommend seeking help. Loneliness or feeling unsatisfied can lead to more serious issues. Start with your college counseling center, as they will be able to help you assess what isn't working. If you suspect you are experiencing an unhealthy friendship — such as emotional or physical abuse or manipulation — seek professional support. Appendix C has more advice on identifying signs of emotional abuse and finding support.

RESOURCES

On Campus

- College counseling center: A counselor can help you identify what is lacking in your current friendships, strategize ways to make changes, and support your efforts. A counselor can also help assess if there are other issues that may need treatment, such as social anxiety or forms of autism, and recommend referrals.
- College chaplain: Chaplains provide mentorship and connection as well as a bridge to campus religious groups.

- College residence staff: Staff are natural connectors who help students meet and can provide friendship themselves.
- College diversity office: This office can provide mentorship and connection to groups that match your culture.

Books

- *Friendship in the Age of Loneliness: An Optimist's Guide to Connection* by Adam Smiley Poswolsky: This book is a loving take on how to add more healthy connection to your friendships.

"I was putting all my focus on being friends with the people on my residence hall floor. I thought that was what I was supposed to do, but I didn't really feel like myself with them, and it was stressful and draining. When I became more honest with myself, I realized how much more fun I had with my physics lab partner. We like to play ping-pong or go on long walks rather than partying."

— LIZAH

Chapter 25

Healthy Relationships with Family Members and Mentors

"All my adviser does is complain about the college administration. He barely asks how my senior project is going."

"My mom texts me about twenty times a day. She's so lonely and has no one else."

"I'm scared to go home for Thanksgiving. Everyone at home is politically opposite to me."

"I feel like no one has my back. I can't talk with my parents because they are already too stressed."

"I'm scared that my professor will judge me if I go to their office hours."

Besides peer relationships, students also come to counseling centers to discuss two other main types of relationships: family and college faculty or mentors.

Family comprises our first set of relationships in life. By the time we enter college, they may remain our most important relationships and represent exactly what we hope for in relationships. Or our relationships with family may be troubled and broken and represent exactly what we don't want in relationships. Most of the time, family relationships exist somewhere in between those two extremes!

Mentors play a significant role, especially in college, as they help guide students on their path and to articulate a vision for their future life beyond college.

WHY FAMILY AND MENTOR RELATIONSHIPS ARE A CHALLENGE

Creating workable and satisfying relationships with family takes intention and consistency over time. If we come from a dysfunctional family — and many therapists feel that the majority of families contain some level of dysfunction — then it will be a struggle to understand the dysfunction and find a way to create decent relationships within the family system. In some cases, that can be impossible.

When our family has let us down, it can be hard to trust that other adults won't do the same. This can make it hard to seek out or accept the help of mentors, whether in college, at work, or in any situation. That said, it's also true that adults in positions of authority can also become untrustworthy mentors.

Obviously, college represents a period of enormous change in family relationships. As students become independent adults, and learn about themselves and their beliefs, and grow into the people they want to be, that impacts their previously established relationships with parents, siblings, and extended family. Sometimes family members are supportive of these changes, sometimes not. Sometimes students affirm the values and beliefs they were raised with, and sometimes they develop new values and beliefs.

Finding a faculty or staff support system is extremely helpful, *if not essential*, in college. Even so, students may find it hard to cultivate mentors. This can happen if a student didn't experience support at home or from parents, and so they don't trust adults in general. Or students might not believe they deserve support, or they might think support is only for the best or worst students, but not for them.

STRATEGIES

Assess Your Family Relationships

The process of becoming more aware of your family relationships takes courage and deep exploration. It's a process that is ongoing, much like learning to recognize your family values (see chapter 7). Consider and answer the following questions. Do so in a journal or talk about them with a trusted friend, mentor, or counselor.

- Do you enjoy spending time with your family most of the time?
- Do you feel comfortable or safe enough to come to family members with problems?
- Do you get support from your family?
- Is everyone in your family respectful to you?
- Do you feel safe in general with everyone in your family, as well as safe to be your true self?
- Do you have an appropriate relationship with all members of your family?
- Is there a balance between you and family members in terms of listening and giving?

If you answered no to any of the above questions, whether about your family overall or individual members of your family, that represents an area of hurt and loss in your life. Review chapter 21, "Grief and Loss," and consider if you need to grieve that relationship. Also consider seeing a counselor to address difficult family relationships.

I use the analogy of a pie to help people conceptualize how they feel overall with their family and what feels like a healthy way to interact. A pie seems appropriate since these issues often come up around Thanksgiving.

A whole pie represents a healthy family, though of course, no family is perfect: This means people enjoy spending a significant amount of quality time together, they discuss many topics of conversation together, they feel loved and cared for, they do a large variety of activities together, they feel safe to be honest about most personal issues, and everyone supports each other.

The pie wedge represents a challenging family, one in which some-one struggles to feel okay: This means they prefer spending less time to-gether (like a smaller wedge versus a whole pie), only certain topics feel safe to discuss (like sports but not politics), only certain activities feel safe together (like eating out but not shopping), only certain topics are safe to be honest about (like opinions about music but not feelings about relationships), and not everyone is supported.

Believe You Deserve Support from Mentors

Many students struggle to believe that they deserve support from profes-sors or other college staff. It is part of a professor's job to mentor students. Even if some teachers and staff do not embrace that role or fulfill it well, *you deserve support!* Remind yourself of this whenever you feel you could benefit from the help of a mentor.

Find Mentors and Build a Circle of Support

College is difficult, but you don't have to figure everything out and suc-ceed alone. Find the support you need. Assess the areas you could use mentorship in and the people available to you who might provide it. Here are some ideas for potential mentors:

- Academic adviser
- Professor of a favorite class
- Administrative staff in your major department
- Teaching assistant or other academic staff
- Supervisor in your work-study job
- Athletics coach
- Arts staff
- Student organization staff member
- Student affairs staff (such as career counselors, multicultural life staff, residence staff)

The best way to develop a relationship with a potential mentor is to chat with them and get to know them. It takes courage, but all it takes is dropping by their office and seeing if they have time to chat.

> "I felt intimidated by my academic adviser and upset that I never got the information I needed from her. One day I mentioned it in a very hesitant way to the department coordinator and was relieved to hear that many students have had that experience. I was also told it wouldn't be hard to switch me to a new adviser. I was grateful that I had been brave enough to speak up because it made me much more comfortable to work with a new adviser."
>
> — LAURA

Be Courteous, Respectful, and Prepared When Communicating with Mentors

Many students are intimidated by the idea of talking to their professors. But most professors regard mentoring students as part of their job, one they enjoy. Every professor was once an undergrad, too.

There is no magic formula for a good conversation. Simply be courteous and respectful, and ahead of time, think through what you want to say or what advice or help you are seeking. Communicating with a professor doesn't need to be in person, either; if you feel more comfortable, contact them first via email. Remember, you have the right to approach every professor, and doing so will help you learn better — that is what you are at college for.

Before contacting them or meeting, write out your concerns or questions. Clarify for yourself exactly what you want to ask or what you hope they can do for you. This will help you communicate more clearly in person. For example, maybe you want help narrowing down the thesis for a paper. If you are really nervous, role-play your conversation with a trusted friend (or in your journal). Here are some examples of how you might approach a professor for help:

- "Hi Professor, I am writing to get some feedback on the paper that is due [on X date]. My main questions are [X and X]. Could we meet to talk about these in person? Thanks, [name]"
- "Hi Professor, I am concerned that I'm not on the right track for the class presentations next week. I'm focusing on [X topic], but I'm worried I don't have enough information about [X and X]. Could we meet to talk about this in person? Let me know what times work for you. Thanks, [name]"

A big caveat: Not all professors are great with people, even if some are geniuses in their field. If a professor isn't helpful, realize that this

happens, and don't take it personally. However, seek help from someone else, like a
teaching assistant or department coordinator, or from the college study center.

Ask for Assignment Extensions When Necessary

You have a right to ask for assignment extensions, just as professors have a right to
decline these requests. But it is not a blight
on your personhood to ask, and sometimes,
students need more than advice; they need
more time to do their best work. Even twenty-
four hours can make a huge difference.

Before making a request, check the
course guidelines. These might specify the
circumstances under which late papers will
be allowed and if grade points will be deducted. Some professors are
very liberal, some not, but it doesn't hurt to ask. Remember that asking
for an extension at the last minute won't be as successful as asking a few
days in advance.

Here are some examples of how you might ask a professor for an
extension:

- "Hi Professor, I am writing because I am struggling to finish my
  paper on time, which is due [on X date]. Could I get an extension
  until [X date]? It would make a big difference so I can finish the
  assignment to the best of my ability. Thanks, [name]"
- "Hi Professor, I am concerned that I'm not on the right track to
  present my class presentations next week. Would it be possible to
  have an extension until [X date], and can we meet to talk about
  it in person beforehand? Let me know what times work for you.
  Thanks, [name]"

> "I am very close with my parents. When I first came to college, they wanted to text and call me all the time to hear every detail of my life and how I was doing. It became too much for me, especially because it took time away from my studies and even from connecting to new friends. It was hard, but it was also a relief when I asked them to wait for me to contact them, and to set up a regular phone call on Sunday afternoons. Today, I am still very connected to my family, but it feels more organized and less invasive to my life in school."
>
> — AMOS

WHEN TO SEEK PROFESSIONAL HELP

Unfortunately, some adults aren't good mentors; even if they are well-meaning, they can be dysfunctional. However, some can be abusive or demeaning. Here are questions to assess mentor relationships:

- Does your mentor put you down about anything, including your work, how you look, or how you live?
- Does your mentor make everything about them and their needs?
- Does your mentor prevent you from working with others or make you feel you have to have their help to succeed, or that they won't recommend you if you leave?
- Does your mentor ask about your personal life in a way that feels uncomfortable?
- Does your mentor ask you to do work for them that is inappropriate?

If you answer yes to any of these questions, it is a sign of an unhealthy mentor relationship. Seek advice and help, such as by confiding in a trusted friend or college staff person. Value your own health over any feelings of loyalty.

RESOURCES

On Campus

- College counseling center: Counselors are a confidential resource, unlike other offices on campus, where you can be completely honest about issues with professors or other college staff without fear that anyone else will find out. Counselors can also help you evaluate and cope with unhealthy family relationships, and they can recommend referrals to off-campus providers.
- College chaplain: Chaplains are also a confidential resource on most campuses, and they can provide support for understanding relationship issues.

- Dean of students office: This office can provide clarity and support for how to navigate an unhealthy relationship with a college professor or staff person.
- Title IX officer: This office is legally mandated by the federal government to oversee harassment cases on college campuses.
- Academic dean: This dean can provide support to help you change an adviser or professor if needed.
- College residence staff: Staff may also provide support and advice for approaching professors.
- College diversity office: Staff can provide mentorship and connection that match your culture.

Books

- *Sex and the Spiritual Teacher: Why It Happens, When It's a Problem, and What We All Can Do* by Scott Edelstein: This book provides a deeper understanding of how and why spiritual leaders can engage in inappropriate relationships. It also gives a path for change and healing. Many of the ideas can be translated to other settings where there is a power differential.

Chapter 26

Intimacy

"I don't feel connected to anyone here at college."

"I know everyone on campus, but I don't feel really close to anyone."

"I don't think that people know the real me."

"Our group has a special connection after surviving that trauma."

"I was so close with my family growing up, I haven't valued being close with friends until now."

Intimacy is defined as "close familiarity or friendship," and it is the core ingredient in connected relationships, which are shown to be as important to mental and physical health as any other factor. Most people tend to think intimacy refers to or includes sexual intimacy, but that's not true. Intimacy is part of every close relationship, whether or not the relationship is sexual. There are many ways of being intimate, which involves two basic aspects: sharing experiences (usually over time) and being vulnerable or honest about ourselves. How this expresses itself differs depending on the relationship and the context.

For example, here is a list of different types of intimacies, in alphabetical order, so this list doesn't imply a hierarchy:

Academic field of study: Sharing ideas and passion for an area of study

Arts: Sharing the creation, experience, and/or appreciation of any creative performance or visual art

Crisis/trauma experience: Sharing a specific trauma event or type of crisis, which fosters connection, trust, mutual respect, and commitment

Family: Sharing family history, culture, ethnicity, cuisine, upbringing, and traditions/activities

Friendship (close friend): Sharing strong affection and enjoyment, understanding, commitment, compassion, empathy, and implicit trust

Friendship (platonic): Mutual affection and compatibility, including shared interests, enjoyment, and appropriate vulnerability

Romantic: Sharing love and emotional closeness, often including special experiences, physical intimacy, and devotion

Roommate: Sharing a collaborative spirit to live in harmony, with mutual support, respect, and enjoyment

Sexual: Sharing a pleasurable, consensual physical connection that often includes romance, love, respect, and trust

Spiritual and religious: Sharing a religious faith and/or spiritual values, which often includes shared participation in rituals or services

Sports: Sharing a mutual passion for participation in a sport or athletics, including shared goals, training efforts, and mutual support and respect

Travel: Sharing a love of experiencing and exploring the world, often including travel together

Work: Sharing workplace goals, efforts, and values, along with mutual respect and support to express talents and succeed

WHY INTIMACY IS A CHALLENGE

Intimacy is often challenging, since it requires the bravery of vulnerability — having the courage to share our passions, our truth, our pain, our hopes. Most people find this pretty hard, since everyone has been let down by others at some point, while some have had their trust truly violated. It is a risk to be honest and present. Intimacy also takes time to develop; it involves regularly showing up for another person and consistently earning their trust.

For college students, who are already feeling vulnerable about their identities, intimacy can feel even more risky and overwhelming.

Our 24/7 media-saturated society also works against true intimacy. It is easy to connect broadly but shallowly with many people. People can cultivate a thousand friends on Facebook, share naked pictures on Snapchat, and broadcast strong feelings on TikTok, and yet still be terrified of face-to-face intimacy. But satisfying relationships require such intimacy.

STRATEGIES

Recognize That Intimacy Requires Bravery

We sometimes judge ourselves if we don't have many, or any, genuinely intimate relationships (of whatever kind). But remember, connection and closeness take not just time and effort but courage, and this applies to others. In time, we will find people who will reciprocate our efforts. Take pride each time you take the risk to foster more intimate relationships in your life.

Evaluate Your Own Fears about Intimacy

Everyone fears rejection, but look more closely. What do you fear being rejected for? Identifying this can help you recognize regular fears that block attempts at intimacy. Pay attention to your self-talk:

> "I'm afraid to say what I think because I want to be socially acceptable."
> "When people invite me out, I always think they don't really want to be friends with me."
> "I'm afraid of being judged by negative stereotypes for being who I am [whatever identity that is]."
> "I always assume everyone is hanging out without me, so why try?"
> "People will think I'm weird once they get to know me."

Remember That Intimacy Takes Time

Deeper emotional intimacy must be built over time and requires patience. Lasting intimacy rarely arises in a week or a month; it's the product of a history of shared experiences. If a relationship seems to be moving slowly, or more slowly than you want, give it time and don't be too quick to abandon it.

Slow Down with Others

When you are with people, take the time to talk and get to know each other. Create a space where you have a chance to be more vulnerable, without rushing to fulfill another agenda.

Be Open in Appropriate Ways for the Situation

What is an "appropriate" level of self-disclosure entirely depends on the other person and the context. If you're unsure, match what the other person is talking about, especially in new relationships. Here are some examples:

- Talk about school, classes, or interesting homework
- Talk about common interests, such as artists, sports teams, books, or movies
- Talk about hobbies, games, and extracurricular activities you participate in

Deepen Self-Disclosure Over Time

As people get more familiar and trusting, they naturally share more serious and intimate aspects of their lives. Once again, when unsure, match the other person's level of disclosure. Take small steps to deepen a relationship over time, and make sure the other person is open and responds in kind. More intimate topics include these:

- Talk about your family
- Talk about important life experiences
- Talk about politics and life philosophy

"My girlfriend was the only person I was truly emotionally as well as physically close with. And once we broke up, I began to understand how disconnected I was from my family and friends. I realized that I had to rebuild my connections to others. I made more deliberate plans to hang out and share more deeply with my roommates; I called home more regularly; I reached out to other friends and took the time to get to know them and let them get to know me. Building a broader base of intimate relationships is the only thing that helped me recover from my breakup."

— JAYDEN

Closeness Comes from Listening and Sharing

What we share with others is important, but listening to what others share is equally if not more important. Developing the skill of listening is so vital it warrants its own chapter (chapter 29).

Intimacy also develops through shared experiences. Often those experiences are built into a relationship — they are the reason two people meet, such as being on a sports team or in a club together. If not, create new shared experiences, like these:

- Eat meals together, both on and off campus, and discover favorite places
- Get coffee or tea together, on or off campus
- Study together in the library or a dorm room
- Attend campus events
- Pursue any mutual interests

Put Away Devices to Focus on Others

Intimacy requires attention, focus, and care. So the other person feels valued by you, put away electronic devices. Be in the moment with others as much as you can.

WHEN TO SEEK PROFESSIONAL HELP

If you struggle to create intimate relationships and feel disconnected from others, seek support. There are many ways to get help, so start where you feel the most comfortable: with residence hall staff, a counselor, a trusted mentor, and so on.

If you suspect something more serious is preventing you from developing trust, vulnerability, or intimacy, seek professional counseling to assess whether social anxiety or a previous harmful experience or relationship is the cause.

RESOURCES

On Campus

- College counseling center: A counselor can be a good place to start to explore how to develop more intimate relationships, and they can recommend referrals to off-campus providers.
- College chaplain: Chaplains can provide connection and support.
- College residence staff: Part of the mission of residence staff is to help students connect with other students, so they might be able to help build connections.
- College diversity office: Staff can provide mentorship and connection that match your culture.

"I'm a shy person. I struggled with loneliness when I first came to college and wanted more close connections. I had made some mistakes in the past — I went too fast and started with deep conversations — instead of honoring the need to start more slowly and build trust. I worked up the courage to invite some friends over for a game night, and to my surprise it was fun. Next, I invited those friends over to cook dinner together. We also made some plans for study breaks and to see a movie at a theater off campus. My friend group was getting closer, and we started to have those deep conversations that I enjoy — disclosing more details about our lives. We had earned some shared trust over having fun experiences together."

— RUTH

Books

- *Daring Greatly: How the Courage to Be Vulnerable Transforms the Way We Live, Love, Parent, and Lead* by Brené Brown: This book describes what it means to be open and authentic and how that fosters better-connected relationships.

Chapter 27

Boundaries

"Whenever he needs me, I drop what I'm doing."

"You mean I can say no but still be a good friend? I didn't think that was true."

"I always feel guilty if I don't answer her calls right away."

"I never let anyone in. I've learned it's safer that way."

"I get sucked into being a therapist, and I'm not. I'm just a college student."

A healthy boundary, both emotional and physical, is the comfortable space between you and another person. Having healthy boundaries facilitates having healthy intimacy. A healthy boundary entails recognizing what feels like the right, authentic level of responsibilities, and then standing by that in whatever way works for the situation.

Boundary issues range on a continuum from having too much distance from others (usually due to a lack of trust) to having little ability to separate one's own feelings and needs from the feelings and needs of another person (enmeshment).

WHY SETTING BOUNDARIES IS A CHALLENGE

Setting and maintaining comfortable boundaries is hard to learn and practice. Most of the time, our culture doesn't provide us with healthy examples of this.

Once students make new friends, they often struggle to maintain a comfortable emotional space between themselves and the friend that feels right. Keeping healthy boundaries comes up in many ways in college relationships: spending too much time with one or two people and not letting in any new friends; feeling at the mercy of one friend and not knowing how to say no; not believing one has the right to say no; taking on a caretaker role with a needy friend; enabling addictive (or self-harming) behavior in a friend; and more.

In general, everyone wants to be a good friend and a good person. This can easily get confused with doing too much for another person. In addition, students also want to be good students, and this might require devoting less time to friendships.

Boundaries aren't just for friendships. Many students struggle with how to keep healthy boundaries with parents and other adults as well as with significant others.

STRATEGIES

Accept the Need for Healthy Boundaries

Every relationship needs to have boundaries, and you have the right to establish boundaries in any relationship that feel good and appropriate to you. This includes your relationship with yourself. You have the power and responsibility to make your friendships work for you.

Listen to Yourself

When relationship boundaries are off, we usually have some little spidey sense or gut feeling that something doesn't feel right. Or we might experience huge, unmistakable feelings of anger, resentment, or overwhelm that indicate we need to set boundaries that are missing. Don't ignore these warnings, even if you are afraid to hurt the other person, and even if the other person is telling you that there is no problem. If a relationship doesn't feel appropriate or healthy to you, trust yourself and readjust your boundaries.

Listen to Your Friends

Sometimes a friend can see what might be too painful for us to acknowledge. If friends are brave enough to say something, it's a good idea to at least consider it.

Identify the Particular Boundary Issue

If you know you need to readjust a relationship's boundaries, take some time to identify the particular issues. Feel free to write about this in your journal if it is helpful. Where is the problem, and how or when does it come up? This will provide a clue to the best, most appropriate solution. Consider these scenarios:

- You drop everything for the friend, no matter what your needs are. You can't say no to them.
- You feel you owe another person all your private information.
- You feel you owe a person or friend group all your energy to help hold the relationship or group together.
- You feel guilty or fearful (versus concerned) when something isn't going right for your friend. You feel their emotions versus your own.
- You feel the need to be available for your friend all the time. You feel it's your duty to be there for them.
- You feel guilty if you want to do something on your own, rather than always being with the friend or group.
- You try to take up the least space so you won't be seen or heard.
- You struggle to engage when others reach out to you. You feel distant most of the time.

If any of these scenarios applies to your life, that signals a boundary that needs readjustment. Sometimes just naming the issue for yourself will be enough to know how to change things. Here are some examples of how you might handle each situation:

- I can say no to certain friends when they ask to study because I never get any work done with them.
- I don't have to tell my roommate everything about my date because it feels private to me right now.
- I can refer my friends to a better source of support when I don't feel I can handle their issues on my own.
- I can say no to the party because I don't like hanging around that friend group.
- I can say yes to going to bed at 10:30 p.m. because my body loves the sleep.
- I can tell my family I won't be traveling home at Thanksgiving because the trip is too exhausting right now.
- I can ask my friend to talk when I am feeling lonely.
- I can say yes when my friends ask me to go to a movie because I deserve to take a break.

Learn to Say No

Saying no is a challenge for most people. Setting a boundary by saying no to an invitation can get misinterpreted by others as meaning the person doesn't value or like others or doesn't consider them important. Or people can believe they aren't a good person if they don't say yes. However, saying no and setting limits are vital for living in a way that supports our values and needs. Otherwise, our life can fill up with things that aren't what we really want.

Mahatma Gandhi said, "A no uttered from deepest conviction is better and greater than a yes merely uttered to please, or what is worse, to avoid trouble."

You might find it helpful to use a mantra. Here are two examples:

"Me and my roommates have been on constant alert and taking care of our other roommate who is depressed and suicidal. We are all at a breaking point because our friend won't seek help and is acting in self-destructive ways, mainly getting blackout drunk or isolating and making suicidal statements on social media. I reached out to the counseling center and made an appointment for all of my roommates, including the depressed roommate who agreed to attend. In the session, we were able to talk more openly and get other college staff members involved, so the responsibility didn't all rest on me and my roommates."

— LENA

Every time you say yes to something, you are saying no to something as well.
What good is your yes if you can't say no?

For example, if you say yes to volunteering at an all-day world peace conference to help out a friend who is coordinating the conference, you might be saying no to study time the day before an important exam. Or if you say yes to a sexual act before you are ready, you are saying no to feeling truly comfortable. If you say yes to staying up late with a friend who needs to talk, you are saying no to your own sleep and self-care, which might make you exhausted. Of course, sometimes we sacrifice our needs for friends, but make sure that is an intentional decision, not an unwilling obligation.

Here are some examples of how to say no:

"I would love to help, but I have another commitment" [even if that's to yourself].

"Thanks for asking. I would love to do it another time, but I can't tonight."

"I want to hang out with my roommate tonight. Let's see each other for lunch tomorrow."

"I would like to do that someday, but I'm not ready yet."

"I'm honored that you asked, but I have to decline. I have too many obligations already."

"I need to study for my exam tonight, so I won't be able to come by your room like usual."

"I'm exhausted and going to bed early tonight. Just so you know, I'm turning my phone off, too."

"No, I'm not interested."

"No."

WHEN TO SEEK PROFESSIONAL HELP

If you have identified a boundary issue but are struggling to make changes, seek outside support, such as from a trusted mentor or counselor.

This chapter has focused on more benign boundary issues, but there are many types of serious boundary violations that students have experienced, whether in their family of origin or other relationships (such as emotional or physical abuse, sexual abuse, emotional or spiritual manipulation, and so on). See appendix C for definitions of abuse and for support resources.

RESOURCES

On Campus

- College counseling center: A counselor can help you recognize and articulate what boundary issues are occurring in your life, brainstorm ways to make changes, and support your efforts to change. A counselor can also recommend referrals to off-campus providers.
- College chaplain: Chaplains can provide mentorship and support for making changes in your life.
- College residence staff: Staff are specially trained in roommate issues and can help provide support when having challenging discussions.
- College diversity office: Staff can provide mentorship and connection that match your culture.

"My mom is going through a divorce and has been depressed for a while. My mom texts me all the time, looking for attention or a chance to complain about my dad, rarely asking about what is going on with me. It is the worst when my mom FaceTime's me at night, crying in her bed. I'm not willing to cut off communication with my mom in any way, I believe that I need to be there for her, but it's too much right now. I am determined to reduce the times I do text with my mom to only a couple of times a day (usually before lunch and dinner); this would allow me to feel emotionally prepared to respond, I'd be able to connect with my friends right afterward, and it wouldn't feel as if it was intruding into my day quite as much. I also plan to send a quick text or call to my mom as a study break around 8 p.m. Although it is difficult, at that later text or call, I will inform my mom that I am very busy with school so will likely have my phone off when I head to bed, in order to avoid the overly painful end-of-day communication. I struggled with feeling like I should be there more for my mom, but I also feel safer and less burdened knowing there were some limits on when I'm connecting with her."

— DANIEL

Books

- *Set Boundaries, Find Peace: A Guide to Reclaiming Yourself* by Nedra Glover Tawwab: This book makes the complex topic of boundaries understandable and relatable.

Chapter 28

How to Make New Friends

"I don't enjoy big parties, but I'm not sure where else to meet people."

"I don't fit in here. It's been hard for me to find friends."

"I feel like the only junior who doesn't have a good friend group."

"I get so overwhelmed at the thought of talking to people that I end up just staying in my room."

"I broke up with my main friend group from last year. I need some new friends."

Making friends comes naturally to many people, but it can be a struggle for others. Luckily, the steps to making friends can be learned!

WHY MAKING FRIENDS IS A CHALLENGE

Humans evolved as social animals, and interaction with others is critical for our health and survival. Yet even though relationships are so important, that doesn't mean it's easy to make and keep friends. It feels risky to be vulnerable and reach out to another person. Developing new friendships takes time and effort, and failure is built into the process. Not everyone becomes a friend, and most people hate the thought of failing.

Part of college is making new friends. Students must do this at the same time that lots of new and unfamiliar things are happening, such as living away from home, managing a college-level course load, and simply learning hard stuff. Some students arrive on campus and realize they haven't really had to make new friends since kindergarten! Some students are commuting to campus and don't spend much time there, some students are transferring to a new school and find it hard to break into existing friend groups, and some folks are living at home and have time-consuming family responsibilities. Some people also take a longer time to warm up and trust others, and people who come from a minority population (especially relative to their campus) may feel out of place or isolated.

For introverts and others who find socializing a challenge, college can be tough, especially the first semester. This period just naturally demands a lot of time spent in social interactions, which can feel exhausting. During the first months, the main way people meet is through big parties, which aren't always the best environments to get to know new people well.

STRATEGIES

Be Open and Nonjudgmental with Yourself

In order to create a new community of friends at college, you may need to go outside of your comfort zone. Be open to new situations, and don't judge yourself if it takes a long time to make new friends. Making deep, intimate connections with new people takes time and shared experience. Know that what feels hard at first will get easier. Be patient.

Keep Making the Effort

Not everyone we meet will become a good friend. If at first you don't succeed in finding "your people," keep trying, even if you have to force yourself. Try new strategies and situations, and keep putting in the time and energy to form new friendships.

For instance, at first, you might not feel comfortable starting a conversation with a stranger, but if you keep going out, showing up, and making yourself available, someone might start a conversation with you. In time, you will become more comfortable connecting with others. Be patient.

Go Where People Are

It's great when you find yourself in a ready-made group, like a sports team, an amazing class, or that lucky dorm floor. But without a ready-made group, you will need to be creative and seek out the type of people you are interested in.

Pick the places where others hang out. It's simple and logical, but it may not feel natural at first. It can feel uncomfortable to show up in places when you don't yet know people, whether that's a lounge, a study hall, a particular eatery, or a park. Our natural inclination is to play it safe, but showing up is half the battle. Arrive early to class so you have extra time to chat with other students. Study in the same area in the library, and you will start to recognize the regulars and they will recognize you. Being in the same place, it's easier to start a conversation about whatever is going on. So hang out where others hang out.

Follow Your Interests

To find people you might want to connect with, look for people who share your interests. Don't do things you think you should like to do. Do what you really like to do. If you prefer to hang out in the student lounge on your dorm floor, do that. If you are passionate about ancient Greece, find a group that matches your interest. If you like a certain cuisine, ask around for people who might want to explore the area's restaurants.

Another way to meet people who share your interests is to join a student organization or two. Most campuses have many options, ranging from career-oriented groups to those focused on social justice or performance. Identity affinity groups such as the Black student union (which goes by different names on different campuses), the LGBTQIA union, and religious groups have been lifelines for many students. Give each one a chance; don't go once or twice and quit. Unless you are absolutely sure the group isn't right for you, stick around until you make a friend. On the other hand, perhaps try a club that does something fun you've never done before, like a knitting club or a volunteer group. If you're unsure about your commitment, choose clubs that are more low-key and casual.

Exhibit Inviting Body Language

Our body language communicates as much as our voice, so consider if you have an open or receptive posture. People can usually tell just by looking whether or not someone feels confident and comfortable and seems interested in meeting others. Display the eagerness to talk rather than worry about what you'll say. Also notice everyone's body language. Scan the room and note what others are doing. If you're unsure what to do, match what others are doing.

Here are some elements of open body language:

- Making appropriate eye contact while talking or listening (not staring past people or gazing in the distance or at your phone)
- Facing others with arms down or open (not with arms crossed)
- Speaking at a normal volume in a friendly, measured tone (not being too quiet or loud, nor talking too fast)
- Steady hands and feet (not jiggling legs or bouncing feet)
- Smiling

If there's one clue to someone's openness, it's their facial expression. If someone is scowling, frowning, or looking afraid, people don't feel invited to approach. And when we're uncertain in a new situation, it's shockingly easy to forget to smile. So smile; practice in a mirror if that helps you smile more confidently.

When People Talk, Listen

Of course, you'll talk to people, and when they ask about you, tell them. But the best way to get to know someone else and make friends is to ask about them and then listen to what they say. Follow up and ask them more about their interests and experiences and history. Seek to find out what makes people tick. (For more, see chapter 29.)

Have a Conversation

There's an art to having a good conversation with someone new. It involves three basic parts: starting a conversation, maintaining and deepening it, and ending it in a friendly way.

It is often best to start with an easygoing topic — such as the weather, weekend plans, homework. But don't dismiss the importance of starting with a compliment. This should be sincere and not too personal, but something that makes the other person feel good and demonstrates your interest in them. Praise their backpack, clothes, or something they said in class.

If someone says something nice to you, don't deny the compliment, even if it makes you self-conscious. The best and easiest reply is a simple thank-you, then return the favor.

After the first time, starting a conversation gets much easier, since you can refer to shared experiences, depending on the context in which you know the person. If you met in the dining hall, discuss the food; if in the residence hall, bring up something that happened last night or last week; if in class, ask their opinion of the professor or what classes they might take next semester.

Once the conversation is started, maintaining it relies on both your curiosity and your listening skills. Ask open-ended questions about what people think or how they feel. That is, not just "How are you?" but their thoughts and opinions about the college you're both at, what they're doing, and what they hope to accomplish. Ask about what music they like, what they like to do for vacation, what their family is like, or what jobs or internships they have. Remember, your goal is simple: just to get to know them better and connect. Of course, if you show genuine curiosity about another person, they usually show curiosity about you. Don't be shy about sharing about yourself in just the way you hope the other person will share themselves with you. Conversations and friendships are two-way streets.

Some conversations end naturally, the same way they can start naturally. But sometimes it can be awkward when you run out of things to say. Don't worry, that happens to everyone. However, make a point to end by saying something positive. That might just be appreciation for talking

"I was miserable because it was the second semester of my first year and I hadn't made one friend yet. I was mostly hanging out in my room between classes and always ate by myself at the dining hall. My counselor urged me to try two things: to study every night in my residence hall floor lounge, and to always eat meals at the same counter in the dining hall. At first nothing happened, and I felt skeptical and lonely. Then I noticed that the same people were always studying and eating near me. After a few weeks, I started to talk to those students. The conversations were brief at first, then became more fun. Finally, I realized these folks were my friends. I now hang out with them outside the lounge and the dining hall counter, and I have to admit that I am much happier."

— STELLA

and the desire to meet again, or wish the person luck with something that's meaningful to them, like an upcoming test.

Reach Out

With people you'd like to meet again or develop a better friendship with, make the effort to reach out. Contact them and make a plan to do something. It doesn't have to be involved or special. Relate it to the context for your friendship, such as getting together to study for a class or meeting for lunch once a week when your schedules match. If you bond over movies, suggest a movie. If you have a mutual interest or activity, do something related to that. Reach out more than once, even if it feels like you are doing most of the inviting at first. As your friendship develops, this will even out eventually. There is no timeline you need to follow. Every friendship develops at its own pace, in its own way.

Expect Some Rejection

Not every friendship works out or is meant to be. If some folks don't reciprocate or show interest in you, it's important to try not to take it personally. When it does happen, let yourself have a moment or two of sadness, then focus on developing your next friend.

Be a Friend to Yourself

Making friends in a new environment can be draining work. So be kind to yourself; give yourself alone time to recharge. Every day make space for an activity you love that you can do by yourself. Do something that you really look forward to. Make a "date" with yourself to do something that will brighten your day. Strive for a balance of social interaction and strategically placed quiet time.

WHEN TO SEEK PROFESSIONAL HELP

If you are feeling alone and isolated and having trouble connecting with others, reach out for support. Know that you are not alone; many students struggle with this issue. Often the best places to reach out and seek help are the closest: residence hall staff, professors and campus mentors, campus counselors, and clergy.

RESOURCES

On Campus

- College residence staff: Part of their job is to help students make connections on campus. Trust your gut and reach out to someone who appeals to you and seems understanding. They can help connect you to others and suggest campus resources like student organizations.
- College diversity office: Staff can provide mentorship and connection that match your culture.
- College counseling center: A counselor can teach new skills and offer support for making new friends, and they can recommend referrals to off-campus providers.
- College chaplain: Chaplains can provide mentorship and connection through a spiritual lens as well as a bridge to campus religious groups.

"I had been isolated and negative, especially on weekends. Back at home, I had one best friend, and I was very close with my mom and little brother, but otherwise I didn't have many friends. I agreed to make two changes: to get out of my room and study at the library each weekend day, and to sit next to (not across the class from) the people I really liked in my favorite class and to get there early so we would have time to talk. It was hard to get to the library on weekends, and I struggled to do it consistently at first. Sometimes I forgot to sit next to my potential friends in class, but I was glad when I did it because we chatted and got to know each other. It took a while for me to establish these habits, but once I did, it turned around the isolation and negativity on the weekends, and I was able to make friends."

— HAMILTON

Books

- *Reclaiming Conversation: The Power of Talk in a Digital Age* by Sherry Turkle: This book is a great argument for the power of face-to-face communication, even though most of us are spending lots more time looking down at our phones making "friends" in cyberspace.
- *What to Say Next: Successful Communication in Work, Life, and Love with Autism Spectrum Disorder* by Sarah and Larry Nannery: Though not all chapters relate to college students, this book, written by someone with autism spectrum disorder, is an invaluable guide to navigating all types of communication if you are on the autism spectrum.
- *Quiet: The Power of Introverts in a World That Can't Stop Talking* by Susan Cain: A thorough and passionate look at how introverted traits have created some of our culture's most important milestones yet continue to be discounted in our extroverted society.

Chapter 29

How to Listen

"When I get in a group of people, I turn on the humor. I never listen to others because I'm afraid that people won't think I'm funny and then I'll be a nobody."

"I'm so afraid of what others are thinking of me that I freeze up and am unable to listen."

"I feel all alone when I can tell my friends are checking their phones and not really paying attention to me."

"I was so worried about what I was going to say in the class discussion I couldn't listen to what other class members were saying."

"Sometimes I just find myself tuning out when my friends are talking. I feel bad about it."

It is impossible for two people to have a quality relationship without being able to listen to each other. Attentive listening facilitates awareness, understanding, and empathy.

WHY LISTENING IS A CHALLENGE

Listening deeply takes intention and focus. Most of the time, we listen lightly or selectively. The goal is to really hear what someone is saying without imposing our perspective and opinion.

This can be hard. We might be afraid of what the other person is saying and what it means for us. We may not know the right thing to say or how to treat them. We may not know what our responsibility is. It takes courage to be truly present with someone and want to hear their truth.

Students are naturally self-focused in college. They are discovering their skills and passions, striving to learn as much as they can in their chosen field of study, experimenting with friendships, and working to understand themselves and their sense of identity. At times, it's hard to remember everyone is doing the same thing and to listen to what others are going through.

We can also worry about how we appear to others, which makes it difficult to really listen. Negative self-talk can make it impossible to focus on someone else. So one goal is to identify when this happens and "quiet" our inner voice so we can hear others.

STRATEGIES

Consider the Quality of Your Listening

Part of valuing and prioritizing our listening skills is to assess how well we listen. In a journal, reflect on these questions:

- Do you usually do most of the talking?
- Do you ask open-ended questions, seeking to learn more about what others are talking about?
- Do you remember what others have said about topics that seem important to them?

Check Your Body Language

Our body language conveys the quality of our listening. Having an open face and body shows others that you are available. Make eye contact if possible. Turn your body toward the person you are listening to. Notice if your arms are crossed, creating a physical barrier between you and the other person. If it feels authentic, nod and gesture to convey that you are listening.

Put the Phone Away

It needs to be said: Phone use gets in the way of authentic listening. If you look down to your phone and send a quick text, you have told the person you are talking to that they do not command your full attention. If you intend to have a deep conversation and listen closely, put your phone on silent and put it away.

Ask Open-Ended Questions

Open-ended questions reflect your own curiosity and intention to learn about the other person. They are invitations for the person to share their thoughts and ideas, to reflect more deeply and broadly. Open-ended questions usually start with *how*, *what*, or *why*. As in: How did it happen?, What do you feel?, and Why did you do what you did? Asking closed yes-or-no questions can sometimes be dead ends: Did you like what happened? So follow those up with *why*, *how*, and *what* questions.

Reflect Back What Others Say

From time to time, restate or clarify what you have heard the other person say. This lets the other person know that they have been heard correctly and prevents you from misunderstanding. Reflecting back is only about confirming your understanding, not giving your opinion or being judgmental. Here are some examples:

> "It sounds like you are saying that you really don't like your computer science classes."
> "From what I'm hearing, you haven't been getting along with your roommate for a long time."
> "Clearly, you are beyond frustrated and don't know what to do" [but said without telling them what to do].

Remember to WAIT

In general, but especially when your intention is to listen deeply, avoid giving advice or expressing your opinion unless the person expressly

"I had a hard time connecting to others in group settings because I used to zone out whenever I felt overwhelmed or worried about how others perceived me. I worked hard to focus on what others were saying, which took some time and practice. After a while, I began to feel calmer in group settings; it was a relief to me that all I had to do was worry about what others were saying and what they were trying to communicate, rather than worrying about how I was coming across. And as I was listening to others, I could easily formulate authentic responses rather than struggling to figure out a clever thing to say."

— ROSALIND

requests it. A good acronym to remember is WAIT, which stands for "Why am I talking?" We all want to jump in and help solve a situation or connect the situation to our own experience. Those aren't bad impulses, but be patient and don't rush in or interrupt the person. Sometimes, the best thing we can do is to allow others to have time and space to express themselves so they can figure out a solution for themselves.

Note that WAIT has a sibling ("Why aren't I talking?"), which I explain in chapter 30.

WHEN TO SEEK PROFESSIONAL HELP

If you are struggling to listen to people, for any reason, consider seeking help, whether from a counselor, clergy, or a trusted mentor. Struggling to listen to others could be a symptom of many issues that can be hard to tease apart, such as anxiety, attention-deficit disorder, autism issues, or depression. If you suspect another cause, be assessed by a mental health professional, who can provide treatment with support groups, individual counseling, and sometimes medication.

RESOURCES

On Campus

- College counseling center: A counselor can provide help with listening better, and they can assess and diagnosis any underlying mental health issues, such as anxiety, social anxiety, autism issues, ADD, and so on. They can also recommend referrals to off-campus providers.

- College study center: This center might provide resources to improve active listening as it relates to the classroom.
- College chaplain: A chaplain can provide a safe space to practice deep listening.

Websites

- Verywell Mind (www.verywellmind .com): This mental health website has published an excellent article called "What Is Active Listening?" (www.very wellmind.com/what-is-active-listening -3024343).

"I have been having a hard time listening and paying attention to classroom lectures. I thought it was partly due to me not totally understanding what was going on with the material, which made me feel very unsure of myself to the point of having low self-esteem in class. This exacerbated my depression symptoms. When I worked with the disability office and borrowed a Smartpen [an assistive technology] to take notes, it removed the emotional burden on me, so I could focus on the learning."

— DYLAN

Chapter 30

How to Communicate Clearly

"I don't know how to tell him that I don't want to live together next year."

"I didn't realize I can just ask a professor for an extension."

"My coping strategy is just to stay quiet and not deal with things."

"I thought she would just know what I was thinking."

"Starting a conversation is so awkward. I hate feeling awkward."

Everyone knows what communication is. As the Britannica dictionary defines it, it's "using words, sounds, signs, or behaviors to express or exchange information or to express your ideas, thoughts, feelings." Also obviously, quality relationships are enhanced with clear communication. What this chapter focuses on is being clear when communication is difficult, such as when we have disagreements, differences, and anxieties about speaking up.

Clear communication includes these attributes:

- It uses respectful language (such as using "I" statements, being assertive but not aggressive).
- It is understandable and uses clear language.
- It is honest (by not avoiding or denying thoughts and feelings).

- It is aware of power imbalances (that is, we are thoughtful about the relative positions or roles of both persons).

WHY CLEAR COMMUNICATION IS A CHALLENGE

If only communication skills were taught in grade school along with basic academics, our world would be a better place. All of us struggle with communication issues to a certain extent, and there are many reasons: It can feel risky to speak our truth. We can think we are speaking clearly and still be misunderstood. We can fear hurting another person. Or our heated emotions can make it challenging to express ourselves clearly.

In addition, every society contains many power imbalances — related to gender, race, class, sexual orientation, and so on — and finding our power to speak our mind, and allowing another person to do the same, can be challenging. Many people struggle with how to be assertive (in respectful ways) without being either aggressive (or disrespectful), passive aggressive (or unclear), or deferential (putting others' needs first).

College students wrestle with all these communication issues. They might not know how to speak up for themselves or how to express frustration, anger, and disagreement in respectful, appropriate ways. Many students struggle with valuing themselves and their needs as equal to others. Further, students who come from cultures where assertive communication is not the norm can struggle on US college campuses, where strong communication skills and being assertive are often considered important for professional development.

Here are some common communications challenges:

- How to express anger or disappointment to friends
- How to talk about deep or challenging needs and feelings in general
- How to say no
- How to talk to people in positions of authority (like professors)
- How to ask for something that might not be easy to ask for (like extensions on projects)

STRATEGIES

Learn Not to WAIT

In chapter 29, the acronym WAIT stands for "Why am I talking?" That's a good reminder to listen to others and not impose our perspective. But WAIT can also stand for the opposite: "Why *aren't* I talking?" This can be a reminder to speak up, rather than stay silent, and express how we feel and what we think and to ask for what's important.

It is not just okay but important to speak your truth. No one is a mind reader, and others won't know what you are thinking unless you tell them. What you think and feel matters.

Knowing when to listen and when to speak up is tricky. Strive to be sensitive in every moment, knowing that sometimes we need to listen and sometimes we need to speak our truth.

Believe That Difficult Conversations Help

Some conversations can be uncomfortable, especially when we say things others don't want to hear. However, in the long run, it's beneficial to be honest and clear with others. In fact, all we can do is be as clear as possible to solve a problem or improve a relationship. We can't control what other people think, feel, or do. Ultimately, relationships are strengthened when people work together to resolve conflicts.

Assess Your Goals or Needs

Before having a difficult conversation, consider what you hope to achieve or ask for. Write about this in a journal. That will help you avoid conflicts that become about winning the conversation rather than solving problems. When either person tries to "win," such as by intimidating the other, it can harm the relationship. The healthiest goals are to try to make ourselves understood, to strive to understand the other person, and to seek resolutions that are acceptable to both.

Make a Plan for the Conversation

Difficult conversations always go better when we plan for them, rather than springing a hard topic without preparation. Arrange a specific time to talk, such as by making an appointment with a professor during their office hours, asking a friend to coffee, or asking a roommate when they would have time to chat during the day. If you wait for the "right moment," that moment might not come. A roommate might return to the room late at night and too tired to talk, or a professor might be too busy immediately before or after class.

In addition, plan for a moment when both of you have enough time to talk fully. This is part of being respectful: Raising a difficult topic when the other person is distracted or too busy to think it through for themselves can set up the situation for failure. If it seems appropriate or necessary, let the other person know the topic you want to discuss, so they can prepare as well.

Write Out What You Want to Say

With difficult subjects or conflicts, write out what you want to say beforehand. You might even practice a speech with a trusted friend. This way, you have a much better chance of saying what you want in the way that you want, rather than going off in a harmful direction. When you actually talk, if it helps (because you are nervous or afraid of forgetting something or saying things the wrong way), it is okay to use your notes. Simply tell the other person that their relationship is so important that you want to get it right.

Be Prepared to Listen

Remember, every successful conversation involves listening as well as talking. While your first goal is to say clearly and appropriately what you want to say, the other main goal is to listen and discover how the other person thinks and feels. Use all the listening and body language skills that I discuss in chapters 28 and 29.

Use a "Difficult Conversation" Communication Paradigm

How we say things is important, especially with difficult topics. We want to speak in a way that others can hear. That is, we don't want our tone, manner, or word choice to upset the other person and close them off to what we have to say. While this communication paradigm works for all conversations, it's especially useful when discussing conflicts or challenging topics.

- **Start with a connecting or fun statement** (unless it's not necessary or more appropriate to jump right to the main topic):

    "I always look forward to lunch with you."
    "You are an awesome roommate."
    "I appreciate you taking the time to talk."

- **"When you…"**: Start by describing in a factual and respectful way the behavior of the other person. Be as neutral as possible and focus on specific events without universalizing (as in, "when you did this," not "when you always do this").

    "When you put me down in front of our friends…" [or made that joke].
    "When we talked politics last night…"
    "When you came in at 4 a.m. and made a bunch of noise…"
    "When you didn't take out the trash all week…"
    "When you stayed out all night without texting me that you would be gone…"

- **"Then I…"**: Using an "I" statement, describe the results of their behavior, or how their behavior affected you. Avoid presuming that the person's intention was to be hurtful, even if that was the result. Be careful to use respectful language, and again, focus on the incident.

    "Then I didn't want to hang out with the group" [or in our room].
    "Then I didn't think you cared about me" [or respected my opinion].
    "Then my sleep was disrupted and I was exhausted the next day."
    "Then I had to be the one to clean up."
    "Then I couldn't sleep because I was anxious about you."

- **"I feel..."**: Next, if it's not already clear, describe how the behavior made you feel. Always use "I feel" or "I felt" to describe this, not "you made me feel." It is very common to want to blame others for our emotional reactions, but remember, the other person probably didn't intend to be hurtful, and we can't control how others react. Be clear about your feelings, and express them as *your* feelings. This helps avoid the other person reacting in a defensive way. For help identifying and naming your emotions, see chapter 17.

"I feel hurt and belittled" [or angry, frustrated, resentful].
"I felt rejected" [or like my opinion didn't matter].
"I felt frustrated to be doing most of the cleaning."
"I felt anxious that you might have been hurt."

- **"I would prefer that you..."**: Finally, name clearly the alternate behavior that you would prefer. What action do you want the other person to take? Be specific, since that gives the other person an active way to fix or resolve the problem.

"I would prefer that you not put me down when we hang out" [or joke like that].
"I would prefer that you be as quiet as possible when you come in late, like after 1 a.m."
"I would prefer that you stick to the cleaning arrangement we agreed to and take out the trash every other week."
"I would prefer that you shoot me a quick text when you know you won't be coming home."

Learn How to Communicate Across Difference

Most students appreciate being able to learn from and connect to students who are different from themselves. This starts with being curious, but we want to be respectful in how we frame our questions to another person. A good way to reflect on how a question will be received is to ask ourselves: Would we be willing to answer the same question if asked of

"I was fearful of breaking my family's expectations that I major in a STEM area. I decided to major in English because I love writing and reading, I have a plan for a senior honors thesis, and I have researched with the career center many potential jobs I could get upon graduation, as well as the statistics for employment of English majors. Although I was afraid to talk to my parents, I worked out what to tell them, wrote it down, and practiced with a friend. They reacted better than I expected. They had questions, but I was ready for them with my research. After I finally talked to my parents about my plans, I was very relieved."

— GRACE

us? Also, it is always nice to ask permission before asking more personal questions, such as by saying, "Do you mind me asking?" As with overall clear communication, listening without making assumptions is essential.

Ask for What You Need

All people deserve to express their needs and wants. That doesn't mean we will always get what we need and want, but we can and should ask. If we don't ask, people won't necessarily know what we need (or feel is missing), and if we ask in a respectful way, we give others a chance to help.

- **"I need…":** Describe in a factual and respectful way the thing you need.

  "I need some alone time in our room."
  "I need help with my math problem set."
  "I need to go home because I'm tired and don't feel well."
  "I need to talk to you."

- **"Can/will you…":** Name clearly and specifically what you would like the other person to do.

  "Can we arrange times when I can have the room to myself?"
  "Will you have any free time this week to help me study?"
  "Can you walk me home?"
  "Can you talk now, or would you prefer talking later? If so, when?"

WHEN TO SEEK PROFESSIONAL HELP

If you are struggling to talk to people in your life, for any reason, seek advice from trusted friends, relatives, clergy, or mentors. If everyday interactions cause significant anxiety, fear, self-consciousness, and embarrassment, this might indicate social anxiety. Meanwhile, difficulties deciphering nonverbal communication (like facial expressions or body language) can indicate an autism spectrum disorder. If you're worried or unsure, visit a mental health professional for an assessment.

RESOURCES

On Campus

- College counseling center: Counselors can provide support to help you develop healthy communication strategies and appropriate assertiveness. They can also assess mental health issues and provide referrals to off-campus providers.
- College student organizations: Joining a student organization will give you a chance to practice your communication skills with the same group of people over time.
- College chaplain: Chaplains can provide a safe space and spiritual lens to work out communication issues.

> "I get along great with two of my housemates, but the fourth has been difficult — not doing his chores, being manipulative, often trying to pick a fight. I usually just avoid this housemate, but it is getting worse, and I know I need to take some action. I worked out some basic phrases to mention to my housemate when a good opportunity comes up. When I finally spoke with him, he reacted badly at first and just avoided everyone for a couple of weeks. Then, to my surprise, he confided that he's been a little down lately and didn't realize he was taking it out on us, his housemates. He was glad that I had said something because he knows that meant I value our relationship. There has been more peace in our house, and I'm glad I took the risk to be honest and clear."
>
> — ARJUN

Books

- *Your Perfect Right: Assertiveness and Equality in Your Life and Relationships* by Robert Alberti and Michael Emmons: This classic assertiveness training book will help you learn how to have respectful and more equal relationships.
- *The Shyness & Social Anxiety Workbook* by Martin M. Antony and Richard P. Swinson: This step-by-step program uses a cognitive

behavior framework to assess and create personal strategies and goals to heal social anxiety.

- *The Subtle Art of Not Giving a F*ck: A Counterintuitive Approach to Living a Good Life* by Mark Manson: The author has a fresh way of helping readers let go of what other people think and drop the fantasy that everyone else has their life figured out.

Chapter 31

Healthy Sexuality

"How often is it healthy to have sex?"

"Should it hurt when I masturbate?"

"I'm not ready to have intercourse, but I like kissing. Is that okay?"

"The sex I have in a hookup is different than the sex I have in a relationship."

"How do I tell my partner what I like and don't like?"

Healthy sexuality involves recognizing where we're at as a sexual being while acting sexually in safe and consensual ways. Sexuality is not one type of activity or behavior. There is no single "right" way to be sexual. What feels right can change from day to day and person to person.

Sometimes we prefer sex with ourselves, and other times we prefer sex with another person.

Sometimes we want to be in a caring relationship to enjoy sexual activity, and other times we might enjoy a hookup without being in an established relationship.

Sometimes we prefer a monogamous sexual relationship, and other times we might enjoy an open relationship.

Sometimes we want to experiment with new sensations, and other times we want to do what is comfortable for us.

Sometimes we want regular sex, and other times we prefer closeness in a nonsexual way.

Sometimes sexual connection feels amazing, and other times sexual connection can feel "meh."

Sometimes we are attracted to one gender, and sometimes we are
attracted to other or multiple genders.

Sometimes our gender expression is fluid, and this may or may
not affect our sexuality.

What isn't healthy when it comes to sexuality?

- Feeling we don't deserve to be sexual because of how we look,
  our body type or shape, or our identity.
- Not exploring and discovering what gives us sensual or erotic
  pleasure.
- Adopting a sexuality because others have dictated what is ac-
  ceptable or allowed.
- Any sexual act we think we "should" do because others do it.
- Any sexual act that doesn't feel good to us.
- Any sexual act that isn't consensual.

WHY HEALTHY SEXUALITY IS A CHALLENGE

Between Hollywood rom-coms and porn, our media culture paints a false
picture of what sexuality is like, one that's intended to entertain us — it
isn't intended to show reality. But we internalize these sexual images and
fantasies all the same. What we need are images of real sexuality that
include a diversity of bodies and styles.

This is hard to find. Sex education in US schools has at times even
been made illegal, and there are few places that provide an honest education about what constitutes healthy sexuality. As a result, a plethora of
myths and mistaken beliefs endures.

Many students come to college with little sexual experience, nor do
they know yet what constitutes a healthy sexuality for themselves. Further, in college, most sexuality education focuses on important issues like
birth control, the prevention of sexually transmitted infections (STIs), and
sexual violence/consent. Sexual pleasure itself is rarely explored.

College students often experience a lot of shoulds about sexuality.

Some students feel pressure to be sexual in only certain ways. Others feel pressure to not be sexual at all. Many feel pressure to hook up and have as many sexual connections as possible.

Students may also come to college with baggage from previous relationships that were unhealthy or abusive. Research shows that people in this situation are more likely to seek sexual relationships as a form of validation rather than as a form of healthy connection.

Identity exploration, one of the cornerstones of the college experience, also includes sexual identity, which can leave students unclear about how they feel or what they want.

STRATEGIES

Get to Know Yourself First

Before we can connect fully with others, we need to know ourselves, and that includes our sexuality. This involves three main areas of reflection and exploration: understanding the values we grew up with, considering the values we hold or consider important for ourselves now, and exploring what we like in terms of sex, sexuality, and physical touch.

Reflect on the Values You Grew Up With

In a journal, write about all the messages you heard about sexuality from your family, your peers, your culture, your religion, and society. What anecdotes, speeches, or judgments do you remember? Was sexuality ignored? Growing up, how did your friends talk about it? If you have a faith tradition or religion, what messages did that convey? What about our culture? Pinpoint the messages you received and where they came from. What have you been taught up to now about sexuality? To help you, here are some prompts and examples of messages:

- **Purpose of sexuality:**

  "Sexuality should only be for procreation."
  "Sexuality is a natural part of being human."
  "Sex means getting laid as often as possible."

- **Masturbation:**

  "Masturbation is okay if it's kept private."
  "Masturbation is each individual's choice."
  "Masturbation is only something that immature people do."

- **Religion and spirituality:**

  "Sexual intercourse should only be between a married couple."
  "Sex between two people is sacred."

- **Sexual orientation:**

  "Sexual orientation is always discovered later in life."
  "You were born with your sexual orientation."
  "Bad parenting causes homosexuality."

- **Birth control:**

  "Birth control is wrong. Abstinence is the only acceptable form of birth control."
  "Birth control is a public health right."
  "Women should be responsible for their birth control. Leave men out of it."

- **Polyamory:**

  "Sexual relations should only be within a committed couple."
  "Each individual gets to decide how they do their relationship."
  "Polyamory is risky, as one person will always get hurt."

Reflect on the Values You Currently Hold

Similarly, in a journal, write and reflect on your current thoughts and feelings about sexuality. Are there values from your upbringing you agree with and retain, and are there ways you disagree with the messages you've received? Here are examples from the same areas:

- **Purpose of sexuality:**

  "Sexuality is for sensual pleasure and connection (and at times procreation)."

  "Sex can mean a lot of different pleasurable sexual acts, not just penetration."

- **Masturbation:**

  "Masturbation is a way to have sensual pleasure and connection with one's self."

  "Masturbation can be a part of a healthy relationship with another person."

- **Religion and spirituality:**

  "Sexual connection can be done with integrity within or outside of marriage."

  "Sexual connection between two people can be sacred."

- **Sexual orientation:**

  "Sexual orientation is on a continuum."

  "People come to understand their sexual orientation at a variety of times, some in childhood and some after they've had some life experience."

- **Birth control:**

  "Birth control is each person's choice and responsibility."

  "Women have a right to control their own bodies."

- **Polyamory:**

  "Both monogamy and polyamory take trust, honesty, dignity, and respect."

  "Polyamory is a legitimate choice if everyone gives consent."

Explore What Feels Good to You

I suggest exploring what you like on your own, independent of sex with others. First, get to know what you like by touching yourself, or masturbating. This can include any and all kinds of touch; there is no one single way to masturbate. Simply be sensual, and touch anywhere on your body, whether or not that leads to orgasm. See this chapter's resources for some excellent guides to masturbation.

You can also explore your sexuality through reflection and journaling. One way is to review a "yes, no, maybe" list. What things have you done, what haven't you done, what would you like to do, and what might you be willing to experiment with? Scarleteen.com (see the resources below) has a good list.

Be Aware of Common Myths about Sexuality

Society, culture, and media promote a lot of misleading myths about sexuality. Most are rarely if ever true. Here are a few to be aware of:

"Good partners will automatically know what the other wants."
"Having an orgasm at the same time is the definition of good sex."
"When people are right for each other, sex is good from the beginning."
"It's okay to fake an orgasm."
"Good partners always want the same things in terms of sex."

Always Confirm Consent Before Sex

When you feel ready, exploring sexuality with others is wonderful, but always make sure it's mutual. Consent means making sure that the other person agrees to sexual touch *before it's initiated.*

Consent is sexy. Consent means getting an enthusiastic yes as a response. Any hesitation, silence, or a no means do not proceed further. Here are some examples of asking for consent:

"Is this okay?"
"May I kiss your neck?"

"Can I take your shirt off?"

"Would you like oral sex?"

"I know we did this last time, but would you like to do it again?"

Nonconsensual sex can apply to a variety of situations. It means that whatever happened was not mutually agreed to before it happened. Here are some examples:

- I wasn't asked if I wanted to be touched.
- I was too incapacitated (because of alcohol, drugs, or sleep) to give thoughtful consent.
- I felt coerced or manipulated into the sex act.
- I didn't know how to get out of the situation (that is, I would have said no if I'd felt safe to do so).

Avoid Mixing Alcohol and Sex

I recommend not mixing alcohol and sex for two reasons. One is, alcohol can mask our true feelings, it can inhibit or lessen our self-control, and this can lead to doing things that don't reflect our values. Further, when either partner is under the influence, it risks behavior that is or might escalate into nonconsensual sex.

Practice Good Sexual Communication

No one is a mind reader. We need to tell partners what we like or would like to do. While it can feel awkward at first communicating about what feels good or not, this leads to more satisfying sex. Here are some examples:

"That felt great to me. I'm so happy we did that."

"What are you into?"

"I really like it when you touch me here."

"I'm glad we tried that, but I don't want to do it again."

"Can you show me with your hand how you like to be touched?"

"I've never done this before."

"I have been thinking about how I approach my sexuality. While I have been raised to keep intercourse for marriage, and I have thought it through and agree with that, I wondered if I could have a satisfying sexual life without intercourse. I thought through sexual acts that fit with my values, such as kissing, massaging erogenous zones, oral sex, and manual sex. It was helpful to talk about my sexual boundaries in counseling because it will make the conversation easier with my future partners."

— BOB

If you are in a relationship, clear communication is a positive aspect of healthy sex. This is rarely portrayed in the media, so few role models exist. Try to develop an open and ongoing discussion about sex: how often to have sex, what types of sexual activities you prefer, what is more or less pleasurable, and so on. These conversations can happen before, during, and after sex, and they are the hallmark of a healthy sexuality and a healthy relationship.

Be Patient and Generous with Yourself and Your Partner

Not every sexual encounter will be amazing. Not every sexual partner will be right. But don't consider anything a "failure." You are exploring, learning, and growing, and every experience teaches us more about what works and doesn't for ourselves. Sexuality is complex and varied. It involves a lot of trial and error, and we learn as much from the ups as the downs. Have patience with yourself and your partners, who are also learning and growing. If you can, approach sexual exploration with a sense of humor, which is super helpful in finding your way.

WHEN TO SEEK PROFESSIONAL HELP

If you are struggling to figure out sexual values or boundaries, or if you are concerned about your current sex life, seek help, whether from a counselor, clergy, or trusted mentor.

If sex is causing physical pain, consult with a doctor. And if you have experienced sexual assault or sexual abuse, seek a professional counselor or therapist. Appendix C includes resources for addressing sexual violence.

RESOURCES

On Campus

- College health center: This center can assess and perhaps treat medical issues related to sex (like pain or STIs), and they can usually provide birth control and contraception.
- College counseling center: Counselors can help you explore your values and sexuality, and they can recommend off-campus providers if needed.
- College chaplain: Chaplains can provide a spiritual lens to help you discover or solidify your values around sexuality.

Websites

- Scarleteen (www.scarleteen.com): This thorough website is focused on everything to do with sex (and relationships). It has a great "yes, no, maybe" list, and it's very LGBTQIA friendly.
- Go Ask Alice! (www.goaskalice.columbia.edu): This site is supported by a multidisciplinary team of Columbia University health professionals. They use a question-and-answer format to address hundreds of questions on every aspect of sexuality in the "Sexual & Reproductive Health" section.
- RAINN (Rape, Abuse & Incest National Network; 800-656-4673; www.rainn.org): RAINN is the nation's largest antisexual violence organization, they operate the National Sexual Assault Hotline, and they have many resources on coping with sexual violence and safety and prevention.
- Day One (866-223-1111; www.dayoneservices.org): This national resource operates a crisis hotline and can direct you to services

"I am in a polyamorous relationship, and I am interested in becoming sexual with a new person. My partner and I have agreed about how to talk about when we want to sleep with someone new, but at times I feel hesitant to talk openly because I don't want to cause my main partner any jealousy. After some reflection, it felt best to me to approach the conversation as an open conversation where the outcome isn't known, rather than just telling my partner what I am going to do, without any discussion."

— SABINE

in your state. They provide services to victims of sexual assault, domestic violence, trafficking, and crime.

Books

- *Guide to Getting It On* by Paul Joannides: A thorough, nonjudgmental, encyclopedic, readable book on all things to do with human sexuality. Topics range from kissing to romance to masturbation to every possible type of sex act, plus sex after sexual violence, nonvanilla sex, and health issues related to sex.
- *I ♥ Female Orgasm* by Dorian Solot and Marshall Miller: This book provides great detail on the how, what, where, and why of the female sexual experience, written for every gender. It has helpful and humorous anecdotes and sidebars on such topics as fantasy, masturbation, intercourse, and losing virginity.
- *The Pleasure Is All Yours* by Rachel Allyn: Allyn says she "wrote this book for anyone who's felt homeless in their body, disconnected from their essence, and conflicted in receiving the pleasures they deserve. I wrote this so we could heal collectively from the body up."

Chapter 32

Healing from a Breakup

"I feel like my world has ended."

"I never realized that 'brokenhearted' is a real thing until it happened to me."

"I know the breakup was the right thing, but I'm way lonelier and sadder than I thought I'd be."

"I hate being on a small campus. I see her almost every day."

"Everyone thinks I should be over it already. It's been a month, but I'm still devastated."

A breakup, when a relationship formally ends, can occur because one person quits the relationship or both parties mutually decide it's over. Generally, the term *breakup* is usually used to refer to romantic relationships, but there are also friendship breakups.

WHY BREAKUPS ARE A CHALLENGE

Breaking up with someone we've loved, or still love, and especially the experience of being dumped, creates a sorrow that is hard to put into words. The pain of a broken heart is unlike any other. It can feel acute like a knife to the heart or be more like a dull ache over the whole body.

On top of the pain of the breakup itself, the loss of a significant other creates a gap in social support, and encountering loneliness may feel very difficult. Feeling lonely can also trigger other issues, such as depression. Nor does it usually work to move right into a new relationship to avoid the pain of the original loss.

In college, many students experience their first serious breakup, which makes the pain of a broken heart even more acute. And this is on top of all the other stressors of college.

Some students experiencing a breakup can struggle to find truly empathetic support. Not every friend will understand the pain, and students are often separated from their previous support system of family and friends at home. This makes it critical to seek the support you need.

STRATEGIES

Know That the Pain Won't Last Forever

It sounds like a truism, but it's important to remember that "this, too, shall pass." No matter how much pain you feel, things will get better. You will eventually make your way through to healing and hope. Remind yourself of this often, but especially in the early, painful days.

Be Gentle with Yourself

Healing is improved with a generous and kind attitude. Be easy on yourself and practice self-care. Eat mild foods, get extra sleep, don't expect your usual output at school and work, and practice calming, kind self-talk. Many students tend to be hard on themselves after a breakup — self-blame and self-hatred are rampant — but it's important to catch this negative self-talk and turn it around. Here are some examples:

"Just because I broke up with one person doesn't mean I won't find love again" (versus "No one will ever love me again").
"I don't want to blame myself, since I did the best I could" (versus "If only I'd been different").

"I'm really hurting right now, but it won't last forever" (versus "I'll never get over this").

"I choose to let go of the relationship, since I recognize it wasn't working" (versus "I need to do whatever I can to get the person back").

Practice Acceptance

Many people don't want to accept that a relationship is over. It might be hard to say it, even to yourself. But denying that the relationship is over is not helpful, even though it is very common. Some would say denial is a stage of the grieving process, but it extends the recovery time. This includes staying in touch with your ex, which can make it difficult to begin the process of healing and often extends emotional pain.

Grieve the Relationship

A breakup is like the "death" of the relationship, and it's the end of your hopes for that partnership, so allow yourself to grieve that loss. Just like with grief of any kind, expect a roller coaster of emotions. Some days will feel easier; some days the pain will return with full force. Expect it to go up and down, so you aren't surprised by the process. Give yourself time to grieve. There is no right way to grieve: We feel loss and sadness, of course, but we can feel rage, anger, numbness, relief, and more. Treat yourself with grace and know that grieving is complicated.

Here are some active grieving strategies to try:

- Cry (sounds obvious but some people don't let themselves cry)
- Take long, quiet walks
- Engage in deep talks with friends
- Journal; write memories about your relationship, the good and the bad
- Write poetry
- Write a letter to your ex (that you *won't send*)
- Put away old photos of your ex (and perhaps burn some)
- Release flower petals into a body of water

Reflect on All That Has Been Lost

In a journal, explore the extent of all that you've lost along with the relationship. Make a list. This might include physical intimacy, mundane daily interactions, and other social activities. Creating this list of specific losses provides a road map you can use to find ways to fill the gaps. For instance, arrange to eat dinner with new people or rebuild your weekend social life. This reflection helps you see how to compensate for the loss of your significant other in your life.

For instance, if your ex was the only person you could complain to about your parents, figure out if you have friends who could play that role for you. Or if you were maintaining a long-distance relationship and let your social network at school suffer, recognize that now you need to reach out to people and create that network.

Reflect on What Wasn't Working in the Relationship

No person or situation is perfect, so make a list of all the things you won't miss now that the relationship is over. This might be annoying traits, like someone who left their dirty clothes on the floor or insisted on controlling what TV shows to watch. Or it might be more serious issues of disconnection and hurtful behavior. It is helpful to list these out in detail, perhaps in a journal.

"When my boyfriend of two years broke up with me, I was completely out of control and all I wanted to do was drink cocktails and play video games. After about a week, I was able to get back to my schoolwork, but I still felt a range of intense loss, a dull ache, confusion, anger, loneliness, and at times hopelessness. I wondered what I had done wrong, questioned what I was doing in school, and struggled to grasp what my career goals were and what I stood for as a person. I guess my world was upside down. I realized that I had been putting all my hopes, dreams, and self-image into my boyfriend, and now that he wasn't in the picture, I needed to rebuild my sense of purpose and self. As I began this work, I admitted to myself that I loved mentoring my high school debate team and started working toward making sure my major would allow a path for me to teach in a high school setting. This helped me move on, and I found it much easier to get out of bed, find joy in the day, and not be totally preoccupied with the breakup."

— HAYDEN

Concentrate on Your Own Growth and Development

One "benefit" of a breakup, though it may not feel that way at first, is that you can focus on your own growth and development, perhaps in new ways. Evaluate your current friendships and make new ones. Consider what your life was like before the relationship. Are there things you haven't done since you broke up that you'd like to do again? Try new things, return to old things, and learn what makes *you* happy. Sometimes you might choose to curb your active grieving and lean into activities that cheer you up.

For instance, maybe you didn't have time to join any clubs during your relationship, but now you can. Or if making time for the relationship impacted your studies, you can now put more energy into academics, such as by joining study groups.

"One of the most painful parts of my breakup was feeling that I had let myself down, since I had promised my girlfriend that we would be together forever. It was hard work for me to accept that the breakup was the healthiest thing for me as a person, and that not all hopes and dreams are meant to last. I had to grieve the loss of my dream of having the 'relationship that defies the odds' as much as I had to grieve the actual relationship. Once I understood that, I found it easier to let go and move on."

— ABE

Move On

Eventually … you will discover that there is life after a breakup. Be careful to take some time to get yourself grounded again before trying to tackle another relationship. Enjoy all the positive ways your life has changed being single, such as more time for friends, old hobbies, new hobbies, and for yourself. Know that the lessons learned from a breakup will benefit your future relationships.

WHEN TO SEEK PROFESSIONAL HELP

It's okay to go into "survival mode" immediately after a breakup, but if the pain of loss is affecting your class attendance or homework, seek help, either from a counselor, clergy, or a trusted mentor.

RESOURCES

On Campus

- College counseling center: Counselors can provide strategies for surviving a breakup and help you recover and rebuild your life.
- College chaplain: Chaplains can provide spiritual counseling and support to heal from a breakup.

Books

- *Tiny Beautiful Things: Advice on Love and Life from Dear Sugar* by Cheryl Strayed: This book is based on essays from Strayed's "Dear Sugar" advice column, so not all of them apply to breakups. The essays that do concern breakups are amazing and heartfelt.

Movies

Here are some films that address breakups.

- *When Harry Met Sally*: This classic is partly about crying over someone you didn't even want.
- *500 Days of Summer*: This is about leaving behind the fantasy of what you thought the relationship was.
- *Love Jones*: This is about being clear about what you want in a relationship instead of playing games.
- *Always Be My Maybe*: This is about not letting fear get in the way of your relationships, and when friendships become romantic relationships.
- *Forgetting Sarah Marshall*: This is about refinding the work passion you had set aside for your ex.
- *How to Be Single*: This is about allowing yourself not to go right into another relationship.

Part VI

YOUR TIME

How we spend our days is, of course, how we spend our lives.
— Annie Dillard, *The Writing Life*

For many college students, time is a frequent source of distress, if not anguish.

How can you make choices about how you spend your time so that you feel good about the work you accomplish? It's all about identifying your values, recognizing your responsibilities, and staying balanced, but this is extremely challenging, not just at college but in our culture.

First, consider the typical college mindset, which is to work to an unhealthy extent during the week and then play to an unhealthy extent during the weekend. If we go for all-out intensity all the time (whether with work, play, or both), or think we are supposed to, that puts our mental health at risk.

Second, our 24/7 connectivity has caused us to experience time differently. Our days no longer have a clear or natural start or end point. The "universe" is available anytime on our devices, so that makes it even more challenging to maintain balance and use our time in healthy, productive ways.

Third, research shows we get good at what we practice. What does this mean? The activities we engage in the most are the ones we will be best at, so we have to evaluate what we are spending the most time doing. If we are on TikTok for hours each day, we will get really good at quickly scrolling through content, but will we be able to focus our attention for more than a few moments at a time? If we pack our day from dawn to bedtime with constant activity but never take breaks, we will be productive, but will we know how to relax and enjoy the moment?

Stress and anxiety over how you use your time can become a mental health issue. Students can be accomplishing a lot and still feel out of control. The goal is to make conscious choices about how you spend your time, which always involves trade-offs, and to accept the limits of each day.

Chapter 33

Balancing Priorities

"I know most students are all about their classes and grades. But for me, it's the extracurriculars that make my life, and they are what I value."

"I really didn't think about what I wanted from college except to get away from home and to party. That's probably why I don't have great grades today."

"I thought it was wrong to get a full night's sleep during college. Now that I am taking better care of myself and getting enough sleep, my grades are great."

"It is my responsibility to get a full-time job after college and support my family. I must prioritize that, even though it feels so challenging to me."

"I struggle with depression and I need to watch my self-care every single day, so my grades aren't perfect, but my mental health needs my attention more than my grades do."

Our values help us figure out how to prioritize our time. However, aligning our values and real life is not always easy. If it were, we'd all be doing it already. Learning to recognize when we aren't living up to our values or priorities is the first step in making a plan to change that.

This book is focused on mental health, so I haven't always emphasized academic and career issues, but they are prominent in this chapter.

Academics are a critical question when it comes to prioritizing, and many students express anguish that academics are not going the way they'd like.

The effort to prioritize our time is always a work in progress. We are rarely fulfilling all our goals and values at once. So how do we determine what to do in any given day? What does balance mean to you?

WHY SETTING PRIORITIES IS A CHALLENGE

It takes hard work, time, and intention to dig deep and identify our priorities. It is easy to get pulled off track and spend our time doing things that are distracting or unsatisfying and that undermine our goals.

Even ancient philosophers grappled with what makes a worthy way to spend one's time. Determining the best way to spend our time is one of those profound issues that can change day by day and that will certainly change over time. There is no perfect answer or formula.

In fact, since college is a time of instability and exploration, priorities have a way of changing frequently. Students find it challenging to weed out what is really important to them from the opinions of others. Plus, college is a time of great demands, while also being a cornucopia of easy, attractive distractions. How in the world is a student supposed to balance academics, career, friendships, family, romance, social activities, parties, sports, media, and all the rest without screwing everything up?

STRATEGIES

Define Your Mission

The first step when it comes to setting priorities in your day-to-day life is to define your personal life mission — this is the big picture that you use to guide the little picture of each day. In chapter 9 ("Write a Mission Statement," pages 95–96), I explain how to write this, and if you haven't done this already, do so now. For example, if your mission is to be "the kind of person people feel comfortable around," then prioritize managing your stress and anxiety in your daily activities. This is one way we make sure that the little things in life are in alignment with what matters most to us.

Assess Your Priorities

In your journal, assess your priorities by reflecting on all the items in the two lists below. One is focused on mental health, and the other on academics and career. For each statement, note whether you agree, disagree, or are unsure. Then jot down one or two specific areas that could use improvement. For each one, I've provided some sample statements as examples.

Be honest with yourself as you reflect on each category. Treat this as a snapshot of where you are right now, and consider using these lists to revisit your priorities each semester. Assessing priorities is ongoing, since as life and our circumstances change, and as we grow, our goals change.

Mental Health Priorities

Physical self-care: My physical self-care is overall helping me feel energized and healthy.

Agree   Disagree   Unsure

Examples of possible areas for improvement:
I only exercise once per week; I can tell my body would like more.
When I forget to eat lunch, I lose all energy by 2 or 3 p.m.

Self-knowledge and growth: I am exploring my identity and growing in my self-knowledge.

Agree   Disagree   Unsure

Examples of possible areas for improvement:
I don't have many friends from my cultural background.
I haven't tried anything new at college yet.

Mental and emotional self-care: I have helpful strategies and support for my mental and emotional self-care.

Agree   Disagree   Unsure

Examples of possible areas for improvement:
I feel anxious on Sunday nights.
I feel like I have no alone time for myself; there are always people around.

Relationships with family: I am satisfied with my relationships with my family.

Agree   Disagree   Unsure

Examples of possible areas for improvement:
I get along great with my sister, but I feel out of touch with my dad.
I want to be honest with my parents, but I'm afraid they'll be judgmental.

Relationships with friends: I have friends I can confide in, hang out with, and identify with.

Agree   Disagree   Unsure

Examples of possible areas for improvement:
I feel good about two groups of friends, but wish I had one more close friend.
I feel close to my boyfriend, but I'm worried I am losing touch with other friends.

Relationships with coworkers and mentors: I get along with my coworkers and have at least one mentor who supports me.

Agree   Disagree   Unsure

Examples of possible areas for improvement:
I don't have a mentor; I'm not even sure where to start.
I'm scared of my adviser.

Academic and Career Priorities

Major: I feel my major reflects my interests and/or my career goals.

Agree   Disagree   Unsure

Examples of possible areas for improvement:
I'm not that happy with my major, but I'm not sure what to switch to.
I like my major but have no idea what I want for my career.

Classes: I enjoy the content of my classes most of the time.

Agree   Disagree   Unsure

Examples of possible areas for improvement:
I love two of my classes but think two are mediocre.
I feel like a fish out of water in one class.

Attendance: I attend all classes, except when I am ill or out of town.

Agree   Disagree   Unsure

Examples of possible areas for improvement:
I have missed my early class twice so far this semester.
I avoid class when I haven't done the reading, which makes it worse.

Participation: I participate in classroom discussions an appropriate amount.

Agree   Disagree   Unsure

Examples of possible areas for improvement:
I am scared others will judge me if I speak up.
Sometimes if no one else is talking in class, I feel like I talk too much.

Homework timing and habits: I usually get my homework done on time, and I'm satisfied with my study habits.

Agree   Disagree   Unsure

Examples of possible areas for improvement:
I turn in papers at the last minute and feel totally stressed out.
I wish I had a way to see the big picture of the semester and manage my workload accordingly.

Homework quality: I think my homework quality reflects my knowledge and work.

Agree   Disagree   Unsure

Examples of possible areas for improvement:
I want my paper to impress my professor, but don't know how to organize my ideas.
I struggle with my problem sets for calculus.

Job/internship: I have a job and/or an internship that supports my needs and goals.

Agree   Disagree   Unsure

Examples of possible areas for improvement:
I like my job, but the hours don't mesh with my schedule.
I would like an internship but I'm not sure how to find one.

Organizations/groups: I am proud of the student organizations and/or campus groups that I participate in.

Agree   Disagree   Unsure

Examples of possible areas for improvement:
I don't really do anything outside of classes.
The student organization I'm involved with has taken over my life.

Set Goals

When you discover things you are *not* happy with among your various priorities, set some specific and attainable goals. These goals should be things that you can control. For example, the goal of "getting an A in organic chemistry" may *not* be possible, since students are not in control of grading, professors are. However, students can control what they do to try to earn an A grade. Here are some goals a student can control:

- Attend every class
- Attend office hours whenever I have a question
- Form a study group
- Get homework done on time
- Seek help at the study center

We also can set goals related to mental health and personal qualities. Perhaps we want to be friendlier or more outgoing, to have more courage, or to foster more discipline. Here are three goals that might foster these three things. Each is something we can control:

- Smile and say good morning to the lady who serves me eggs every morning.

- Ask for help with homework when I get stuck.
- Show up on time for class.

For each category below, write one or two goals in your journal, with concrete actions you can take. I've provided a couple of examples for each one.

Mental Health Goals

Physical self-care:
Add a walk once a week with my lab partner.
Plan to eat lunch with friends, so I won't be tempted to skip lunch.

Self-knowledge and growth:
Make an appointment with the career center for career exploration.
Ask a friend if I can attend their student organization with them.

Mental and emotional self-care:
Stop doing homework by 7 p.m. on Sunday nights, and watch a comedy with my roommate by 8 p.m. to help relax.
Read a book for pleasure twenty minutes each night before bed.

Relationships with family:
Make a regular time to talk with Dad once each week.
Text my little sister something fun every other day.

Relationships with friends:
Reach out to a good friend and set up a weekly dinner date.
Stop reaching out so much to a friend group that feels toxic.

Relationships with coworkers and mentors:
Visit my professors' office hours once this semester.
Visit the campus employment office to see what other job opportunities are open for next semester.

Academic and Career Goals

Major:
Reach out to an upper-class member within my major to see what the best classes are in our department.

"I love all the people in my diversity office work-study job, and I was given the task of creating posters for events, which sounded great at first. It didn't take long for it to feel overwhelming, as I received a lot of judgment from all sides. It seemed as if I could never make everyone happy. I spoke to my department coordinator, and she added two more staff members to the poster team. I felt so supported by this change and liked that I had a team around me to develop ideas as well as to help handle the critical pressure. I felt I could meet my goal to be a part of the diversity office without the anguish of feeling like a failure with the posters."

— XIMENA

Classes:

Schedule a meeting with my adviser, tell them which classes are working for me and which aren't, and ask for advice.

Attendance:

I will ask a friend to go to breakfast before my early class to help motivate me to get up.

I will be kind and forgiving of myself whenever I do miss class and not "give up" on that class and stop trying.

Participation:

I will try to speak up at least once per class (in discussion classes) and prepare notes to help make that easier.

I will meet with my professor to get their opinion on how I am doing with class participation.

Homework timing and habits:

On my calendar, I will set aside times for homework and name the location where I will do it.

I will bring my backpack full of study materials to dinner and then head right to the library after dinner, so I don't waste time returning to my residence hall.

Homework quality:

I will attend the campus study center to get writing help.

I will create a study group to get support for tough problem sets.

Job/internship:

I will plan a buffer zone of downtime before my internship, so I'm not exhausted or rushed during my shift.

I will talk to my work supervisor about changing my schedule so it doesn't conflict with class and study time.

Organizations/groups:

> *I will make time to join the club soccer team;*
> *it may not "look good" on my résumé,*
> *but I'm passionate about athletics.*
> *I will step down from my leadership role in*
> *my student organization, since it is get-*
> *ting in the way of my coursework.*

WHEN TO SEEK PROFESSIONAL HELP

Understanding our priorities and setting realistic goals takes time and reflection. No one can do this for us, but if you are struggling with this, reach out for help. Choose whoever feels the most comfortable or safe to you. That could include family, friends, spiritual leaders, academic advisers, career counselors, or student life staff. Further, if anyone displays judgment or impatience, seek support from someone else!

"In the spring of my first year at college, I started to feel anxious every Sunday night after dinner. My body became tense, and my mind started racing. I learned that there was a multifaith prayer group on Sunday evenings, but I was hesitant about adding another activity when my goal was to lessen my anxiety about my busy week ahead. When a friend mentioned that they attended the meeting, I decided to give it a try. I found community and a reconnection to something greater than myself, which helped put my academic anxieties in perspective. I met my main goal to lessen my Sunday anxiety, and also my goals of building community and developing a richer spiritual life."

— ELIJAH

RESOURCES

On Campus

- College counselor: Counselors can provide nonjudgmental listening and support to help identify your personal priorities.
- College career center: This center can provide career counseling and help set goals.
- College chaplain: Chaplains can provide spiritual counseling to help identify your priorities through the lens of faith.
- College diversity office: Staff can provide supportive discussions that help you identify priorities through the lens of your culture.

Books

- *Year of Yes: How to Dance It Out, Stand in the Sun, and Be Your Own Person* by Shonda Rhimes: Half memoir and half motivation guide, this book will help you make choices that benefit you, even if they are frightening.

Chapter 34

Time Management for Mental Health

"I just didn't pay attention when professors said three to four hours of study time per class. I didn't make a schedule to study that amount of time, and I got behind."

"I'm glad I play a varsity sport, as I don't have enough time to fool around and get off track."

"My day is scheduled from 8 a.m. to 11 p.m., and I have no time for myself. I feel anxious all the time."

"I'm trying to go for a balance of gentle *and* accountable."

"I had no idea when I came to college as a first year how important managing my schedule would be."

Time management for mental health boils down to planning. It means exercising conscious control of your schedule so that you stay on top of your obligations without sacrificing wellness, social engagement, and self-discovery.

Time management is critical for mental health, as evidenced by the huge number of students who seek counseling to address it. In essence, it's hard to feel good about ourselves if we don't feel good about our work and study habits, if our social time is suffering, and if we aren't making time for self-care. These things don't "just happen." We have to plan for them. This is part of the metric of life.

WHY TIME MANAGEMENT IS A CHALLENGE

Many people don't make the time to plan. Even when we have a plan, it can be hard to stick to it because life happens. We are not robots programmed to follow instructions. We are complex humans who have many competing demands. Further, college students are still learning how to identify priorities, set goals, and then anticipate the skills and effort required to accomplish them.

Time management is a learned skill. We aren't born knowing how to make reasonable schedules that balance everything: study, work, play, social connection, and self-care. The process itself is easy to understand, but doing it well is actually quite nuanced and takes trial and error. Further, our schedules continually evolve over time. But with practice, everyone gets better.

For students, this is a big transition from high school, where schedules are often rigid and established by others; in school, teachers give regular tests and assignments. At college, classes might only have one or two tests (a midterm and final exam), and only a few written assignments (or maybe only one huge research paper) — and professors don't monitor student progress. Students who excelled in high school can flounder in college when faced with huge blocks of open time that they have to schedule for themselves. Online classes demand a special kind of time management and discipline because the classes are often offered asynchronously.

It's no mystery why balancing all the elements of life in college is so hard. In a way, it's the reason for this book: College students try to pack as much as they can into every day to try to achieve the most they can on every level. Yet there are only twenty-four hours in each day.

Here are some practical strategies for managing your time to make the most of those twenty-four hours.

STRATEGIES

Start with a List of Goals

As I recommend in chapter 33, make a list of your goals, or what you need to do to achieve your priorities. This is like naming the destination you are trying to reach during the journey of each day, week, and month. Your time management plan and schedule is your map or blueprint for how to get there. For instance, a goal might be "to eat three meals a day and exercise three times per week" or "to meet my deadlines and not procrastinate." Now that you've named your priority, you know what you need to make time for.

Create a One-Week Calendar

It doesn't matter what type of calendar you use, but choose the program or format that is easiest for you to work with. Then jump right in and fill in your schedule for one entire week: This is your main time-management tool, your blueprint for the semester. At first, only focus on one week at a time, but as you figure out what schedule works best, you can plan further ahead, so that you can manage bigger assignments that take more than one week of planning and work. See the next page for an example of a one-week calendar.

Start by inputting all school-related activities with established times: classes, labs, study groups, tutoring, office hours for professors, work and internship shifts, volunteer obligations, student organization meetings, team practices and games, and so on. These are the obligations that you've already committed to.

Next, focus on self-care. We also have daily obligations to take care of ourselves, so write in when you will eat meals, sleep, groom, exercise, meditate, follow a spiritual practice, and so on. Estimate how much time each activity will take. For now, develop the habit of being specific: not just "sleep," but "sleep from 11 p.m. to 7 a.m."

Next, consider socializing. Block off times when you know you will want to hang out with friends, even if you don't have specific plans yet. This might be weekend nights, Sunday brunch, and so on. If you don't end up making plans for those times, then that becomes "free time" you can use for something else. And if other social plans come up, you can shift other activities around. Also estimate how long you expect each social activity to be.

Finally, assess the blocks of time that are left over and create a studying/homework plan. For each time slot, be specific about what class you

	Monday	Tuesday	Wednesday	Thursday	Friday	Saturday	Sunday
6 – 7							
7 – 8	wake/prep	wake/prep	wake/prep	wake/prep	wake/prep		
8 – 9	breakfast	breakfast	breakfast	breakfast	breakfast	wake	wake/prep
9 – 10	FRENCH	prep for lab	FRENCH	study french	FRENCH	brunch	VOLUNTEER/ SPIRITUAL
10 – 11	PSYCH	PSYCH LAB ↓	PSYCH	FRENCH LAB	PSYCH	↓	LIFE
11 – 12	free	– – – free	free	free	free	laundry	↓ lunch
12 – 1	lunch	lunch	lunch	lunch	lunch	clean room	↓
1 – 2	STATS	study religion (library)	STATS	study religion (library)	STATS	study – varies	free
2 – 3	study stats (Science bldg)	↓	study stats (sci bldg)	– – ↓ – – review todo	study stats	(coffee shop)	(or study)
3 – 4	KARATE	RELIGION	KARATE	RELIGION	free	(or library)	(or social)
4 – 5	– – – –	↓	– – – –	– – – –	↓	review to do for next week	– – ↓ – –
5 – 6	dinner	dinner	dinner	WORK	dinner	dinner	WORK
6 – 7	study psych (library)	study psych (library)	prep stats	off-campus job	free	↓	off-campus
7 – 8	↓ study french	review to do	STATS STUDY		KARATE	social	job
8 – 9	(French lounge) review todo	ANIME CLUB	GROUP ↓		CLUB		↓
9 – 10	social	– – ↓ – – social	social	↓	social		buffer zone
10 – 11	buffer zone	buffer	buffer zone	buffer zone		↓	bed
11 – 12	bed	zone bed	bed	bed	buffer zone bed	buffer zone bed	

Sample one-week calendar

will study for, what you will do to study, how long you will study, and where you will study (see below for more on this). Remember, studying doesn't just happen. You have to plan for it.

Once you've done all this, you may find several things. First, not everything you want to do might fit, and so you will need to immediately prioritize; some things might need to be put off until the following week or let go of altogether. Or you might fit everything in but with no time left over. That's okay for now; live the week and see what happens. Or you might have several blocks of "free time." Again, that's okay for now, just make sure you've accounted for everything you need to accomplish. Having some open blocks is good because they give you wiggle room if something unexpected comes up, and something unexpected always comes up.

Follow this plan for a week — *knowing there is no way this will go exactly as planned.* Treat this as an experiment. Notice what works and what doesn't work. Be honest about what isn't working and figure out why. Perhaps you need more time to study for a certain class, or everyone goes out to dinner together after student organization meetings, and you need to account for that in your schedule.

Each week, repeat this process and keep fine-tuning your schedule to meet your needs, while also understanding that every week won't be exactly the same. You can keep your original weekly plan as a blueprint, and input it into your electronic calendar, which can be easily filled out for the whole semester so that you can also input big homework assignments that take more than one week to prepare for.

End Each Day by Planning Ahead

Every evening, spend half an hour reviewing your schedule for the next day and writing out a to-do list. A good time to do this is at the end of the last study time for the day (and before socializing or starting your buffer zone before bed). This way you can stay current on what you were able to accomplish that day and what still needs to get done, and you can adjust the next day's schedule if necessary. This is great for mental health, as it lessens anxiety to keep our to-do list on paper instead of in our head.

Make Use of Small Chunks of Time

Don't discount the benefits of small chunks of time. We can get a lot done in half an hour if we're prepared. As you create your schedule, you will probably find short "transition times" between classes, meetings, and so on. Utilize those odd hours during the day, even if it's just fifteen minutes. Sure, you could scroll social media, but maybe you could make a phone call, do some research from the library, get a few pages of reading done, shop for dinner, or checking off another small but essential task from your to-do list. Several short sessions of studying can produce great results. Another great bonus of making it a habit to use every chunk of "free time" during the day is that it frees up more time at night to socialize or unwind.

Determine Your Most Productive Study Times

As you schedule, consider when you work best so study times are as productive as possible. Students can struggle with this. Many people find that their concentration is usually higher earlier in the day, and so that can be the best time to tackle the most challenging coursework. A side benefit of doing hard stuff earlier is that it can relieve anxiety later, since you know it is done. On the other hand, if you're most productive at night, then reserve evenings for study. For example, you might find it's better to tackle math in the morning (when your energy is higher), but extended reading goes better at night, when you have a longer chunk of time.

Coordinate Study Times with Class Times

Set up study times that make sense with your class schedule. This is not only so that homework gets done on time, but so you study as close to class time as possible. That way, what you study will be fresh in your mind. While you could study on Monday for a Friday class, it might be better to study on Thursday for it. Also, many students report great benefits from attending a weekly study group for tough classes. Plan time to review notes or readings the hour before an especially challenging class. All of this helps with feeling more confident about speaking up in class.

Consider Where You Study

Students find that *where* they study also impacts their productivity, and this can vary depending on what they're doing. Part of this is developing a routine: When we study in the same place at the same time every day, we automatically shift into "study mode" during those times. Study routines are incredibly helpful. They make it much easier to create and keep to schedules, and we tend to get more work done, since we train ourselves to be ready to work at those times and places.

Another strategy to consider, however, is not studying in the same place all the time or for extended stretches. For instance, if you have a four-hour block of time, consider breaking it up into two two-hour blocks and switching your location and subject. For instance, for two hours, read in the library, then move to the student center to draft a sociology research paper. "Location switching" can provide a short break and keep focus and motivation fresh over long periods.

Also consider "creative" locations to keep study time interesting. Discovering what works for you will take some trial and error.

- Study in a coffee shop with a favorite beverage. Some find this very motivating (unless the café hubbub is too distracting).
- Study in your academic department's lounge, which may have free tea or coffee, some great sofas, and a motivational vibe.
- Study in a building you don't usually enter. For instance, English majors might head to the biology building. Sometimes a nonfamiliar place frees up the mind to focus better.
- Minimize or avoid studying in your dorm bedroom. Ideally, the bedroom should be a relaxing, calming space that is conducive to sleep, but the stress of studying can undermine that. Also, the presence of roommates who are not studying can get in the way.

Plan Study Dates

Another way to increase motivation and maintain a study schedule is to make regular study dates with friends. Knowing others will be expecting us, say, in the library at 5 p.m. can give us the motivation to go. The supportive camaraderie of others can also help us focus, that is, unless "study time" morphs into "social time." If that tends to happen, decide to meet in "quiet only" locations.

Don't Overdo It

There is such a thing as too much. One reason to schedule each week ahead of time is to be able to see when we're overdoing it and either cut back or find a better balance.

If you are studying six to seven nights per week, all day on weekends, and feeling anxious about giving yourself a break to talk with a friend or attend a campus event, then your overall quality-of-life balance is out of whack. Consider scaling back on some of your studying, or add short twenty-to-thirty-minute blocks of downtime for yourself or for socializing to break up studying. In fact, taking short "mental health" breaks not only makes us calmer and happier, but it can improve our focus and productivity when we get back to work.

> "In general the only way I finish big assignments is with tons of stress and pain because I am disorganized and don't get to my work until the last minute. College feels like a roller coaster of emotions for me, mainly because I get blindsided by the due dates or underestimate the amount of time it will take me to write a paper. I agreed to meet with the time management specialist in the study center and create a better homework schedule. Forming a daily routine to review my week and look ahead, and having the mindset to stay on top of things, has been a game changer."
>
> — CARTER

Don't Underdo It

On the other hand, sometimes students create a schedule and find they have more "extra" time than they expected. This might not happen every semester, but for some. If that's the case, consider filling that time with a new campus activity — whether the focus is academic, social, or personal. Make the most of your time and seek the richest college experience possible. Most college campuses have literally hundreds of extracurricular options.

Join a student organization, play a club sport, or volunteer. Of course, consider the size of the commitment you will be taking on. Make sure it fits within your current schedule and doesn't cause conflicts or stress. So long as students don't overbook themselves, joining groups is healthy and enriching.

Vary Types of Socializing

With surprising frequency, students come into the counseling center asking for advice on how to balance partying with other types of socializing. This is something you can tackle when creating the week's schedule, so that you balance a variety of types of socializing in a healthy way.

Some students love to attend parties several nights a week and suffer no ill consequences, while others find too much partying leaves them exhausted, less connected to friends, and less motivated about their studies. Many students report that they really can only handle going out to a bigger party one night a week. If that's you, vary your socializing to avoid feeling burned out.

Social time can happen in many places and ways during the day. Meals are often a primary source of social time, and so are study groups, volunteering, athletics, social organizations, and paid jobs. Ideally, every day should include some time for hanging out and catching up with friends, and that shouldn't only focus on rowdy, crowded events.

Sometimes we need quiet conversation and face-to-face intimacy. Sometimes we prefer playing games or watching movies with only a couple close friends. As you make each week's schedule, create a balance of all types of socializing, whether that involves inviting someone for coffee, organizing a movie or game night, meeting someone for dinner, going out to a concert, and/or attending the big party half of campus will be at.

"I always used to feel disorganized and overwhelmed at all I have to do. I decided to try using a journal that contains my academics to-do list as well as other lists that help me, such as positive affirmations. It takes three to five minutes to rewrite the to-do list every week, which I try to do on Mondays, sometimes with the help of a counselor in the study center. Having this overview of the week helps me feel like I have an image of the bigger picture, so I'm not just running from place to place on autopilot. Since I started using the journal consistently I've been getting my homework done in a timelier manner, studying for exams more thoughtfully and in a less rushed way, and feeling calmer about school in general."

— RACHEL

WHEN TO SEEK PROFESSIONAL HELP

Time management is a learned skill that takes time and experience to get good at. However, if you are struggling to make or maintain a productive schedule, seek help from a mentor, counselor, or campus career center.

That said, an inability to manage time and stay focused might also signal an underlying issue, such as attention-deficit disorder, a learning disability, anxiety, depression, or a sleep disorder. If you worry about any of this, seek an assessment from a professional counselor, therapist, or doctor.

RESOURCES

On Campus

- College study center: This center can provide help with time management and scheduling. They often offer workshops on time management as well as one-on-one time management counseling.
- College health center: Come here for further assessment of any underlying conditions (like ADD); staff can provide referrals to off-campus resources if needed.

Websites

- Bullet Journal (www.bulletjournal.com): Developed by Ryder Carroll, bullet journals are an organization and time management system that promotes itself as "a mindfulness practice disguised as a productivity system." Many students love this system, as it is flexible and allows them to track homework and self-care goals together.
- National Institute of Mental Health, "Attention-Deficit/Hyperactivity Disorder" (www.nimh.nih.gov/health/topics/attention -deficit-hyperactivity-disorder-adhd): This webpage gives a thorough overview of ADHD, with a description of symptoms and the variety of treatments available.

Books

- *The Power of Habit: Why We Do What We Do in Life and Business* by Charles Duhigg: This *New York Times* reporter provides great examples about bad habits and how to change them.
- *Atomic Habits* by James Clear (www.jamesclear.com/atomic-habits): The author guides readers to be more aware of and to consciously choose the actions they take. His four-step paradigm helps build good habits, and his website is full of great ideas.

Chapter 35

Healthy Media Use

"Once I get on Hulu, it can be hours before I get off. Just one more episode is so seductive, especially in comparison to my dreaded research paper."

"I'm on Instagram at least two hours a day. But that's not what I want. I want to be a good student."

"I get into bed at night and I just start scrolling. It can be hours before I finally turn it off. It totally messes with my sleep goals."

"When I see a friend's name pop up in a chat, I can't help but answer, and it can be a long time before I get back to work."

"I just want to kill one bridge troll before I get back to work, but then a river troll comes up, and it is hard to get away from that magical world."

Many of the greatest minds of our generation are concerned and grappling with the issue of screen use. While our technological age has produced many positives — including the democratic sharing of information and broader social connection — media use has its share of negative aspects, such as loss of social or work time and divisions due to toxic influences on social media platforms.

The jury is in on the topic of smartphones being addictive. No one doubts that now, and phone makers admit that creating addiction was part of the design process. The jury is still out on how to cope with it.

This will be one of the defining issues of this and upcoming generations: how to find a balance between being plugged in and unplugged.

WHY HEALTHY MEDIA USE IS A CHALLENGE

Phones and social media are designed to keep our attention. It's just easier and more fun to look at one of the millions of truly fascinating items on our phones than attend to all the items on our to-do lists.

It helps to understand why our screens are so seductive. The technology uses an intermittent reward system (based on research by behavioral psychologist B. F. Skinner), which is incredibly addictive. This also explains why slot machines in casinos are so addictive as well. The quick potential hits of pleasure are much more immediately seductive and rewarding (to our brain chemistry) than the delayed pleasure of getting a good grade after hours of slogging through challenging homework.

What's more, it has become socially acceptable to pull the phone out and check it continually.

Many students keep their phones next to them with the ringer on at all times, including at night. They want to be available in case a friend needs them, and they don't want to miss any updates. This habit creates a state of vigilance that interrupts sustained focus (on homework, work, friends) and disrupts life in general, especially face-to-face relationships and sleep.

Many students are stressed, and phones provide an easy moment of escape, and so turning to a screen becomes an instantaneous path to stress relief.

Many students are also fearful of awkward moments, either in social connections or just in general. Once again, turning to a screen is an easy "out" in any situation, providing a known and nonawkward moment of connection to whatever is happening on the screen.

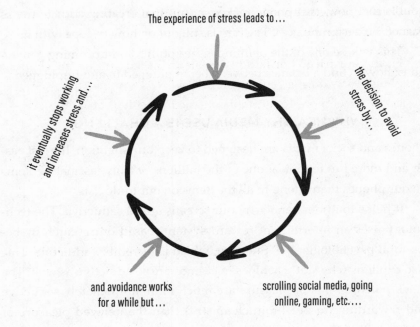

The experience of stress leads to...

the decision to avoid stress by...

scrolling social media, going online, gaming, etc....

and avoidance works for a while but...

it eventually stops working and increases stress and...

The Stress-Go-Round

STRATEGIES

Assess Your Use and Determine If It's Problematic

Of course, we use phones for all sorts of necessary communication and for work and study. So this is about assessing your nonacademic screen time and whether it's getting in the way of important aspects of your life. If it helps, reflect on the following questions in a journal.

For instance, consider the impact of media use on classwork:

- Do you struggle to stay with a hard homework assignment and often find yourself shifting your attention to your favorite social media or content?
- Do you frequently check your phone while you are in class and wonder why you aren't learning the course content?

Consider whether nonacademic screen time is getting in the way of connecting authentically with friends:

- Have your friends or family repeatedly asked you to put your phone away during conversations?
- Do you feel more comfortable interacting with a screen in your room than hanging out with friends in person?

Consider whether nonacademic screen time is getting in the way of self-care:

- Are you scrolling through your phone for hours late at night when you wish you had let yourself go to sleep?
- Do you often miss a chance to take a walk outside or attend a fun activity because you got caught up in something online?

If screen time is a problem in any of these or other ways, simply admit it. This is often the hardest step. No one wants to admit they are overinvolved or even addicted to media use.

Track Your Usage

Explore how and when you are using screen time in ways that negatively affect you. You could use a page in your journal to keep track of your screen time. You might use a phone app to track how much time you are spending on your phone, and a computer app to track nonacademic computer time (for apps, see resources below). Find out specifically when and how much screen time is affecting your day.

Set Media Use Goals

Set goals for media use related to your studies, social life, and self-care. This issue has already been raised in various places throughout this book. This doesn't mean never using screen time for entertainment, socializing, or stress relief. Rather, challenge yourself to be thoughtful, proactive, and creative about your media use. For example, you might decide to keep your phone off the table at meals, to put the phone in airplane mode

"I have been getting lost on my phone every night before bed, due to feeling overwhelmed with schoolwork and sad from missing my boyfriend. I can tell that it interferes with me getting to bed on time and also causes my sleep to be less restful. So I brainstormed some other activities that would bring me comfort at night: taking a warm shower before I got into bed, bringing extra stuffed animals near my bed, and turning out all the lights except the reading light near my bed. I found a great soothing background noise playlist, but I put my phone out of reach so I wouldn't be tempted to check it. Then I settled into bed with one of my favorite middle school books that I found at the library. It worked. I felt like I was treating myself, rather than just trying to escape my sadness."

— VALERIE

when going to sleep, or putting the phone on silent (and putting it away) while studying, and then only checking it on breaks.

Limit Media Interruptions

Here are some strategies for limiting interruptions from media use and phones:

- Turn off all audio and vibration alerts on your phone and computer. Check your phone at the times you choose, rather than reacting to alerts.
- Put your phone into airplane mode.
- Close your email and chat programs, and only keep open the actual page or search you need to work with.
- Put paper or a sticky note over any corner of your computer screen to block a tempting area.
- Hide your phone for a preset amount of time. If necessary, text folks first to tell them you are going offline for an hour. Personally, I hide my phone under my tissue box. It sounds stupid but it helps!
- Use a computer program to disable what you don't want on your computer for periods of time (see resources below).

Proactively Plan Media Use

Explore scheduling media use the way you schedule any other activity:

- Establish a routine that certain times/places are just for class-work. As you develop the habit of not accessing your phone while studying or writing, this will become second nature.

- Establish a routine of putting the phone away for set time periods, like for half an hour to study. Set an alarm, work as hard as possible for thirty minutes, then reward yourself with a five-to-ten-minute break.

Practice Creative Avoidance

Develop your own unique strategies for preventing your media use from interfering with your studies or life:

- When possible, work with paper and pencil, not on a screen.
- When writing, turn the computer screen off and start typing. This is a classic technique to overcome writer's block (typing errors are easy to correct later), but it is also helpful to block out everything else on the screen.
- Study in public. You can't watch television or play console video games if you aren't at home.
- Give your phone to a friend while you study.
- Study with a friend who is coping with the same issue and be accountability partners.

Take Extreme Measures

When all else fails, go to extremes. These ideas might seem drastic, but they can help:

- Delete your social media apps; delete your bookmarks.
- Turn off all notifications. Pick a maximum number of times each day when you allow yourself to check the sites you like.

"I was getting anxious from my morning routine. The first thing I did before even getting out of bed was to check my phone and all my notifications. I felt jittery when I saw who had and hadn't replied to me, let alone from reading the news headlines of the day. I decided to experiment with not checking my phone each morning until after I'd showered and eaten breakfast. I'm amazed that, with this new practice, I feel much more positive about the world. I feel in control of my life rather than being reactive to everything around me."

— FOSTER

- Turn your screen to black and white (versus in color).
- Every time you log into an app or site, log out!

WHEN TO SEEK PROFESSIONAL HELP

If you have trouble taking control of your media use, and it's affecting your ability to study, socialize, or get to sleep, then seek help. For study issues, go to your college study center. If you feel your media use has an emotional component, such as feeling awkward around others or using media to cope with emotions, talk to a counselor.

RESOURCES

On Campus

- College counselor: A counselor can assess any emotional issues and help you develop media use strategies. They can also provide referrals to off-campus resources.
- College study center: This center may provide classes, workshops, or other resources for managing media use to improve study skills.

Books

- *Indistractable: How to Control Your Attention and Choose Your Life* by Nir Eyal (www.nirandfar.com): This book, as well as Eyal's website, offers many strategies for developing social antibodies — defenses against new harmful behaviors that have arisen from phone use.
- *Futureproof: 9 Rules for Humans in the Age of Automation* by Kevin Roose: This smart book makes clear the costs of remaining ignorant to the power of AI in our lives, and it gives practical and doable strategies for how to live a more humane life.
- *Dopamine Nation: Finding Balance in the Age of Indulgence* by Anna Lembke: This book explains addictive or excessive media use

as imbalances in our brain chemistry due to the overwhelming abundance of pleasurable activities in our world.

Apps

- Freedom (www.freedom.to): This free app helps manage or block media use.
- OffScreen (for both Google and Apple): This free app can block unwanted media sites, track your screen time, and also has attractive timers for studying.
- one sec (for Google and Apple): This free app delays the opening of social media apps instead of blocking them, giving you a little time to interrupt a habitual behavior.
- Screen Time (find in Settings on the iPhone): This phone setting provides insights about screen use and has the ability to limit the apps you specify.

Afterword

Your Future

A journey of a thousand miles begins with a single step.

— Lao Tzu

Dear Student,

Here are some words to remember:

You deserve to love yourself just as you are. Right now, no changes.

You deserve to embrace the journey you are on, which includes learning about yourself and learning about your academics and career.

You deserve to measure yourself by the growth you've already accomplished and to value how hard you are working right now.

Your life is not set in stone the way it is today. Life is always changing; let yourself change with it. Small steps matter, persistence matters.

You are not alone on your journey. Others are with you, including family, friends, mentors, professors, and even resources like this book.

Reaching out to and being vulnerable with another person can feel like the hardest thing in the world, but it is worth the risk and it gets easier with practice.

Wishing you a mentally healthy college career,
Mia

Appendix A

Calming Strategies

BREATHING TO BRING CALM

Square Breathing

Square breathing is a simple method to slow breathing down. It's popular with many students because it is easy to remember. As you breathe, visualize a square shape, and use your finger to trace a square on your arm or leg to help you stay focused on your breathing.

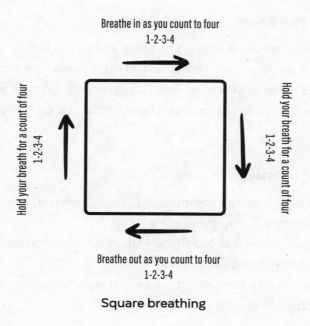

Breathe in as you count to four
1-2-3-4

Hold your breath for a count of four
1-2-3-4

Hold your breath for a count of four
1-2-3-4

Breathe out as you count to four
1-2-3-4

Square breathing

1. Breathe in for four counts (the first side of the square).
2. Hold your breath for four counts (the second side of the square).
3. Breathe out for four counts (the third side of the square).
4. Hold your breath for four counts (the fourth side of the square).

Alternate-Nostril Breathing

Alternate-nostril breathing slows your breath by covering one nostril at a time as you breathe in and out.

Sit in a comfortable position with your legs crossed, place your left hand on your left knee, lift your right hand up toward your nose, exhale completely, and then use your right thumb to close your right nostril. Then inhale through your left nostril, close the left nostril with your fingers, and remove the thumb to exhale through the right nostril. Inhale through the right nostril, close the right nostril with the thumb, and remove the fingers to exhale through the left nostril.

Continue this cycle for up to five minutes or as long as you want. End the practice by finishing with an exhale on the left side.

Counting Your Breath

As you breathe in, count slowly up to four, and as you breathe out, count slowly back down to one. However, you can increase the count to five or ten or as much as you want. You can also count a certain number of breaths, such as up to ten (or down from ten); count each breath on the exhale.

Visualizing an Image

Visualize a dot going up a line on the inhale, and down on the exhale (like an Etch A Sketch).

Visualize a balloon or ball filling with air on the inhale and reducing to a dot or going flat on the exhale.

Visualize the Hoberman sphere (an expandable sphere) expanding and contracting in time to your breath.

Repeating a Word or Phrase

It can be calming to repeat words or phrases in your mind in time with your breathing. Here are several possibilities. The first word is for the inhale, the second for the exhale.

- *in / out*
- *I am / at peace*
- *I am / enough*
- *Let / go*
- *Be / here / now* (repeat in a cycle as you breathe in and out)

Focusing on Your Breath

- Focus on your breath coming into your nostrils, feeling cool or warm.
- Focus on your breath caressing the back of your throat.
- Feel your lungs expanding and contracting with each breath.
- Feel your diaphragm and belly expanding and contracting with each breath. Perhaps keep a hand on your belly.

BODY SCANS

During a body scan, you focus your mind on each region of the body, from your feet to your head, as simple as that.

Regardless of what happens, it's okay. Some people fall asleep, lose concentration, feel bored, or don't feel anything. If your mind wanders, or strong feelings arise, simply acknowledge the thoughts or physical sensations and bring your focus gently back to the area of the body that you are working with. Let go of ideas of success or failure, of trying to do well or feel something specific. Just do it with an attitude of openness and curiosity.

This body scan moves through the body from toes to head. You can also focus on only one part of the body, such as the legs, arms, or head.

Find a comfortable position, either lying on a bed, rug, or yoga mat or sitting in a comfortable chair. Let gravity control your arms and legs and gently close your eyes if that is comfortable for you. Notice what it feels like to be resting comfortably. Notice the temperature of the air in the room, how your body feels held up in this time and space. Bring your attention to your breath. Don't manipulate or control the breath; simply direct your attention to your belly rising on the inhale and falling on the exhale.

Move your attention to the toes of both feet. You don't need to move your toes, just bring your focus to your toes. You may feel tingling, warmth, coolness, or no sensations; that is just fine. You might feel your clothing on your toes, the floor beneath them, or just the air. Let your mind stay on your toes for a moment with a sense of curiosity and exploration, not judgment. Remember, if your mind wanders, simply acknowledge the thoughts and bring the mind gently back to the body scan.

Move your attention to the bottoms of both feet. As before, don't move your feet, just focus on the bottoms. Whatever sensations you feel are fine. For a moment, focus on the bottoms of your feet with curiosity and exploration, not judgment.

Move upward slowly and focus on the next areas of your body, repeating this process one area at a time: Focus on the tops of both feet and ankles; then the lower legs, calves, and shins; then the knees and kneecaps; then the thighs; then the hips and hip bones; then the back and shoulder blades; then the abdomen and stomach; then the chest and lungs; then the shoulders and arms; then the wrists and hands; then the neck; then the face; and finally the top of the head. Each time you focus on a new area of the body, do not move it; just bring your focus to it. Notice any sensations, such as tingling, warmth, or coolness, or if there are no sensations. Let your mind stay focused on that area for a moment with curiosity and exploration, not judgment.

To finish, take a deep breath that ripples from the top of your head and out the bottom of your feet. When you are ready to end, gently stretch your body before getting up, and move slowly to maintain your relaxed state.

VISUALIZATIONS

Visualizations can be helpful to shift our minds to more positive, calm, or pleasant thoughts, especially if we feel stuck in a negative headspace. This can be especially useful at night when trying to get to sleep. In the visualization, imagine a place that you enjoy, whatever brings you peace and happiness. Our brains are powerful, and imagining an event impacts us in the same ways as actually experiencing the event.

As you practice your visualization, if difficult emotions arise at any time, or something becomes painful, know that you can simply end the visualization if you wish.

Find a comfortable position, either lying on a bed, rug, or yoga mat or sitting in a comfortable chair. Let gravity control your arms and legs, and gently close your eyes if you wish. Take a few slow breaths.

Imagine a place that you know well and enjoy. This can be any place, inside or outside, imaginary or real. Use your five senses to experience this place. How does it look? Note the details, such as colors or shapes. How does it smell? Breathe in the smell. Is the temperature warm or cool? What are you wearing and how do your clothes feel on your skin? What sounds do you hear? Is it quiet or loud? Are you tasting anything?

Here are some ideas for visualizations that students have come up to help them foster peace of mind:

- Taking a familiar hike in the woods
- Watching the ocean waves from the beach
- Walking to a coffee shop
- Browsing a bookstore
- Watching penguins slide down a hill
- Ice skating
- Sitting on a porch swing and slowly swinging
- Walking through a garden and noticing the flowers

PROGRESSIVE MUSCLE RELEASE

A progressive muscle release is like the more active sibling to a body scan. In a similar way, you shift your focus from toes to head, moving slowly through your body, but instead of just focusing, you intensely clench the muscle group for a few seconds, and then release and relax that body part. The process of briefly restricting and then allowing blood flow can feel very relaxing.

As you practice your progressive muscle release, if difficult emotions arise, or something becomes painful, know that you can simply stop at any point.

Find a comfortable position, either lying on a bed, rug, or yoga mat or sitting in a comfortable chair. Take a couple of slow, deep breaths. Notice your breathing through the whole exercise.

Curl the toes of both feet as tightly as you can. Hold for five seconds (slowly count to five), while noticing the feeling of tension in your toes. Then release your toes and notice the feeling of relaxation.

Next, flex both feet from your toes to your shins and calves. Hold for five seconds (slowly count to five), while noticing the feeling of tension in your calves. Then release your calves and notice the feeling of relaxation.

Proceed with each body area in the same way, squeezing and holding for five seconds, and then releasing, while noticing both the tension and the relaxation. After your calves, squeeze your legs together and tense your thighs; then clench your stomach muscles; then squeeze your forearms and biceps up to your shoulders; then make tight fists with your hands; then squeeze your shoulders up to your ears; then squeeze your shoulders down your back and clench your back; then open your mouth as wide as possible; and then squeeze your eyes tight and clench your face. Finally, tense your whole body from top to bottom. As before, hold for five seconds, then release.

To finish, take a deep breath that ripples from the top of your head and out the bottom of your feet. Notice if you feel more relaxation in your body, or where you might still feel tense. When you are ready to end, gently stretch your body and get up slowly.

MEDITATION

Meditation is a dedicated time to practice doing nothing other than noticing the physical reality of the present moment in a nonjudgmental way. Some religions use meditation as a form of prayer, but it can also be used in a secular, nonreligious way.

An abundance of research shows the benefits of meditation for a slew of issues: pain management, deeper sleep, anxiety and depression management, improved focus, better self-compassion, less reactivity, more self-awareness, and more.

Why Meditate?

People meditate to slow down their mind and cultivate calm and focus. It helps lessen the "monkey mind" that jumps constantly to a million places.

People also meditate because it helps them learn to tolerate discomfort. The practice of noticing the moment, over and over, is similar to practicing weightlifting for an athlete. It builds strength of mind that can then be used toward whatever goal a person has.

People also meditate because it provides time and space for self-acceptance, which leads to acceptance of others. When we "just sit there" being nonjudgmental about what we notice, we help foster self-acceptance. It's hard to accept and love others if we don't first accept and love ourselves.

What Is Meditation Like in Practice?

Typically, people meditate either sitting or lying comfortably, and they focus their attention on their breathing. Some people do this for about twenty minutes per day. Over and over, the breath provides a convenient focus point for what is happening in the present moment.

However, we have amazingly complex brains, and our thoughts are ever-present. These thoughts inevitably arise and pull away from our focus on our breathing. The goal is to nonjudgmentally bring our focus back to our breathing each time. In addition, our physical bodies provide us with an ache here or a pain there. When we become aware of this, the goal is to patiently let that sensation just be and return our focus back to our breathing.

Does Meditation Always Feel Good?

No, meditation doesn't always feel good. The closest metaphor is a physical workout. Some days we feel great after a workout, and some days we feel disappointed or stressed by it. Overall, we know that working out gets easier when we practice consistently, and it's okay to have a disappointing workout once in a while. It's the same with meditation, which can feel different every day.

QUICK STRETCHES TO DO WHILE STUDYING

When we spend long hours hunched in front of our computers, our bodies are not getting the movement they need, and this can end up affecting mental health. So develop the habit of doing some quick stretches at least once per hour. It's even better to stretch every half hour.

Sitting Stretches

- Hold your shoulders up to your ears for a few seconds, then release. Repeat three times.
- Hold the seat of your chair with your hand, roll your shoulder blades back trying to touch each other, and gently look up.
- Tilt your right ear to your right shoulder, let it hang there for a few seconds. Tilt your left ear to your left shoulder, let it hang there a few seconds. Repeat.
- Flex your feet so your toes reach toward your shins but your heels stay on the ground. Repeat a few times.
- Hold one arm out in front of you and gently pull your fingers back with your opposite hand to give your wrist and forearm a gentle stretch. Repeat on the other side.

Standing Stretches

- Reach for the sky. Grab your right wrist with your left hand and lean to the left a few seconds, then straighten up. Grab your left wrist with your right hand and lean to the right for a few seconds, then straighten up.
- Hold your arms out to your sides. Twist and swing to the right, gently hitting your right arm behind you while your left hand taps your right shoulder, then twist to the left, gently hitting your

left arm behind you while your right hand taps your left shoulder. Repeat a few times.

- Gently bend forward and touch your shins or toes. Let gravity work; let your head be as heavy as it can. Hold for a few moments, then gently roll back to standing.
- Hold on to your chair with your left hand. Bend your right knee and lift your right foot behind you. Grab your right ankle with your right hand and gently stretch and hold for thirty seconds. You should feel this in the front of your right thigh and in your right hip flexor. Repeat on the left side.

Stretches for the Privacy of Your Room

- Get down on all fours. Breathe in and arch your back and gently look up, then breathe out and curl your back and look at your knees. Repeat a few times. This is called cat/cow in yoga.
- Lie on your back and stretch your arms overhead and your feet away from you. This is a classic full-body stretch.
- Lie on your back, with your butt flush against a wall, while putting your legs straight up against the wall. Stay here for a few minutes, or as long as you wish.

PRAYERS — RELIGIOUS AND OTHERWISE

Many studies have shown that prayer is positive for mental health. While prayers are used primarily by religions, they can be used in a secular, nonreligious way as a form of well-wishing, expressing gratitude, generosity, and so on.

Prayer can help you feel more at peace and grateful and to be kinder to others. Prayer can help you focus on your day and clarify your intentions. Here are some prayers you might consider using:

May you truly be happy.
May you live in peace.
May you live in love.

May you know the power of forgiveness.
May you live in recognition that your life has deep meaning and
    good purpose.

> — DALAI LAMA

God, grant me the serenity
to accept the things I cannot change,
the courage to change the things I can,
and the wisdom to know the difference.
Amen.

> — REINHOLD NIEBUHR

Dear God, please give me strength when I am weak, love when
I feel forsaken, courage when I am afraid, wisdom when I feel
foolish, comfort when I am alone, hope when I feel rejected, and
peace when I am in turmoil. Amen.

> — UNKNOWN

May the road rise up to meet you.
May the wind always be at your back.
May the sun shine warm upon your face,
and rains fall soft upon your fields.
And until we meet again,
may God hold you in the palm of his hand.
May good luck be with you wherever you go, and your blessings
    outnumber the shamrocks that grow.
May your days be many and your troubles be few, may all God's
    blessings descend upon you, may peace be within you, may
    your heart be strong, may you find what you're seeking wher-
    ever you roam.
May you have the hindsight to know where you've been,
the foresight to know where you're going,
and the insight to know when you're going too far.

> — TRADITIONAL IRISH PRAYER

Appendix B

Counseling

Counseling is the process where a person seeks support from a trained professional to help make life changes and/or treat mental health issues. It's the same as seeking help from nurses and doctors for physical health issues. Mental health counselors usually have a master's or higher degree in psychology or social work, and they hold a license from the state in which they operate (same as your college).

An important aspect of the counselor-client relationship is that it isn't equal or reciprocal. The counselor is hired to help the client; that is their job. In other words, the relationship is one-sided and only focuses on the client, you. That is part of what makes it effective.

In a personal relationship, we expect reciprocity, equality, and give-and-take: Each person cares about, listens to, and tries to help the other. This can certainly involve counseling, but the relationship is about more than counseling. Indeed, since relationships with friends and family exist within a larger context, we might not be fully honest or forthcoming with them, since we might worry how they might treat us, or how our relationship might change, if others knew all the details or if we admitted all our feelings.

This raises another critical fact that makes counseling effective: Counseling is confidential, which means your privacy is protected by law. This helps create a safe space in which you can be honest and say anything without worrying who else might find out. Counselors must keep information private. The main exception is if a student expresses a plan or intention to harm themselves or others. That information is no longer considered private, and counselors are ethically obligated to do what's necessary to save someone's life.

WHAT DO PEOPLE TALK ABOUT IN COUNSELING?

People talk about anything that is bothering them — any and all problems, worries, and anxieties, anything that doesn't feel right in their life. Students also seek counseling support for problems and anxieties directly related to being a student. This can include homesickness, adapting to college, making friends, making healthier sleep habits, roommate issues, recovering from a breakup, coping with family issues, self-esteem issues, assertiveness, career issues, and learning to communicate clearly.

Students seek counseling for support around coming out, transitioning genders, or coping with a painful disability. Students come to counseling to cope with painful events, such as experiencing racism or other discrimination, death of a family member, recovering from a sexual assault, and recovering from an accident or injury.

Finally, students come to counseling to be assessed, diagnosed, and treated for mental health issues. This might include anxiety, social anxiety, depression, obsessive-compulsive disorder, bipolar disorder, attention-deficit disorder, borderline personality disorder, eating disorders, and drug or alcohol addictions.

What do students get from counseling? Here are some quotes from students:

"Counseling slowed me down and helped me take the time to go deeper with myself and understand myself. I never took the time before to get to know what makes me tick."

"The first place I could speak my truth and not feel judged was in the safety of a counseling session. My counselor is the least judgmental person I've met."

"I felt that all parts of me could be seen at the same time when I was in counseling. My counselor provided that security and support for me."

"In counseling I could be more direct about the details of issues that I simply glossed over with my friends. My counseling encouraged honesty and that was so helpful."

"My counselor was creative and supportive with problem-solving my different issues. I also knew that I was going there to check in, and it ended up being a place to be held accountable for changes I wanted to make in my life."

"I learned new skills to help cope with painful issues with my counselor, such as recognizing and interrupting my negative thoughts, how to speak up for myself, and some social skills."

HOW TO FIND ON-CAMPUS COUNSELING

Most college campuses have at least one mental health counselor on staff, and some universities have a large counseling center.

How to make a counseling appointment will vary from school to school, but the website will have detailed information. Usually, you need to call or email, or if you are at a big university, you might even be able to make an appointment through the website.

Expect paperwork. You will be expected to fill out a few forms before your first session. This is standard procedure, as it helps your counselor know who you are, and it helps the counseling center and the college itself be responsible in treating you appropriately.

Not all colleges offer ongoing counseling. You might be invited for one or a few sessions, then be encouraged to find long-term counseling off campus.

HOW TO FIND OFF-CAMPUS COUNSELING

Most people need to make sure private counseling is covered by their health insurance, so review your insurance's mental health coverage. They may have a list of counselors in your area that take your insurance.

Your on-campus counseling center can also recommend off-campus providers, or use *Psychology Today*'s "Find a Therapist" webpage (www .psychologytoday.com/us/therapists). Confirm that the counselor takes your form of insurance, and make sure the counselor is located conveniently to where you live.

Contact your top choices and request a brief phone meeting to see if you connect to each person. In addition to double-checking that they take your insurance, here are some questions you might ask:

- Do you feel comfortable working with a college student on issues of [fill in the blank]?
- What is your counseling style, and what does a session look like?
- What is your fee per session? How do you accept payment?

If you have a first session and don't like the counselor, for any reason, you are under no obligation to stay with them. Make sure only to continue with a counselor you feel respected by, who listens well, and who meets your goals for counseling. Your counselor should never do any of the following:

- Make you feel shame about an issue
- Talk about their personal problems
- Want a friendship or sexual relationship with you
- Pressure you to do any treatment you don't want to do

COPING WITH A PANIC ATTACK

Panic attacks can be frightening and painful, so much so that some folks head to the ER believing they are about to die. Panic attacks may last a few minutes or a couple of hours. Afterward, it may take days to recover and restore a sense of equilibrium.

Here are a few common physical panic attack symptoms:

- Racing heart or feeling your heart is missing beats
- Trouble getting your breath and feeling your chest is tight
- Shaking hands or legs, sweaty palms, legs feeling like jelly
- A headache or feeling a tight band around your head

Here are a few common thoughts or emotions that arise during a panic attack:

- A sense of impending doom or dread
- Fear that you are going to die
- Uncontrollable sadness and crying
- Fear that the panic attack will never end

After a first panic attack, a major issue for people is fear of having another panic attack. This is a logical reaction to a traumatic experience.

Panic attacks get much better with counseling and cognitive behavior therapy. However, right now, even if you've never had one, you can practice two main ways for coping with a panic attack: calming self-talk and physical calming techniques.

How we talk to ourselves matters greatly. Fearful, catastrophizing self-talk will rev a panic attack into high gear, while calming self-talk will help keep an attack from escalating. Here are some examples of calming self-talk:

- "I can survive this using my breathing techniques" (see "Breathing to Bring Calm," pages 313–15).
- "My body is having a strong anxiety reaction and I can let this pass."
- "I can handle these symptoms. I can ride the waves knowing it will end soon."
- "A panic attack is my body reacting to unconscious fear."
- "A panic attack cannot kill me. It just feels bad for a little while."

Using physical calming techniques can reduce the intensity and length of a panic attack. Our job is to calm our body down in whatever way that works for us. Here are some ideas:

- Lower your heart rate by slowing your breathing (See "Breathing to Bring Calm," pages 313–15).
- Open a window or go outside. This may seem counterintuitive, but many people say fresh air is essential. Have a fan blow air on your face.
- Use a method that is physically grounding. If it's comfortable, try physical touch, such as holding someone's hand or having a friend gently rub your back. Try drinking something hot or cold. Sometimes gentle stretching can help soften tight muscles.

JOURNALING

I recommend journaling for all students. It is a simple and effective tool for self-expression. The process of writing helps transform mere wisps of thought into solid forms that can help us better understand ourselves. A journal is a good listener, patiently hearing all our feelings, from joy to anguish, and it never judges.

What Is Journaling?

Journaling is writing down our thoughts, goals, positive messages, experiences, and more, so we can reflect on them and keep track of them. The act of life review and naming aspirational goals strengthens learning and positive messages in our brain. Referring back to what we have written helps us practice new learning.

There are really no rules for journaling. Journal in any way that works for you: Write in a fancy blank book or a cheap spiral notebook, open a document on your computer, use a journaling or notes app on your phone, or scribble on scraps of paper that you stuff in a jar. Write with a fancy pen and artful colors or the stub of a pencil — or type away on your phone or computer.

Some people write daily at a special time as part of a ritual, such as first thing in the morning, or as a destressing routine at night. Some people keep their journal with them all the time so they can jot down thoughts and reflections whenever they come up.

Others journal less often or only when something prompts the need, such as to understand difficult emotions or to react to significant events. Journaling is a resource to use whenever it feels helpful, even if you only do it rarely.

How Journaling Can Help

I encourage all readers of this book to journal in response to the topics it raises. This will help you work through the strategies sections. Here are other things you can write about:

- New coping strategies you want to try
- How you have personally experienced common issues and problems
- Responses to journal prompts that help you gain self-acceptance
- Reflections on your sense of self and identity
- Your perspective on cognitive distortions and negative thoughts that arise for you
- How your relationships impact you and what you need or want from various people

Journaling can help anyone's mental health in many ways:

- Expressing our inner thoughts helps build our self-awareness of thoughts.
- Being honest with ourselves in a journal is a safe and effective way to express our feelings.
- Writing what we have gratitude for is a way to combat negativity.
- Clarifying thoughts through writing is a helpful way to practice before having a difficult conversation.
- Writing out daily or weekly to-do lists can help with organization and anxiety.
- Making lists of positive affirmations and life goals helps us remember our ideal vision for our lives.

About the only way that journaling won't help is if it becomes simply a dumping ground for our worst thoughts and feelings. Without self-reflection, that could make those feelings stronger. That is, journaling provides a safe space to be honest about all our thoughts and feelings, even difficult, traumatic, unwanted ones. But the goal is to foster self-awareness so we improve our lives, cope with negativity better, and solve any problems that hinder us as we pursue our desired path.

Finally, many students worry about the quality of their writing. They fear being judged if their writing isn't perfect. But journaling isn't about the writing itself, and it isn't for anyone else. The beauty of a journal is that no one will ever see it unless we share it. Journaling is about our own self-expression and self-awareness, and what matters is the process of transforming our thoughts into written words.

A Gratitude Journal

As discussed in chapter 15, keeping a gratitude journal is a style of journaling that helps us focus on the good things in our lives. The approach is simple: Every day, write about one or two things that we enjoy, appreciate, and are grateful for. This can be anything, from the mundane (having food to eat) to the profound (the love of family). The act of affirming the good things in our lives helps amplify positive emotions, and studies show gratitude journaling increases well-being and satisfaction. If you are interested, here are some prompts you might respond to:

- What made you smile today?
- What is something new you learned today?
- Describe something beautiful in nature.
- When has someone shown you kindness, today or in the past?

SUICIDE PREVENTION CHECKLIST

If you or someone you know is struggling with suicidal thoughts, please reach out for help immediately. Don't hesitate to take action. Suicide is irreversible, but emotional and mental distress are temporary and treatable.

The advice in this section is adapted from the Jed Foundation (www .jedfoundation.org), which is a student-focused mental health resource center. Here is advice if you or someone you know needs immediate help.

- For confidential counseling and advice, contact 988 Suicide & Crisis Lifeline (text/call 988; www.988lifeline.org). This national organization (previously the National Suicide Prevention Lifeline) provides 24/7, free, and confidential support to people in suicidal crisis or emotional distress. If you are calling on behalf of someone else, they can help you take the appropriate actions.

- Text the free Crisis Text Line from anywhere in the United States, anytime, about any type of crisis (text HOME to 741-741; www .crisistextline.org). A real-life human being will receive the text and respond, all from a secure online platform.
- If you need immediate assistance, call 911. Tell the operator that you or someone you know is suicidal and having a mental health emergency. Often, the college's own emergency services also respond to 911.
- Go to the nearest hospital's emergency room. Ask a friend to drive if possible.

If you are helping someone else in crisis, know your limits and don't place yourself in physical danger. The best way to help is to connect the person to a mental health professional. Don't try to solve the crisis yourself. If you can and feel comfortable doing so, stay with the person until they can get to or receive help.

If you are hesitant to use a crisis text or hotline for any reason, or unsure what will happen, read the article "What REALLY Happens When You Reach Out to Crisis Lines?" on the Active Minds blog (www.active minds.org/blog/what-really-happens-when-you-reach-out-to-crisis -lines). This excellent article busts myths and clarifies what happens when you call or text a crisis line.

Warning Signs of Suicide Risk

Here are some common warning signs that someone is contemplating suicide or might be at risk of suicide. These could be things they say or that they post on social media. Reach out for help especially if you notice a pattern of suicidal talk or any mention of how to get potentially lethal means, like access to pills or weapons.

Depending on your relationship, either talk to the person (see below) or alert someone more appropriate about what you suspect.

- If someone expresses intense and urgent emotional despair, intense guilt or shame, or feels trapped:

  "I can't take it anymore."
  "There is no way out."

"I'm done."
"I'm so sorry for all the trouble I've caused everyone."

- If someone expresses rage or a desire for revenge:

"I'll show you all."
"She'll be sorry."
"No one would care if I were gone."

- If someone says goodbye and perhaps gives away personal possessions:

"I'll miss you all."
"You won't have to worry about me anymore."
"Everyone will be better off without me."

- If someone glorifies or glamorizes death, if they focus on death in general, or if they make death seem heroic:

"Death is beautiful."
"I didn't choose to be born but I can choose to die."
"Better to live for eternity than live in reality."

How to Talk to a Friend

If you suspect a friend might be suicidal, reach out to them. You don't have to do it perfectly. The main thing is to let them know you notice and care about their distress, while giving them the option to talk if they want to. If they do, listen without judgment or assumptions. Let them know you believe them. See "How to Help a Friend" (pages 333–34) for more on having the conversation. Here are some ways to approach it:

"Hi, I'm just reaching out because I'm concerned about you."
"Do you want to talk? You seem troubled lately, and I care about you."
"I've noticed your mood has been really dark. Are you okay? I'm willing to listen if you want to share what's going on."

Appendix C

Relationships

HOW TO HELP A FRIEND

There is no perfect way to help a friend who is struggling, whether in general or with mental health issues. The main thing is to let them know you care and want to help in whatever way they want. Here is some advice for how to start or conduct that conversation, but use this for inspiration, not as a step-by-step guide. Don't worry if you feel awkward or unsure about what to say. Try to be the friend you want to be.

That said, it's important to remember that you are a peer and a friend, not a professional psychologist. You can't fix the other person, make them talk, or make them want to change. In fact, the most important role you can play is to make sure the friend is getting the appropriate help they need, whether from friends, counselors, doctors, teachers, family, and so on.

- To initiate the conversation, reach out by calling, dropping by their room, or texting to meet up at a particular time and place:

  "I miss you and want to hang out."
  "I care about you."
  "I'm thinking about you and wonder if we could talk."

- Once together, be clear about what worries you. Specific examples are often helpful:

  "I've noticed that you didn't hang out with us to play board games the past week."

"I haven't seen you in class for a few days."
"You seem to get angry over little things lately."

- Use "I" statements so your friend knows how their behavior affects you:

  "I'm worried that you are struggling."
  "I'm concerned that something is wrong."
  "I'm sad that you might be hurting."

- Focus mostly on listening. Allow your friend to talk, and reflect back what you hear them say, without judging or blaming them:

  "I'm listening. Take your time. I'm not in a hurry."
  "I hear you. What you're going through is challenging."
  "Can you explain more about why you feel that way?"

- If it seems warranted, offer to help them connect to professional support:

  "Counseling would probably help. Would it be easier if I walked over to the counseling center with you?"
  "It's too much to handle alone. I think you can get help for this issue at the dean of students office."

- However the conversation goes, make sure to offer your continued support in whatever way fits your relationship:

  "Want me to come get you on my way to dinner?"
  "We could study at the library together tonight."
  "We are ordering pizza Friday night and I want you to be there."
  "Know that I'm always here for you. You don't have to go through this alone."

CHECKLIST OF RELATIONSHIP AND EMOTIONAL ABUSE

While there are exceptions, most new relationships don't start off in abusive ways, and partners who become abusive can at first be caring, loving, and even ideal. Further, possessive and controlling behaviors usually emerge in small ways at first and only intensify as the relationship continues.

Every relationship is different, and abuse doesn't always look the same. However, the central feature or attribute of most abusive relationships is that the abusive partner tries to establish or gain power and control over the other.

If you feel you are in an abusive relationship, the most important thing is your safety; either end the relationship or seek advice and help. It is often very difficult to leave an abusive relationship, so seeking help is often an essential step. Below is a checklist of abusive behaviors (adapted from the National Domestic Violence Hotline). Even one or two of these in a relationship is a red flag of a potentially abusive partner.

- The partner tells you that you never do anything right.
- The partner displays extreme jealousy of your friends or time spent away from them.
- The partner prevents or discourages you from spending time with friends, family members, or peers.
- The partner is insulting, demeaning, or shaming, especially in front of other people.
- The partner prevents you from making your own decisions, including about work or attending school.
- The partner pressures you to have sex when you don't want to, or to perform sexual acts you're not comfortable with.
- The partner pressures you to use drugs or alcohol.
- The partner intimidates you through threatening looks or actions.
- The partner insults your parenting or threatens to harm or take away your children or pets.
- The partner intimidates you with weapons, like guns, knives, bats, or mace.
- The partner destroys your belongings or your home.

Crisis Services

- National Domestic Violence Hotline (800-799-7233; www.thehot line.org): This national hotline provides 24/7 counseling, and their website can help you find local resources.

- *The Gaslight Effect: How to Spot and Survive the Hidden Manipulation Others Use to Control Your Life* by Dr. Robin Stern: This book defines and gives clear instructions for how to break free from one of the most common and insidious forms of emotional abuse.

CHECKLIST OF SEXUAL ASSAULT AND HARASSMENT

Sexual harassment and sexual assault can take many different forms, but one thing remains the same: It's never the victim's fault.

Sexual harassment includes unwelcome sexual advances, requests for sexual favors, and other verbal or physical harassment of a sexual nature, whether in the workplace, school, or any environment. Sexual harassment does not always have to be specifically about sexual behavior or directed at a specific person. For example, negative comments about women as a group may be a form of sexual harassment.

Sexual assault refers to sexual contact or behavior that occurs without the explicit consent of the victim. Here are some forms of sexual assault:

- Attempted rape
- Fondling or unwanted sexual touching
- Forcing a victim to perform sexual acts, such as oral sex or penetrating the perpetrator's body
- Penetration of the victim's body, also known as rape

Recognizing Sexual Harassment

Sexual harassment includes a wide variety of behaviors, and it can occur in a variety of circumstances. The harasser can identify with any gender and have any relationship to the victim, such as being a direct manager, indirect supervisor, coworker, teacher, peer, or colleague.

Here are some forms of sexual harassment (adapted from the Rape, Abuse & Incest National Network):

- Making conditions of employment or advancement dependent on sexual favors, either explicitly or implicitly
- Physical acts of sexual assault
- Requests for sexual favors

- Verbal harassment of a sexual nature, including jokes referring to sexual acts or sexual orientation
- Unwanted touching or physical contact
- Unwelcome sexual advances
- Discussing sexual relations, stories, and/or fantasies in inappropriate environments, like work and school
- Pressuring someone to engage sexually
- Sharing unwanted, sexually explicit photos, emails, or text messages

Crisis Services

- RAINN (Rape, Abuse & Incest National Network; 800-656-4673; www.rainn.org): RAINN is the nation's largest anti-sexual violence organization, they operate a national 24/7 hotline, and they have many resources on coping with sexual violence and safety and prevention.
- Day One (866-223-1111; www.dayoneservices.org): This national resource and crisis hotline can direct you to services in your state. They provide services to victims of sexual assault, domestic violence, trafficking, and crime.

CHECKLIST OF MENTOR, SPIRITUAL, AND FAITH LEADER ABUSE

At their best, relationships with mentors and religious and spiritual leaders can be sources of great support in our lives. However, any relationship with an unequal power dynamic has the potential for abuse, since the mentor or leader may misuse their power, influence, and trust.

Most of all, we enter these types of relationships trusting that mentors and spiritual leaders will act in our best interests, provide what they promise, and not exploit our trust. For example, church members trust pastors to teach them what's necessary to live by their faith; yoga students trust their yoga instructors to teach them how to pursue the practice and do the poses correctly.

How can we recognize abuse in these relationships? The Reclamation

Collective has a great definition of the term *spiritual abuse*, though this can refer to any context in which a leader is imbued with power:

> Spiritual abuse is the conscious or unconscious use of power to direct, control, or manipulate another's body, thoughts, emotions, actions, or capacity for choice, freedom, or autonomy of self, within a spiritual or religious context.

Similar to emotional abuse, mentor, spiritual, or faith leader abuse can take many forms. Typically, the victim is made to feel special while simultaneously needing something they can only get from the leader. This creates a dependency in which access to the desired need or support can only be achieved through relationship with the leader.

Unfortunately, mentor abuse can be common in colleges. Some adults really aren't meant to be mentors. Here are a few of the signs that a mentor relationship is not healthy:

- The mentor puts you down about anything, including your work, how you look, or how you live.
- The mentor makes everything about them and their needs.
- The mentor prevents you from working with others or makes you feel you have to have their help to succeed (such as by refusing a recommendation if you leave).
- The mentor asks about your personal life in ways that feel uncomfortable.
- The mentor asks you to do work for them that is not on your job description or is uncomfortable for you.
- The mentor requires you to share their same beliefs, opinions, emotions, and thoughts.
- The mentor directly or indirectly communicates or fosters dependence upon them.
- The mentor uses your relationship, or the threat of loss of the relationship, as a way to control you.

At the end of the day, a safe relationship with a mentor, as well as a faith or spiritual leader, is one in which you can have and express your own thoughts, emotions, and self without fear of being controlled, dismissed, or manipulated. Relationships with power differentials are only safe when we have access to our autonomy. Here are some questions to ask to explore both power and safety within these relationships:

- Do I have the option to get out of this relationship or community if needed?
- Are there systems of accountability in place for me to report any misuse of power or abuse?
- Am I able to set my own boundaries, personally and/or professionally?
- Are my boundaries respected within this relationship?
- Am I aware of where this supportive relationship begins and ends?

Crisis Services

- Reclamation Collective (www.reclamationcollective.com): This nonprofit community advocacy agency provides support groups, training, and workshops around topics of religious trauma and spiritual abuse.
- Religious Trauma Institute (www.religioustraumainstitute.com): This organization provides education, training, and resources related to spiritual abuse, power dynamics, and religious trauma.

Acknowledgments

Thank you to Scott Edelstein, publishing professional extraordinaire. Your enthusiasm for this book, attention to detail, insights about the human condition, and general kindness helped get the book to the finish line.

Special thanks to these colleagues who took time out of their busy work lives to review and provide a prepublication endorsement for me: Sha Bradley, Dan Buettner, Henry Emmons, Jim Hoppe, Lisa Landreman, Holly Rogers, Robin Hart Ruthenbeck, and Karla Benson Rutten.

Thanks to all the team at New World Library, especially Jason Gardner for seeing the worth in my book, and Jeff Campbell for making the book the best it can be. Thanks also to Tanya Fox, for her amazing proofreading, as well as Monique Muhlenkamp, Kristen Cashman, Tona Pearce-Myers, and Tracy Cunningham.

Thank you to my many colleagues at Macalester College, too numerous to list, especially in the Health and Wellness Center and the student affairs division, as well as to my Wednesday consultation group, who taught me so much about being an effective mental health counselor and a better human being.

For their encouragement and generosity, special thanks go to: Cathy Broberg, first copy editor; Julia Hutchinson for subtitle help; Michael Khune for your insights on community college students; Jodi Leirness for your heartfelt read; Missy Lundquist for your insights on loss and grief; Alison Morse for referring me to Scott Edelstein; Karla Benson Rutten for your diversity read; Debbie Sheets for your early read of the manuscript; and Kendra Snyder for help with the Checklist of Mentor, Spiritual, and Faith Leader Abuse.

Thank you to my kind friends who, in the early days, believed I could write this book: Julie Dean, Patty Diamond, Julie Eisenberg, Carolyn Friedhoff, Miriam Garcia, Suzanne Garfield, Carla Hagen, Janet Lawson, Jane Leonard, Lori Lippert, and John Whitehead. And thank you to the folks of Barnes/Carleton, St. Anthony Park, and Mt. Zion for being my caring communities.

Thank you to my mom, Barbara Field, for being a role model as a writer, and to my dad, Lewis Nosanow, for being a role model as an investigator. Cheers to all the Nosanows, Fields, and Levins for being my loving family community.

To my sons, Aaron and Ethan, you inspire me to be my best and fill my heart with love.

And thank you to Seth, my partner in all things.

Index

About the Author

Mia Nosanow, MA, LP, is a licensed psychologist and mental health therapist who specializes in college students. For twenty years, Mia worked as a mental health counselor at Macalester College in St. Paul, Minnesota, seeing thousands of students for individual and group counseling. Macalester is one of the most culturally diverse undergraduate colleges in the United States, with students from every state and ninety-nine countries, including many first-generation college students. In addition to one-on-one therapy, Mia has designed and facilitated innovative group therapy and mental health programming for college students and administrators, and she has presented at several national and regional professional conferences. Mia is passionate about helping young adults understand themselves and find resources so that they can thrive. She holds a BA from Carleton College and an MA in Counseling and Student Personnel Psychology from the University of Minnesota. She is the mother of two adult sons and lives with her husband in St. Paul.

MiaNosanow.com